THE ART OF
TED HUGHES

Ted Hughes in Persia, 1971

THE ART OF
TED HUGHES

KEITH SAGAR
Senior Staff Tutor in Literature
Extra-Mural Department, University of Manchester

SECOND EDITION

CAMBRIDGE UNIVERSITY PRESS
CAMBRIDGE
LONDON · NEW YORK · MELBOURNE

Published by the Syndics of the Cambridge University Press
The Pitt Building, Trumpington Street, Cambridge CB2 1RP
Bentley House, 200 Euston Road, London NW1 2DB
32 East 57th Street, New York, NY 10022, USA
296 Beaconsfield Parade, Middle Park, Melbourne 3206, Australia

First published 1975
Second edition and first published in paperback 1978

Printed in Great Britain
by W & J Mackay Limited, Chatham

Library of Congress Cataloguing in Publication Data

Sagar, Keith M.

The art of Ted Hughes.

Bibliography: p. 246

Includes indexes.

1. Hughes, Ted, 1930– –Criticism and interpretation. I. Title.
PR6058.U37Z87 1978 821'.9'14 77–90217
ISBN 0 521 21954 X hard covers
ISBN 0 521 29321 9 paperback

CONTENTS

ACKNOWLEDGEMENTS

I welcome this opportunity to acknowledge my debt to the following: Walter Stein, Mrs A. Schofield and Michael Black for detailed constructive criticism of the work in progress; Philip Hobsbaum for allowing me to draw on his vast knowledge of Cambridge poetry in the 1950s; Craig Robinson for suggestions for background reading; Gerald Lacy for helping with much of the spadework on the bibliography, particularly the American side; Pat Hughes for help with the proofs and the indexes; and all the students with whom I have studied the work of Ted Hughes. K.S.

The author and publisher are grateful to the following for permission to use copyright material: Faber and Faber Ltd for extensive quotation from the works of Ted Hughes published by them – *The Hawk in the Rain*, © Ted Hughes 1957, *Lupercal*, © Ted Hughes 1960, *Wodwo*, © Ted Hughes 1967, *Crow*, © Ted Hughes 1970, *Selected Poems*, © Ted Hughes 1972, *Season Songs*, © Ted Hughes 1976, *Gaudete*, © Ted Hughes 1977 – as this book went to press Faber announced a trade edition of *Cave Birds* containing both additional poems and extensive revisions to the Scolar Press text; Victor Gollancz Ltd and Curtis Brown Ltd for the Kingsley Amis poem 'Against Romanticism' from *A Case of Samples*; Harper & Row Publishers, Inc. for extensive quotation from the works of Ted Hughes published by them – from *Selected Poems 1957–1967* by Ted Hughes, Copyright © 1972 by Ted Hughes, from *Wodwo* by Ted Hughes, Copyright © 1967 by Ted Hughes, from *Lupercal* by Ted Hughes, Copyright © 1960 by Ted Hughes, from *Crow* by Ted Hughes, Copyright © 1971 by Ted Hughes, from *The Hawk in the Rain* by Ted Hughes, Copyright © 1956, 1957 by Ted Hughes; the poems from *Season Songs* by Ted Hughes, Copyright © 1968, 1973, 1975, by Ted Hughes reprinted by permission of The Viking Press; William Heinemann, Ltd, Laurence Pollinger Ltd, the Estate of the late Mrs Frieda Lawrence and The Viking Press for the D. H. Lawrence poem 'A Living'; lines from 'The Heaven of Animals' (which first appeared in *The New Yorker*), Copyright © 1961 by James Dickey are reprinted from his

Poems 1957–1967 (1968) by permission of Wesleyan University Press and Rapp and Whiting Ltd; Olwyn Hughes for extensive quotation of the Ted Hughes poems published by the Rainbow Press, 100 Chetwynd Road, London NW5 – *Poems: Fainlight, Hughes, Sillitoe*, © Ted Hughes 1971, *Eat Crow*, © Ted Hughes 1971, *Prometheus on His Crag*, © Ted Hughes 1973, and for those published by other private presses, and those not yet collected in book form including 'Where did we go?' (p. 140), 'In the little girl's angel gaze' (pp. 159–60), 'If searching can't find you' (p. 216) and 'A Lucky Folly' (p. 236).

PREFACE TO THE SECOND EDITION

Any study of a living writer, especially one at the height of his powers is bound to be out-of-date before it is published. Works too recent to have been taken into account will have opened up new territory in unforeseen directions. I hope with each edition of this book to bring it as up-to-date as possible.

Since the first edition in 1975, Hughes has published three major books: *Season Songs* (1976), *Gaudete* (1977) and *Cave Birds* (1978). All three represent important new stages in his development, and *Gaudete* is perhaps the summit of his achievement so far. I have added to this edition a chapter on each of these. The final chapter on *Gaudete* is now the most important in the book. I have also made minor revisions in the earlier text, and brought the bibliography into 1978.

Manchester 1978 K.S.

Man is always, all the time and for ever, on the brink of the unknown. The minute you realize this, you prick your ears in alarm. And the minute any man steps alone, with his whole naked self, emotional and mental, into the everlasting hinterland of consciousness, you hate him and you wonder over him. Why can't he stay cosily playing word games around the camp fire.

(D. H. Lawrence)

INTRODUCTION

I began reading Ted Hughes in 1957 when my attention was drawn to *The Hawk in the Rain* by a couple of enthusiastic reviews I happened to see. My admiration grew with each succeeding book. After *Lupercal* I began to teach Hughes; after *Wodwo* to write about him; and after *Crow* to think of him as a major poet of the first rank. His subsequent work, especially *Gaudete*, has confirmed him as the natural successor to the great English poets of the first half of the century, Yeats, Lawrence and Eliot. To have followed his development step by step over twenty years has been one of the richest experiences literature has yet given me. Every step seems bigger than the last, and Hughes may yet have far to go.

Ever since the appearance of *The Hawk in the Rain*, large claims have been made for Ted Hughes. Yet there is still no consensus about his importance, because there is no consensus about the nature, meaning and relative value of his poems. Since this is the first book on him, it must focus primarily on individual poems, all the important or representative ones, trying to take possession of them (or be possessed by them), asking what they are, what they mean, how they relate to each other, to the tradition, to the work of other contemporary and recent writers, to the experience of living in our time or in any time.

F. R. Leavis says of the business of the critic: 'He endeavours to see the poetry of the present as continuation and development; that is, as the decisive, the most significant, contemporary life of tradition' (*Revaluation*, 1–2). Hughes has a vital relationship with tradition. He draws heavily upon it; but he transforms what he draws. And he enters into a dialogue with it, both consciously and unconsciously. It is surely very significant that the set of names one finds oneself continually invoking in response to Hughes' earlier work – Hopkins, Yeats, Lawrence, Wilfred Owen, Dylan Thomas – should be gradually replaced, in reading his later work, by a quite different set – Blake, Kafka, Eliot, Beckett and Vasko Popa. In his latest work there seems to be a further move towards much older influences – folklore, mythology and religion, the Greeks, Shakespeare, Milton – or, it may well be, towards a territory wholly his own which happens to overlap the territory of all great writers who were preoccupied with the problem of man's relation to the powers of the non-human universe. In his very best recent work he seems to move even further back, to the roots and sources of the myths and legends in the depths of the human psyche.

The objectives I have set myself in this book and the standards by which I should like to be judged are finely set out by Eugene Ionesco in 'A Writer's Problems':

> A criticism or an interpretation is good in so far as the interpreter approaches the work freshly, sincerely and objectively, in so far as he is prepared not necessarily to abandon his criteria, but to call them perpetually into question ... The critic who describes the work, to be precise, someone who follows the work following it step by step, throws light on it; this is, in fact, the only way to do so. This is the way to tell whether it is possible to move through the universe of the work; we see where it leads, whether it leads anywhere, whether it contains culs-de-sac or blind alleys, and whether it has a coherence transcending its incoherences and contradictions. To write, also, is to think while in motion; to write is to explore. The critic must repeat the itinerary of the poet. Often the poet has moved forward in a kind of darkness or twilight. The critic covers the same ground with a lamp in his hand and illuminates the path. (*Encounter*, September 1964)

There will be many contradictions or inconsistencies in my interpretations. Partly this will be due to the inadequacy of my own insight, but partly it will be due to the fact that Hughes is not very interested in consistency. He is not attempting to formulate a philosophy or any fixed attitudes towards life. The poems are explorations, 'reconnaissances', bulletins from an internal internecine battleground.

All great writers are mapping unknown lands, that is, bringing more and more of the unknown into consciousness. These maps are then available for later writers. But the great writer will eventually reach a point where the old maps will take him no further. He is on his own. The old maps may even become an encumbrance or begin to divert him from his true path – the path which leads to the centre. They must be jettisoned, with everything else. It is, as P. Strauss has put it, 'a technique of exhaustion':

> It's as though man can only find back to himself after hurling himself up against all the closed doors of the universe, and finally, exhausted, of force having to give up. Hughes shows Crow exhausting all avenues – testing all

the possibilities of illumination, transcendence, freedom, escape, and being rejected by them all – and this has the effect on the reader of a different kind of exhaustion: an exhaustion physical, mental, nervous and emotional. The experience is like having gone through some terrible destructive fight.

His most difficult task is to remove the obstacles, the clichés of thought, feeling and expression to bring himself into a state of full awareness, openness, excitement, concentration. The rest is a gift, but a gift not so uncommon as the emphasis of our education and culture on language as rational discourse has led us to believe.

The gift is partly metaphor:

Metaphor, for the authentic poet, is not a figure of rhetoric but a representative image standing concretely before him in lieu of a concept . . . All one needs in order to be a poet is the ability to have a lively action going on before one continually, to live surrounded by a host of spirits (Nietzsche, *The Birth of Tragedy*).

I believe Hughes to be a great poet because he possesses the kind of imagination which issues in the purest poetry, charged poetry, visionary, revelatory poetry that sees into the life of things, that takes over where all other modes of apprehending reality falter. Words, though controlled up to a point, are allowed to retain a life of their own and express more than the poet consciously knows. His imagination, which draws on his unconscious, on the racial unconscious, on his sixth sense and perhaps innumerable further senses, speaks through him. He is, in a word, 'inspired', though the word is not now fashionable. He performs a function essential to the race, a function analogous to that performed in more 'primitive' cultures by the shaman, whose function is to make the dangerous journey, on behalf of his society, into the spirit world, which is to say, into his own unconscious:

In preparing his trance, the shaman drums, summons his spirit helpers, speaks a 'secret language' or the 'animal language', imitating the cries of beasts and especially the songs of birds. He ends by obtaining a 'second state' that provides the impetus for linguistic creation and the rhythms of lyric poetry. Poetic creation still remains an act of perfect spiritual freedom. Poetry remakes and prolongs language; every poetic language begins by being a secret language, that is, the creation of a personal universe, of a completely closed world. The purest poetic act seems to re-create language from an inner experience that, like the ecstasy or the religious inspiration of 'primitives', reveals the essence of things. It is from such linguistic creations, made possible by pre-ecstatic 'inspiration', that the 'secret languages' of the mystics and the traditional allegorical languages crystallize. (M. Eliade, *Shamanism*, 510–11)

The 'secret language' is partly metaphor; it is also 'the animal language' in the sense that words can communicate as sheer sound beneath their meanings. They can, as Lawrence put it, 'sound upon the plasm direct'. It is the language of another being within us buried much deeper than the repressed self psycho-analysis seeks to let speak; the being Lorca called the *duende* and Castaneda the *nagual*.

> And in fact this other rarely speaks or stirs at all, in the sort of lives we now lead. We have so totally lost touch, that we hardly realise he is absent. All we know is that somehow or other the great, precious thing is missing. And the real distress of our world begins there. The luminous spirit (maybe he is a crowd of spirits), that takes account of everything and gives everything its meaning, is missing. Not missing, just incommunicado. But here and there, it may be, we hear it.
>
> It is human, of course, but it is also everything else that lives. When we hear it, we understand what a strange thing is living in this Universe, and somewhere at the core of us – strange, beautiful, pathetic, terrible. Some animals and birds express this being pure and without effort, and then you hear the whole desolate, final actuality of existence in a voice, a tone. There we really do recognise a spirit, a truth under all the truths. Far beyond human words. And the startling quality of this 'truth' is that it is terrible. It is for some reason harrowing, as well as being this utterly beautiful thing. Once when his spirits were dictating poetic material to Yeats, an owl cried outside the house, and the spirits paused. After a while one said: 'We like that sort of sound.' And that is it: 'that sort of sound' makes the spirits listen. It opens our deepest and innermost ghost to sudden attention. It is a spirit, and it speaks to spirit. ('Orghast: Talking Without Words', *Vogue*, December 1971)

From the beginning Hughes is searching for a way of reconciling human vision with the energies, powers, presences, of the non-human cosmos. At first his main concern is to identify these energies and describe them, not only in human terms but in their own, that is in Nature's terms. And the discrepancy between these two descriptions gives the most powerful of his early poems, for example the hawk and jaguar poems, their characteristic tension. Hughes is also concerned to discover whether negotiations are possible between man and Nature, that is between man and his Creator, and, if so, why they have so completely collapsed in our time and what the consequences of this collapse have been and may yet be. The destructiveness of Nature is so clearly seen and deeply felt that it seems in many of the poems in *Wodwo* and *Crow* that negotiation is impossible, but in some there are hopes and intimations and in most a determination to go on trying. After the descent into destruction he goes forward a step, and a step, and a step. And, slowly, something begins to come clear. The faces of things are transformed and inner meanings revealed. The imagination begins to yield its secrets, and with this renewed vision, neither negotiation nor, indeed, reconciliation seems quite beyond the scope of man.

I am advancing no dogmas about what poetry should be. But it is surely necessary to have in every generation at least one poet who is at the limit, concentrating extraordinary intellectual psychic and linguistic resources on the effort to get clear of all contingencies and explore that territory which only the poetic imagination, in one form or another, can reach. And those who are exclusively concerned with the contingencies and with the civilized human world, and who deny the need for the larger awareness won by the visionaries, have no foundation more substantial than a heap of begged questions.

If we never step back from our 'civilized' life to ask who we are, what life is, what nature, what our necessary connections with the whole non-human world, what ground have we for answering questions about human relationships and practical activities? It is because all the decisions are made without this grounding that we are making the world uninhabitable. Man has long worshipped false gods, and desecrated himself, his fellow men and nature; but it is only now that he has reached the point where his survival is in question.

It is to the great poet, more than anyone else, that we should look for diagnosis and healing, since science, philosophy and religion are all themselves symptoms of the chronic, perhaps terminal condition. And a great poet's work has its greatest value for us the moment it is written, which is, of course, the moment it is least likely to be recognized as such, according to the rule that all great poets are dead poets, or at least senile. It is a critic's greatest responsibility and challenge to evaluate the work of his contemporaries, and reviewers have much to answer for. It would be an unlucky generation which had no great poet ahead of it. What more often happens is that the great gift is delivered, and we are too lazy or afraid to open it.

BEGINNINGS

Edward James Hughes was born on 17 August 1930, in Mytholmroyd, deep in a sodden valley of the Yorkshire Pennines, near the Brontë country.

From the beginning, as he recalls in 'Poetry in the Making', he was fascinated by animals, first collecting toy lead animals until they went right round the fender, then drawing them and modelling them in plasticine, then acting as retriever when his older brother (who was later for a short time a gamekeeper) went shooting magpies, owls, rabbits, weasels, rats and curlews; and finally, and best, capturing them by writing poems about them.

Ted was the youngest of three children. His father, William Hughes, a carpenter, was one of the seventeen men from his entire regiment who returned from the Dardanelles. The boy's imagination was filled with images of Flanders in the First World War (vividly recalled in 'Out') which closely matched those implanted there by his own experience of the bone-strewn moors and the farms which fringed them.

The valley seemed always dark, under the shadow of a huge, almost vertical, looming cliff to the north, a mere corridor between the cotton towns of south Lancashire and the woollen towns of the West Riding, a shadow trap imposing on the growing boy the need to escape, upwards, onto the high moors, exposed and bleak. Hughes' spirit responded to that of the moors 'the peculiar sad desolate spirit that cries in telegraph wires on moor roads, in the dry and so similar voices of grouse and sheep, and the moist voices of curlews'.

Everything in West Yorkshire is slightly unpleasant. Nothing ever quite escapes into happiness. The people are not detached enough from the stone, as if they were only half-born from the earth, and the graves are too near the surface. A disaster seems to hang around in the air there for a long time. I can never escape the impression that the whole region is in mourning for the first world war. The moors don't escape this, but they give the sensation purely. And finally, in spite of it, the mood of moorland is exultant, and this is what I remember of it.

From there the return home was a descent into the pit, and after each visit I must have returned less and less of myself to the valley. This was where the division of body and soul, for me, began. ('The Rock')

This shut-in, in-bred, industrial community of the Calder Valley has bred strong values – dignity and decency, cleanliness and honesty, hard work and thrift, good neighbourliness, solidarity. This shaped Hughes, and he has much to be grateful for. But the opposite side of the coin is stifling respectability, a self-righteous and self-denying puritanism, and an aggressive self-congratulatory materialism and philistinism. Against the realities of work and muck and brass, all intellectual or artistic activity is traditionally scorned as effeminate and wasteful. For a child to use an unfamiliar word in the playground is to risk being mocked for having 'swallowed a dictionary'.

Yet the familiar words were a rich inheritance. The West Riding dialect has remained Hughes' staple poetic speech, concrete, emphatic, terse, yet powerfully, economically, eloquent. It is a speech in which a spade is called a spade; facts are looked in the face, especially the unpleasant facts; and a saving humour is never far from reach to ward off all self-indulgence, evasion or pretentiousness. The regional anthem of the West Riding is a comic song in dialect about a man who catches his death of cold on Ilkley Moor, is buried, eaten by worms, which are eaten by ducks, which are eaten by his mates. The song ends with the grisly pun:

> That's wheer we gets us oan back.

When Hughes was seven, the family moved to Mexborough, in South Yorkshire, where his parents kept a newsagent's and tobacconist's shop until they returned to the Calder Valley in 1952. In Mexborough, like Lawrence before him in a similar area, Hughes was obliged to lead a double life, one with the town boys, sons of miners and railwaymen, the other in his bolt-hole – a nearby farm or a private estate with woods and a lake.

At fifteen he was writing poems, in galloping Kiplingesque rhythms, most of them about Zulus or the Wild West. One of his heroes, Carson McReared the terrible killer, the man with a hide like an armadillo, was 'shot to hell' in the Grand Canyon after shooting 1,200 men,

> And knee deep in blood, where he had to paddle
> Stood Diamond Ace, with an empty saddle.

A succession of perceptive English teachers at Mexborough Grammar School (culminating in John Fisher, who was able to do a great deal for him) fostered his interest in poetry. Before he left school, he had matured to the point where he could write these lovely lines:

> O lady, consider when I shall have lost you
> The moon's full hands, scattering waste,
> The sea's hands, dark from the world's breast,
> The world's decay where the wind's hands have passed,
> And my head, worn out with love, at rest
> In my hands, and my hands full of dust,
> O my lady.
>
> ('Song')

In 1948 Hughes won an Open Exhibition to Cambridge, but before taking it up he did two years of National Service as a ground wireless mechanic in the RAF on an isolated three-man radio station in east Yorkshire where he had 'nothing to do but read and reread Shakespeare and watch the grass grow'.

Hughes went up to Pembroke College, Cambridge, in 1951. His supervisor was M. J. C. Hodgart (an expert, of course, on the ballads) whom he found very sympathetic. He rarely attended lectures, though he occasionally went to hear F. R. Leavis whom he found fascinating and highly entertaining. But the intellectual ethos of Cambridge and of the English tripos in particular he found sterilizing, and wrote no more poetry. Hughes was probably speaking for himself in 'Dully Gumption's Addendum':

> The colleges stooped over him and night after night thereafter
> He dreamed the morphine of his Anglicising:
> Dreamed his tongue uprooted, dreamed his body drawn and quartered
> High over England and saw Thames go crawling from the fragments –
>
> And fell, and lay his own gravestone, which went on all night
> Carving itself in lordly and imperturbable English.
> So he woke numbed.

W. S. Merwin has recorded a remarkable story:

> At Cambridge he set out to study English Literature. Hated it. Groaned having to write those essays. Felt he was dying of it in some essential place. Sweated late at night over the paper on Dr. Johnson et al. – things he didn't want to read. One night, very late, very tired, he went to sleep. Saw the door open and someone like himself come in with a fox's head. The visitor went over to his desk, where an unfinished essay was lying, and put his paw on the papers, leaving a bloody mark; then he came over to the bed, looked down at Ted and said, 'You're killing us,' and went out the door. (Carroll, *The Poem in its Skin*, 149–50)

In his third year Hughes changed from English to Archaeology and Anthropology. His grounding in these disciplines has proved of immense and growing value in his creative work. His imagination is at home in the world of myth and folklore. Cambridge also gave him time to read a great deal.

Hughes graduated in June 1954, the same month in which his first poem appeared in a Cambridge periodical, 'The Little Boys and the Seasons' in *Granta* under the pseudonym Daniel Hearing. It is a pleasing poem, but too much under the influence of Dylan Thomas for the true Hughes to show through. During the next two years Hughes worked briefly as a rose-gardener, night-watchman in a steel works, zoo attendant, schoolteacher, and reader for J. Arthur Rank. Most of the time he lived in London or Cambridge, kept up his friendships there, and published a handful of poems in the Cambridge poetry magazines. In the early and middle fifties Cambridge was rich in budding poets, but the two Hughes poems published in the November 1954 number of *Chequer*, 'The Jaguar' and 'The Casualty', attracted an unusual amount of attention. The jaguar,

> hurrying enraged
> Through prison darkness after the drills of his eyes...

was the first of Hughes' beasts to be captured in all its vivid otherness in a poem. The last two stanzas were originally quite different from the version in *The Hawk in the Rain*. At the end it is the crowd of spectators who stare out through bars at the greater reality,

> But what holds them from corner to corner swinging,
> Swivelling the ball of his heel on the polished spot,
> Jerking his head up in surprise at the bars
> Has not hesitated in the millions of years,
> And like life-prisoners they through bars stare out.

The central impulse of 'The Casualty' is also to lay open the reader to a wider, deeper reality than he is normally aware of. The witnesses

> ... stand, helpless as ghosts: in a scene
> Melting in the August noon, the burned man
> Bulks closer greater flesh and blood than their own ...

Early in 1956 Hughes and some of his friends decided to launch a poetry magazine of their own, the *St Botolph's Review*. The first and only issue contained four poems by Ted Hughes, 'Fallgrief's Girl-friends', 'Law in the Country of Cats', 'Soliloquy of a Misanthrope' and 'Secretary'. The Misanthrope looks forward to death when he will see 'every attitude showing its bone'. But he will 'thank God thrice heartily'

> To be lying beside women who grimace
> Under the commitments of their flesh,
> And not out of spite or vanity.

Fallgrief is this same Misanthrope who, seeking to

> stand naked
> Awake in the pitch dark where the animal runs,

determines to choose 'a muck of a woman' to match 'this muck of man in this Muck of existence', but finds, by chance, 'a woman with such wit and looks He can brag of her in every company'.

At the party held to inaugurate the *St Botolph's Review*, on 25 February 1956, Hughes met Sylvia Plath and within four months he had married her.

Sylvia Plath was a Bostonian, two years younger than Hughes, at Newnham on a Fulbright. She had had an illustrious academic career, both at school and college. Her first published work appeared in 1950 in *Seventeen* and the *Christian Science Monitor*. In 1953 some of her poems were accepted by *Mademoiselle* and by *Harper's*. But between acceptance and publication had come her '6 month crash' – breakdown, attempted suicide, hospitalization – the experience she later recorded in her novel *The Bell Jar*. By 1956, however, her recovery seemed complete. She married Hughes not only because of their mutual attraction and shared commitment to poetry, but also because 'he was very simply the only man I've ever met whom I could never boss . . .' He seemed like a faun to her, able to call owls to him, able to teach her 'the vocabulary of woods and animals and earth'; she felt like 'adam's woman'. (*Letters Home*, 234–8) In May Sylvia wrote to her mother:

> Ted has written many virile, deep banging poems . . . We love the flesh of the earth and the spirit of that thin, exacting air which blows beyond the farthest planets. All is learning, discovering, and speaking in a strong voice out of the heart of sorrow and joy. (*Letters Home*, 248)

His was the stronger, surer poetic voice, and the immediate effect was of ventriloquism. Her 'Spinster', one of the first poems she wrote after their meeting, is a variation on his 'Secretary' and echoes the vocabulary of 'Fallgrief's Girl-friends':

> But here – a burgeoning
> Unruly enough to pitch her five queenly wits
> Into vulgar motley –
> A treason not to be borne. Let idiots
> Reel giddy in bedlam spring:
> She withdrew neatly.

And another poem of that period, 'Strumpet Song', ends with a passage of pure Hughes, the wrenched syntax, the savage consonants, the pounding monosyllables:

> Walks there not some such one man
> As can spare breath
> To patch with brand of love this rank grimace
> Which out from black tarn, ditch and cup
> Into my most chaste own eyes
> Looks up.

Hughes introduced her to the work of John Crowe Ransome, whom he and his friends admired unreservedly at that time, and for a while she adopted a few of his mannerisms. But Sylvia was, on the whole, resistant to influences, and the most important effect Hughes had on her was to increase her concentration on poetry and to supply her with a fully worked out belief in the poetic mythology of Robert Graves' *The White Goddess*.

Sylvia was able to act as a guide to American poetry for Hughes, and he could hardly have had a better one. Apart from Ransome he knew little of it at that time. Also she helped him to get his poems published, sending out beautifully typed manuscripts in a very efficient American way.

That summer of 1956, much of it spent in the Spanish fishing village of Benidorm, they began their remarkable creative partnership. Each had poems accepted by the *Nation*, *Poetry* and the *Atlantic*. Her scholarship was extended for a further year. They took a flat neighbouring Grantchester Meadows. He taught English and drama at a nearby secondary school. They would get up at five in the morning to do their own writing. By the time she graduated and they left for the United States in the spring of 1957, *The Hawk in the Rain* was finished.

THE HAWK IN THE RAIN

Ted writes with color, splendor and vigorous music about love, birth, war, death, animals, hags and vampires, martyrdom, and sophisticated intellectual problems, too. His book can't be typed. It has rugged, violent war poems like 'Bayonet Charge' and 'Griefs for Dead Soldiers', delicate, exquisite nature poems about 'October Dawn' and 'Horses' – powerful animal poems about Macaws, Jaguars, and the lovely Hawk one which appeared in the *Atlantic* and is the title poem of the book. He combines intellect and grace of complex form, with lyrical music, male vigor and vitality, and moral commitment and love and awe of the world. (Sylvia Plath, *Letters Home,* 298)

Early in 1956 the Poetry Centre of the Young Men's and Young Women's Hebrew Association of New York sponsored a competition for a first book of poems in English. The prize was immediate publication by Harper. Hughes would never have dreamed of entering, but Sylvia typed up a manuscript of his pieces and sent it off. There were 287 entries. The judges, W. H. Auden, Stephen Spender and Marianne Moore, chose *The Hawk in the Rain.* In a brief Introduction to the American edition, Marianne Moore wrote: 'Hughes' talent is unmistakable, the work has focus, is aglow with feeling, with conscience; sensibility is awake, embodied in appropriate diction.'

The early fifties had been a thin time for English poetry. Dylan Thomas was dead; Eliot no longer writing poetry. We think of Eliot and Dylan Thomas as at opposite poles – classical and romantic. But what they had in common is far more important than what superficially distinguished them. Each handled the biggest themes he could reach – the relation of man to time, Nature and God; each knew poetry to be a unique language capable of supra-rational insights and more akin to music than to purely rational forms of discourse; each relied heavily on symbolism as the most powerful weapon in poetry's armoury; each assumed the poet to be a privileged being with a god's eye view of the world; each wrote complex, allusive, often obscure poetry with no concessions to the common reader.

The fifties brought a reaction against all this 'pretentiousness', a deflating scepticism. The mood of the post-war poets was best caught in Robert Conquest's 1956 anthology *New Lines.* The poets of the fifties, Conquest claimed, were 'down to earth', rooted in common experience with a reverence for the real person or event; men speaking to men in a manner in which they could hope to be generally understood about matters human, humane and rational. Clearly poetry must not be allowed to disappear into the clouds. Some poets may need someone to hang on to their legs. But isn't this a function for critics rather than other poets? And a man whose feet are on the ground need not fix his eyes upon his feet. Many of the poems in *New Lines* were not rooted in experiences one could feel to be important; they were commonplace. Too many of the poets represented there spoke like common men speaking to common men of common things in common language, all congratulating each other on their refusal to be taken in, aggressively provincial and slangy, disenchanted to the point of affectation. Most disabling was their refusal to handle or even acknowledge a dimension of human experience beyond the merely local and day-to-day. In the words of Charles Tomlinson: 'They show a singular want of vital awareness of the continuum outside themselves, of the mystery embodied over against them in the created universe' (*Essays in Criticism*, April 1957). The anthology, he concluded, testified to 'a total failure of nerve'.

A poem typical of *New Lines* was 'Against Romanticism' by Kingsley Amis, which reads like a prophetic attempt to keep Ted Hughes at bay:

> A traveller who walks a temperate zone
> – Woods devoid of beasts, roads that please the foot –
> Finds that its decent surface grows too thin:
>   Something unperceived fumbles at his nerves.
> To please an ingrown taste for anarchy
>   Torrid images circle in the wood,
> And sweating for recognition up the road,
>   Cramming close the air with their bookish cries.
> All senses then are glad to gasp: the eye
>   Smeared with garish paints, tickled up with ghosts
> That brandish warnings or an abstract noun;
>   Melodies from shards, memories from coal,
> Or saws from powdered tombstones thump the ear...
>   Over all, a grand meaning fills the scene,
> And sets the brain raging with prophesy...

Hughes was younger than any of the contributors to *New Lines*, on average by several years. With the exception of Thom Gunn, who was already famous at university and whose poems Hughes greatly liked, he was quite unaware of them, wrapped up as he was in the exclusive world of *The White Goddess*.

They had come to maturity during the war, and that, perhaps, had something to do with the sense one gets from so much of *New Lines*, of having had enough of the big themes of Nature and metaphysics. Philip Larkin records no 'Blinding theologies of flowers and fruits' ('I Remember, I Remember'), and Kingsley Amis asks:

> Why drag in
> All that water and stone?
> Scream the place down *here*,
> There's nobody *there*.
> ('Here is Where')

Hughes, on the other hand, had not had enough:

> I was all for opening negotiations with whatever happened to be out there.
> (*London Magazine*, January 1971)

It might seem then, if Conquest was right, that the time was unpropitious for *The Hawk in the Rain*. But, in the event, the reviewers, in the words of Calvin Bedient, 'flocked to the book like ghosts to a pit of blood'. Here was no deficiency of force, rather a superabundance. The poems crackle with surplus energy. The words leap off the page to strike or grapple the reader. Even the most grotesquely exaggerated poems are inordinately there, and alive.

Hughes is a master of hyperbole. Hyperbole is deliberate exaggeration, not intended to be taken literally, to express strong feeling or make a strong impression. It is as essential to poetry as metaphor, and is responsible for the power of many of the most admired passages of English poetry, particularly in the sixteenth and seventeenth centuries. Its rarity in the twentieth is part of the failure of nerve. The metaphysical conceit is both metaphor and hyperbole. The first lines of the first poem in Hughes' first book plunge us into hyperbolic verse of a kind scarcely heard since Marvell:

> I drown in the drumming ploughland, I drag up
> Heel after heel from the swallowing of the earth's mouth,
> From clay that clutches my each step to the ankle
> With the habit of the dogged grave...

Here the exaggeration in the description of a man through mud seems to generate its own conceit: the ea habituated to its primary relationship with man – his grav it knows no reason to wait for him to die, but is, from th hungry for him, pulling him down with a force stronge gravity – mortality. Yet so closely does the language mime the physical experience of dragging across a ploughed field in a rainstorm that we are hardly aware of it becoming either hyperbole or metaphor until it is too late to resist.[1]

'The Hawk in the Rain' stands appropriately at the threshold of the book, for it announces the major themes – man in relation to the animals, the earth, the weather, time and mortality. As in many poems by Hopkins the imagination is hauled from the depths to the heights, from pole to pole, in this case from the turbulent circumference to the still centre. The 'I' of the poem, the narrator, is completely overwhelmed by the elements. He flounders like one drowning at sea, or struggles like the prey already in the predator's mouth. In contrast the hawk effortlessly rides the storm:

> His wings hold all creation in a weightless quiet,
> Steady as a hallucination in the streaming air.

The man envies the hawk its apparent centrality and poise. It is so different in its steadiness from the streaming chaos around it that it looks like a hallucination. In fact it is the only reality:

> For it is the break effected in space that allows the world to be constituted, because it reveals the fixed point, the central axis for all future orientation. When the sacred manifests itself in any hierophany, there is not only a break in the homogeneity of space; there is also revelation of an absolute reality, opposed to the nonreality of the vast surrounding expanse. The manifestation of the sacred ontologically founds the world. In the homogeneous and infinite expanse, in which no point of reference is possible and hence no *orientation* can be established, the hierophany reveals an absolute fixed point, a centre.
> (Eliade, *The Sacred and the Profane*, 21)

It is only by such a 'master-fulcrum' that man, swimming for dear life in the ocean of time and mortality, can take his spiritual bearings.

The 'eye' of the hawk hangs as still as a polestar, at the eye of the storm, the still centre round which all that violence threshes. The poet's eyes are his most vulnerable part, thumbed by wind and rain, but the hawk's eye seems as impervious as immortal diamond. It is always the eye at which Hughes stares, from this hawk right through to Crow. The jaguar hurries 'after the drills of his eyes'; the macaw 'suffers the stoking devils of his eyes'; the thought-fox is 'an eye' –

> A widening deepening greenness,
> Brilliantly, concentratedly,
> Coming about its own business...

The eye is the 'I', the window of the soul, the outward expression of the hawk's innermost being, its unquestionable identity, its concentrated, inflexible purpose.

To the man, all too conscious of his own relativity, the hawk appears as an absolute, inviolable. We know that the hawk will ultimately die and enter the same grave as the man, 'the mire of the land'. The difference is that the hawk's time is up only by an internal clock. He does what he is programmed to do. Even as he plummets to a last suicidal kill, he believes that, by relaxing his will, he has let the earth fall upon his head.

> That maybe in his own time meets the weather
>
> Coming the wrong way, suffers the air, hurled upside down,
> Fall from his eye, the ponderous shires crash on him,
> The horizon trap him; the round angelic eye
> Smashed, mix his heart's blood with the mire of the land.

To die in your own time and your own way and without knowledge of death as a violation, but simply as the next of the programmed instructions from life, is, relative to man, to be free of it. Or, as Yeats put it:

> Nor dread nor hope attend
> A dying animal;
> A man awaits his end
> Dreading and hoping all...
> Man has created death.
> ('Death')

The images of inviolability – diamond, polestar, master-fulcrum – culminate in that of 'the round angelic eye'. There is a strikingly relevant passage in Yeats' *A Vision*:

> Even the drilled pupil of the eye, when the drill is in the hand of some Byzantine worker in ivory, undergoes a somnambulistic change, for its deep shadow among the faint lines of the tablet, its mechanical circle, where all else is rhythmical and flowing, give to Saint or Angel a look of some great bird staring at miracle.

Angels in Hughes are always staring and unseeing.[2] 'Angelic' suggests not only inviolability but also purity and innocence. But we know that the hawk's eye is rounded the better to see distant prey, so that the phrase becomes a paradox like Yeats' 'the murderous innocence of the sea'. The paradox is extended by 'smashed' – angels have no blood to spill.

What is unambiguous is the totally non-human vision of the hawk. 'Angelic' suggests that it is a superhuman vision seeing through life and death – staring at miracle. But it could equally be an inferior vision, the superior poise possible only through sheer ignorance or madness, so that what the man sees as absolute and enviable is only, after all, a 'hallucination'. In the very next poem the jaguar's eye is 'satisfied to be blind in fire'.

The poem owes a great deal, as we have seen, to Yeats, Hopkins and Dylan Thomas, and this is perhaps why Hughes has not included it in his *Selected Poems*. But it seems to me that he has succeeded in making a thoroughly Hughes poem, an expression of his distinct feel for life. No one else could have written it. A poet has no obligation to be an original thinker. The war between vitality and death goes on. There will always be a need for reporters to go to that front line.

It did not occur to any of the reviewers to discuss Hughes as an 'animal poet'. There are only five animal poems, the first five, in *The Hawk in the Rain*. Of these 'The Thought-Fox', however vividly present in the poem the fox may be, is purely metaphorical. 'The Hawk in the Rain' and 'The Horses' are both primarily about the 'I', the narrator. The macaw is simply an image of what the Little Miss and her grandmother have done to the principle of maleness. Which leaves 'The Jaguar' as the nearest thing to an orthodox 'animal poem', but we find that the phrase fits it about as well as it fits Blake's 'Tyger':

> a jaguar hurrying enraged
> Through prison darkness after the drills of his eyes
>
> On a short fierce fuse. Not in boredom –
> The eye satisfied to be blind in fire,
> By the bang of blood in the brain deaf the ear –
> He spins from the bars, but there's no cage to him
>
> More than to the visionary his cell:
> His stride is wildernesses of freedom:
> The world rolls under the long thrust of his heel.
> Over the cage floor the horizons come.

The jaguar is enraged not only because he is caged, but because Nature has set him on this terrible treadmill, turning the world beneath his stride, following the drills of his eyes, blinded by the fire of his eyes, deafened by the beating of his own heart, with the fearful symmetry of some machine forged in furnace and on anvil, and with no more freedom than a machine, whether in prison darkness or the forests of the night. Or with the total freedom of a machine which is so self-contained that it cannot be imprisoned. The poem has it both ways. Either way this machine cannot be switched off, cannot be disconnected from the power source as man was disconnected at the Fall for the sake of that other freedom, the freedom to eat of the fruit of the tree of knowledge, knowledge (as Lawrence puts it) of the self-apart-from-God.

By invoking the jaguar the poet invokes also the God (or Goddess, or demon) of the machine:

> A jaguar after all can be received in several different aspects...he is a beautiful, powerful nature spirit, he is a homicidal maniac, he is a supercharged piece of cosmic machinery, he is a symbol of man's baser nature shoved down into the id and growing cannibal murderous with deprivation, he is an ancient symbol of Dionysus since he is a leopard raised to the ninth power, he is a precise historical symbol to the bloody-minded Aztecs and so on. Or he is simply a demon...a lump of ectoplasm. A lump of astral energy. The symbol opens all these things...it is the reader's own nature that selects.
>
> (*London Magazine*, January 1971)

And it is the poet's task, having invoked all these feelings and energies, to try to 'resolve the whole uproar into as formal and balanced a figure of melody and rhythm' as he can.

All great poetry is inspired; which is only another way of saying that it is a product of the imagination, not the intellect, though the imagination draws freely upon the intellect as it draws upon every other human faculty, and is subject, afterwards, to the judgement and ordering of the intellect.

In *Poetry in the Making*, the best book I know about the writing (and reading) of poetry in schools, Hughes compares writing poems to capturing animals:

> The special kind of excitement, the slightly mesmerized and quite involuntary concentration with which you make out the stirrings of a new poem in your mind, then the outline, the mass and colour and clear final form of it, the unique living reality of it in the midst of the general lifelessness, all that is too familiar to mistake. This is hunting and the poem is a new species of creature, a new specimen of the life outside your own. (17)

The secret is to 'imagine what you are writing about. See it and live it.... Just look at it, touch it, smell it, listen to it, turn yourself into it. When you do this, the words look after themselves, like magic.' Thus you breathe your own life into the poem, whose words, images and rhythms 'jump to life as you read them'.

Most Hughes poems testify to the efficacy of this ancient magic. 'The Thought-Fox' is both a description of the process and a splendid example of it. The language mimes in sound and rhythm what it describes:

> Cold, delicately as the dark snow,
> A fox's nose touches twig, leaf;
> Two eyes serve a movement, that now
> And again now, and now, and now
>
> Sets neat prints into the snow
> Between trees, and warily a lame
> Shadow lags by stump and in hollow...

The delicacy is there in those light consonants – *d*s and *t*s and *f*s, and in the tentative rhythm of that second line. The poem has already set neat prints upon the page in the line before we are told that the fox sets them into the snow. The noun 'shadow' has to drag itself across that gap between the lines which separates it from its adjective. And the alliteration of 'lame' and 'lag' upon a long palatal consonant mimes the meaning to a degree which becomes obvious if we try to find a substitute for either word.

The poem is about writing a poem, about poetic inspiration, not about a fox at all. But the blank page is like a snowy clearing in the middle of a dark forest inhabited by 'things which have a vivid life of their own, outside mine'. The marks he makes on his paper as he records himself imagining this remind him of footprints in snow moving more and more boldly towards him. Suddenly, out of the unknown, there it is, with all the characteristics of a living thing – 'a sudden sharp hot stink of fox'. A simple trick, like pulling a kicking rabbit from a hat, but only a true poet can do it: 'And I suppose that long after I am gone, as long as a copy of the poem exists, every time anyone reads it the fox will get up somewhere out in the darkness and come walking towards them' (20).

Not all Hughes' animal poems are about predators. But his horses share with his hawk their stillness and their trust in nature, even in its most extreme manifestations. 'The Horses' begins with the world, an hour before dawn, 'cast in frost', 'A horse sheltering from the rain', says Hughes in 'The Rain Horse', 'generally goes into a sort of stupor, tilts a hind hoof and hangs its head and lets its eyelids droop, and so it stays as long as the rain lasts.' These horses have gone into just such a stupor against the cold, 'with draped manes and tilted hind-hooves' 'megalith-still', as though they had never moved and never would, with the invulnerability of huge stones.

From the ridge of the moor the narrator watches the dawn:

> Then the sun
> Orange, red, red erupted
>
> Silently, and splitting to its core tore and flung cloud,
> Shook the gulf open, showed blue,
>
> And the big planets hanging –

then stumbles away 'in the fever of a dream'.

If we have responded fully to the language of that description – 'red erupted', 'splitting to its core', 'tore and flung', 'shook open', all this done to the grey sky and about to be done to the grey world (the tops already kindling, the frost showing its fires, the stone horses stirring) – we can feel what might be done to a mere flesh and blood man exposed to such extremes, to such 'red levelling rays'.

> Dazzling and tremendous how quick the sun-rise would kill me

wrote Whitman,

> If I could not now and always send sun-rise out of me.
> ('Song of Myself', 25)

But Whitman is speaking for Nature herself. Hughes speaks for mortal man all too aware of the lack of anything in himself to set against the sun-rise. In him is no fire, but only a fever. The word has many strong associations for us: 'Life's fitful fever', 'the weariness, the fever and the fret'. . . He hopes that the memory of these patient all-suffering horses will sustain him, teach him patience, as he finds himself again caught up in the busy time-conscious world of men.

The poem is Hughes' most Wordsworthian. 'Resolution and Independence' is its model. That poem too begins with the evocation of a sun-rise and of all the creatures which seem to be at one with it. But Wordsworth thinks only of the years to come, of

> Solitude, pain of heart, distress and poverty

madness and death. At this moment he comes upon the Leech-gatherer on the moor, an old man who seems, like the horses, to be in a 'sort of stupor' – 'not all alive nor dead, nor all asleep'. His stillness immediately reminds the poet of 'a huge Stone'

> Couch'd on the bald top of an eminence.

He seems like one met with in a dream. Wordsworth's poem ends in trite banality:

> 'God', said I, 'be my help and stay secure;
> I'll think of the Leech-gatherer on the lonely moor.'

And Hughes' ending

> May I still meet my memory in so lonely a place

though less tritely phrased, is almost as banal in sentiment, and sadly lets the poem down.

Hughes sees human beings as predatory not so much when they fight or kill as when they love. *The Hawk in the Rain* moves straight from animals to lovers. Men and women given over to desire are, almost by definition, incompatibilities:

> Each, each second, lonelier and further
> Falling alone through the endless
> Without-world of the other, though both here
> Twist so close they choke their cries.
> ('Incompatibilities')

To possess the other wholly, to penetrate to the very 'star that lights the face' (if that were possible), the innermost selfhood and integrity of the other, would be to extinguish that star. This kind of love is hardly to be distinguished from hate. Such love released is fire and flood, a hawk in a dovecote.

'The Dove-Breeder' had devoted his life to breeding and showing fantails and pouters (the very names suggest the spite and vanity of women, rejected by the rude Misanthrope of the previous poem). His doves are his carefully cultivated, perfected attitudes and complacencies which enable him to be so mild-mannered. He has known, perhaps, gentle affections, but has never been driven by the desperation which is love. Love, the raider, makes his well-groomed attitudes show their bones. But the dove-breeder does not then go to the opposite extreme and walk the town naked as the truth:

> Now he rides the morning mist
> With a big-eyed hawk on his fist.

He does not allow himself to become hawklike. He neither rejects the hawk nor surrenders to it. He trains it. He canalizes its violence into the controlled, civilized, ritualized activity of falconry.

We see the same process again in 'A Modest Proposal'. Here the lovers are like two wolves rending each other in their obsessive rivalry to possess each other, each rent showing 'the red smelting of hatred'.

> Suddenly they duck and peer.
> And there rides by
> The great lord from hunting. His embroidered
> Cloak floats, the tail of his horse pours,
> And at his stirrup the two great-eyed greyhounds
> That day after day bring down the towering stag
> Leap like one, making delighted sounds.

These beautiful measured lines, with all the stateliness of a medieval tapestry brought to life, are not what we have come to expect from Hughes. Suddenly the violence gives way to grace, the claustrophobia, heat and darkness of the thicket, to cool air, light and space. The two greyhounds embody what the wolves can hardly conceive, a relationship of absolute concord. The wolves for fear of each other are unable to hunt, and therefore to live. The greyhounds, in partnership, bring down the towering stag every day. Their freedom is a condition of their service to the great lord to whose leash of love they submit. He has tamed them, not by violating them, but by releasing creative energies through the discipline of co-operation and respect and ceremony. The embroidery, the stylization, the flourishes, are all part of the evocation of a life lived by a high chivalric code, all air, pride and plume.

The modest proposal of the title is, perhaps, the lover's proposal that they should try to become the greyhounds of his story, not the wolves, by submitting their desire ('a vicious separator') to the yoke and leash of marriage.

The belief that violent energies might be controlled and diverted into creative channels by ceremony is not one we find again in Hughes after 'The Dove-Breeder' and 'A Modest Proposal'. The insistence that every attitude must show its bone takes over.

But here Hughes seems equally drawn to the lover who says

> Love you I do not say I do or might either.
> I come to you enforcedly –
> ('Billet-Doux')

and the more courtly lover who makes his modest proposal of marriage.

The destructive/creative 'love' of these poems is not only the love of man and woman; it is also the relationship between the poet and his Muse:

> The poet is in love with the White Goddess, with Truth: his heart breaks with longing and love for her. She is the Flower-goddess Olwen or Blodeuwedd; but she is also Blodeuwedd the Owl, lamp-eyed, hooting dismally, with her foul nest in the hollow of a dead tree, or Circe the pitiless falcon, or Lamia with her flickering tongue, or the snarling-chopped Sow-goddess, or the mare-headed Rhiannon who feeds on raw flesh. Odi atque amo: 'to be in love with' is also to hate. (Graves, *The White Goddess*, 448)

The poems in the middle of the volume, 'Egg-Head' and 'The Man Seeking Experience Enquires his Way of a Drop of Water', are more overt in their metaphysic than the rest. 'Egg-Head' is a savage frontal attack on man's complacency and pride. The title refers not only to intellectuals, but to all men, for every man's brain is protected from 'the flash of the sun, the bolt of the earth' by a skull as fragile, in relation to those forces, as an egg-shell. Many men, heroes and poets, have taken the terrible risk of exposing their sense to the outside world:

> A leaf's otherness,
> The whaled monstered sea-bottom, eagled peaks
> And stars that hang over hurtling endlessness,
> With manslaughtering shocks
>
> Are let in on his sense:
> So many a one has dared to be struck dead
> Peeping through his fingers at the world's ends,
> Or at an ant's head.

Many have not dared, but have set out to wall in the brain, to seal up the senses, deliberately to blind, deafen and numb themselves, until the skull becomes a monad, a sealed world, feeding upon itself and feeling safe. It is not this Hughes derides. Man cannot help his 'dew-drop frailty'. What angers him is that such a creature, far from recognizing his frailty and peeping through his fingers if he dares to peep at all, sets himself up as master of the world, brags and preens, thinks to defeat mortality itself ('the looming mouth of the earth') with his tiny skull, his nonentity, his petty calculations:

> Spurn it muck under
> His foot-clutch, and, opposing his eye's flea-red
> Fly-catching fervency to the whelm of the sun,
> Trumpet his own ear dead.

Unfortunately, the poem itself stupefies us with its sleights of syntax, benumbs us with its insistence, and deafens us with its trumpeting, so that the many incidental felicities are almost lost in the clamour. The language works mainly as a loud-hailer. What I tell you loudly enough is true! The meaning remains what could have been put in plain prose; was, in fact, put in plain prose by Shakespeare's Lafeu:

> They say miracles are past; and we have our philosophical persons to make modern and familiar things supernatural and causeless. Hence it is that we make trifles of terrors, ensconcing ourselves into seeming knowledge when we should submit ourselves to an unknown fear.
>
> (*All's Well That Ends Well*, III, ii)

'The Man Seeking Experience' is a much better poem. This man is the opposite of the egg-head, knowing himself 'all droplet kin', composed largely of water whose history is much the same as that of the drop he addresses, and containing within himself the accumulated experience of the race.

Every drop of water in the world contains water which has been through every possible experience and has existed in some form or other since the world began. The drop which has just condensed on his kitchen wall is thus an 'ancient eye' which has seen all

> and there is no place
> His bright look has not bettered, and problem none
> But he has brought it to solution.

That last pun betrays him. The man's mistake is in assuming that such experience results in wisdom (or at least knowledge) which can be expressed in language. But the droplet has solved no problems, merely dissolved them. The droplet has been changed by experience not in the least:

> This droplet was clear simple water still.

His grand address is as lost upon it as upon a new-born baby.

> Unconscious under the shock of its own quick,
> After that first alone-in-creation cry
> When into the mesh of sense, out of the dark,
> Blundered the world-shouldering monstrous 'I'.

The droplet too is utterly self-contained and always new-born as what it always was – 'clear simple water'. Every new birth removes the skull for a moment from the egg-shell head, exposing 'the yolk's dark and hush' in all its 'dewdrop frailty' to an earth-staggering shock, a bolt from the blue, a descent of angels.

The man wants 'a plain lesson', the Word of God spelled out. Experience will never yield him that.

This poem has all the qualities its predecessor lacks. It is clear, coherent, progressive, powerful, varied and delicately handled in tone. No prose account could match this poetic evocation of the droplet's chequered history or of the miracle of birth (already that phrase has reduced it to cliché). In this little drama, this dialogue of one, Hughes finds a perfect objective correlative for his theme, an object and a situation to give it body and life. Yet if we compare this poem with 'How Water Began to Play' in *Crow* we will see how far Hughes has come since *The Hawk in The Rain.*

'Meeting' is essentially a much better version of 'Egg-Head'. But here the bragging, preening solipsist, instead of being merely subjected to Hughes' abuse, is exposed for a moment to the 'hurtling endlessness' of the universe, seen in the eye of a black goat. In 'Meeting' the man is content to think himself the measure of the universe. His image in a mirror seems to him that of Faustus, a demi-god to whom the secrets of the universe are an open book. So blind is he to 'the whelm of the sun' that 'the whole sun-swung zodiac of light' is no bigger to him than a trinket, the dazzling and tremendous sun-rise as nothing compared to 'the rise of his eye'. His arrogant eye reduces the world to the point where he can feel himself to be gigantic, a Gulliver in Lilliput, until the day when

> A black goat clattered and ran
> Towards him, and set forefeet firm on a rock
> Above and looked down
> A square-pupilled yellow-eyed look,
> The black devil head against the blue air . . .

Nature confronts him in the form of a goat in whose utterly non-human eye he sees himself reduced to his real insignificance and frailty, like Gulliver in Brobdignag, in a giant hand under an eye like a huge sun, but cold as a star, the eye of some god or demon who has his fate in its hands.

> What gigantic fingers took
> Him up and on a bare
> Palm turned him close under an eye
> That was like a living hanging hemisphere . . .

He might well have cried like Faustus:

> O soul, be changed into little water-drops,
> And fall into the ocean – ne'er be found.

The whole meeting with the goat, occupying some fourteen lines, is one sentence which accumulates great power without in the least straining for it, using so many monosyllables that the longer word, when it comes, has tremendous impact:

> And watched his blood's gleam with a ray
> Slow and cold and ferocious as a star . . .

The poem makes no attempt to interpret the man's experience. The matter-of-fact last line

> Till the goat clattered away

trusts the poem to have done enough to make further comment superfluous. Hughes' rhetoric is impressive; but he is even more impressive when, as here, he generates equal or even greater power without it.

In the best poems in *The Hawk in the Rain* we find a language characterized by its faithfulness to the facts, the evidence of the senses, shaped by a strong inspiration into images which, like those of Henry Moore, seem to have been waiting for aeons within the living rock, the living language, and now, released, will stand for aeons and could not be otherwise. It is a language spiced with great relish for experience, even when that experience is unpleasant or horrifying. Most distinctively it is a language able to cope with the biggest things; it can generate energies equal to the great primary energies of the world. In 'October Dawn' it is the irresistible coming of winter. 'October is marigold'. (Mari is the goddess of fruitfulness.) October is rich and mellow, but vulnerable as a solitary flower when the whole 'whistling green shrubbery' is doomed. Wine, that distillation of autumn's superflux, left outside by careless evening revellers, dreams 'a premonition of ice across its eye':

First a skin, delicately here
Restraining a ripple from the air;

Soon plate and rivet on pond and brook;
Then tons of chain and massive lock

To hold rivers. Then, sound by sight
Will Mammoth and Sabre-tooth celebrate

Reunion while a fist of cold
Squeezes the fire at the core of the world,

Squeezes the fire at the core of the heart,
And now it is about to start.

We know it is 'only' winter, but perhaps each winter is Nature flexing its muscles, rehearsing for the next ice-age. Whatever reunion was celebrated here last night, we know that humanity is doomed ultimately to hand back these lawns and shrubberies to creatures of the great cold. But it is not in these dramatic mammoths and sabre-tooths that the poem's power lies so much as in that relentless rhythm, that ruthless march of monosyllables, and the stark finality of that last full rhyme after so many half-rhymes. And all that weight falling on the word 'start'! No one since Hopkins had used rhythm and rhyme so powerfully.

This is a language uniquely fitted to express a 'vital awareness of the continuum' outside human life, of the mystery embodied in the created universe. The mystery takes many forms. There is no mistaking it when it takes the form of a gale. A house is a place of refuge, keeping out the elements, creating a sheltered environment where man can pursue his civilized activities undisturbed. A man's house is his impregnable castle. The earth under his feet, terra firma, is the most solid, stable, permanent thing he knows, a sure foundation of eternal rock. In 'Wind' this security of houses and hills is without warning pulled from under our feet.

This house has been far out at sea all night,
The woods crashing through darkness, the booming hills,
Winds stampeding the fields under the window
Floundering black astride and blinding wet

Till day rose

The first stanza is a description of a storm-tossed ship at sea, but the ship is this house, the sea these crashing woods, booming hills and stampeding fields. The hills, so much more immovable than the house built of their stones, seem as flimsy as a flapping tent held by one guyrope.

The fields quivering, the skyline a grimace,
At any second to bang and vanish with a flap:
The wind flung a magpie away and a black-
Back gull bent like an iron bar slowly.

The wind has the strength to dent eyeballs, bend iron bars. It can shatter the house, it would seem, by sound alone.

Within the house, how can the occupants, their security gone, hearing those 'wandering elementals' outside, continue with their civilized and complacent reading, thinking and conversation.

Now deep
In chairs, in front of the great fire, we grip
Our hearts and cannot entertain book, thought,

Or each other. We watch the fire blazing,
And feel the roots of the house move, but sit on,
Seeing the window tremble to come in,
Hearing the stones cry out under the horizons.

They can only grip their hearts, hold desperately onto their integrity which is under siege. If the window gave and the wind came in, the whole charade of civilization would be swept away.[3]

The wind is representative of all those natural forces we try to shut out of our lives, which, if let in on our sense would leave us blind, floundering or mad. The wind is

Flexing like the lens of a mad eye

and the window 'trembles' to come in. A window is, etymologically, the wind's eye. The eye we think of as the window of the soul. The window is like a delicate membrane holding back

The huge-eyed looming horde from
Under the floor of the heart, that run
To the madman's eye-corner...
('Childbirth')

holding back demons, dark, anarchic forces which inhabit what we prefer to think of as the safely locked cellar of the unconscious.[4]

Hughes was only fifteen when the war ended. His knowledge of war derived almost entirely from his father's stories and the poems of Wilfred Owen, which is why his war poems all feel like the First World War. 'Bayonet Charge' is good imitation Owen. The second stanza generates deliberate, controlled formulations of a kind we are to grow familiar with in mature Hughes:

He was running
Like a man who has jumped up in the dark and runs
Listening between his footfalls for the reason
Of his still running...

But there is that false note of the 'patriotic tear' in the first stanza to which he returns in the last; and he doesn't know how to finish the poem, or rather, how to go through with it, as Owen would have done. To compare it with Owen at his best, as in 'Spring Offensive', is to recognize it as falling short of that deeper poetry of Owen's which is in the pity.[5]

Hughes is much better when he writes of war from a distance, when he writes of what we at home make of death in war when we are forced to confront it, either at the time or long after. 'Griefs for Dead Soldiers' is in three parts, each expressing a different form of grief. The mightiest grief is the public grief expressed at the unveiling of a cenotaph. Part I has the sonority and large gestures which are the order of the day. It resembles many another poem which might be spoken by some VIP on Remembrance Day – Binyon's 'For the Fallen', for example:

Solemn the drums thrill: Death august and royal
Sings sorrow up into immortal spheres.
There is music in the midst of desolation
And a glory that shines upon our tears.

'For the Fallen' is a tissue of lies and sentimentality and portentousness. There is nothing so blatant in Hughes' handling of the public grief, but one becomes uneasily aware that the large gestures are dwarfing or replacing the actual deaths. If the mere unveiling ceremony is like a 'cataclysm', an end-of-the-world 'terror', a 'monstrousness', what were the actual deaths like? There is a disproportion between the thin bugle, the 'dead drum tap', the marching and the shouting, all 'blown about by the wind', and the sheer size and weight of what, in theory, is being constructed, a block of stone which will

Make these dead magnificent, their souls
Scrolled and supporting the sky, and the national sorrow...

Between these extremes of air and stone, mere flesh is overlooked, discarded. This magnificent grief which so quickly transforms itself into stirring affirmations of

Permanent stupendous victory

is part of the process whereby the nation promises to remember for one day a year in order to be able to forget with a clear conscience for the other three hundred and sixty-four; the process whereby the nation accepts with pride the slaughter of a whole generation of its youth. The rhetoric of the cenotaph ceremony is a continuance in solemn guise of the lying jingoism which prompted Wilfred Owen to write three months before his death: 'I wish the Boche would have the pluck to come right in and make a clean sweep of the pleasure boats, and the promenaders on the spa, and all the stinking Leeds and Bradford war-profiteers now reading John Bull on Scarborough sands.' The bitterness of that prose is clearly absent from this poem. The disproportion is detectable, but many readers will still be able to take the poem at its face value. Its inadequacy only becomes evident when we pass on to the other, truer, griefs.

The smallest, most secret grief is that of the lonely widow:

> She cannot build her sorrow into a monument
> And walk away from it.

Yet even hers is not the truest grief. Her sorrow is for the severing of their love. She grieves for the smashing of her world, not, purely, of his body. She never sees or imagines the smashed body. Her greatest horror is watching her own hands, automatic, numb with apprehension, opening the telegram. Her grief is private grief, true for herself alone.

There remains the truest grief, and the only grief which does justice to the dead by confronting the bald reality of their deaths:

> thud of another body flung
> Down, the jolted shape of a face, earth into the mouth

Here grief can be measured by its exact weight in corpse-flesh and calmly buried. There are no flags and trumpets, no monuments, yet the sight 'could annihilate a watcher'. Perhaps the poem fails, at this point, quite to substantiate that horror. The reader has to imagine for himself why he would find that moment annihilating. Hughes needs a whole poem to develop his thought. That poem is 'Six Young Men'.

In Parts II and III of 'Griefs for Dead Soldiers' Hughes shows that he is not dependent on sound and fury, on exaggeration and strenuous muscular language. The image of the telegram 'opening of its own accord' really is more terrible by far than that of a bomb 'that dives to the cellar and lifts the house'. Gradually Hughes is to gain confidence in the just style as sometimes truer than the mightiest.

In his Introduction to the *Selected Poems of Keith Douglas*, Hughes wrote of the truth which kills everybody:

> The truth of a man is the doomed man in him or his dead body....The murderous skeleton in the body of a girl, the dead men being eaten by dogs on the moonlit desert, the dead man behind the mirror, these items of circumstantial evidence are steadily out-arguing all his high spirits and hopefulness.

In 'Six Young Men' Hughes adds his own evidence, a photograph of his father's, six young men on a Sunday jaunt, each as alive as any man you can confront

> And shake by the hand, see hale, hear speak loud.

Yet they all died within six months and forty years ago.

> To regard this photograph might well dement,
> Such contradictory permanent horrors here
> Smile from the single exposure and shoulder out
> One's own body from its instant and heat.

'Exposure' is a perfectly chosen word. The camera which cannot lie exposed them as forever alive and young. Six months later they were exposed to the horrors of war which exposed their bones. And one's own vivid life, for all its bulk and weight, is equally flimsy. We are no more alive than they were, than, here in this photograph, they still are, as by a bilberried bank, a thick tree, a black wall 'which are there yet and not changed' they listen to the waterfall that roars yet in that valley. Yet we know that they are as dead as dinosaur or dodo, dead and rotten. If I have my photograph taken today, someone will look at it forty years hence and be looking at the photograph of a dead man. It is like seeing one's own tombstone, like becoming aware of one's own skeleton which will one day shrug off its flesh.

War, childbirth, the weather, love, and animals, are Hughes' chosen themes here because they all afford us, whether as participants or witnesses, moments of contact with a deeper reality than that we normally inhabit, with a dimension of existence where life is not insulated against the vast currents of energy which flow and drive everywhere in the non-human world: 'Any form of violence – any form of vehement activity – invokes the bigger energy, the elemental power circuit of the Universe' (*London Magazine*, January 1971).

Such experiences don't have to be 'galvanized into the improbable' as one critic put it; they are already, if we can be made to confront them, miracles, manifestations of forces we do not in the least understand or control, which can destroy us, mind or body, in a flash.

At the moment of childbirth, for example,

> The commonplace became so strange
>
> There was not looking at the table or chair:
> Miracle struck out the brain
> Of order and ordinary...
>
> ('Childbirth')

The opening through which a new life can come, that breach in the barrier between being and not-being, he imagines as death's door through which all the dead might have got back from their underworld 'under the floor of the heart'. It is as though all barriers were, for a moment, down, all strongholds breached, the whole world let in upon the sense as though the skull had been removed. All to let one child pass through into this life out of the dark. One would have thought some monster had shouldered the earth out of its path. Perhaps each

> Frowning ten-toed ten-fingered birth

is monstrous in its assumption of arrogant selfhood as its birthright.

> This six-day abortion of the Absolute

he is later to call Man –

> This monstrous-headed difficult child!
> ('The Perfect Forms')

To watch an animal, particularly a predator, about its business; to watch a pair of lovers, or a woman in labour, or a man dead, dying, or at great risk, is, clearly, to be a watcher of violence, but not a voyeur. Hughes watches, and makes us watch, such violence, not for frisson, but for estrangement. He wants to undermine our sense of the ordinary and let in a sense of the miraculous, a shock of recognition of ourselves as animals, as killers, as newborn babies or as corpses. If the violence we are made to confront is reality, or even a fundamental part of it, then the reality most of us think we inhabit must be relatively or wholly unreal. For Hughes, the poet cannot see too much or experience too much. He tries to find 'words that live in the same dimension as life at its most severe, words that cannot be outflanked by experience', and out of them to forge a vision which evades as little as possible and which the soul must learn to bear as best it can.

At this date it is perhaps most instructive to look closer not at the many enthusiastic reviews but at the reservations some of the favourable critics expressed, and at the criticisms of the few unfavourable ones.

The commonest criticism was that so many of the poems were derivative. This is of course true, and to be expected in a first book. These influences are not diffuse, but tend to be concentrated in single poems, as if Hughes had consciously attempted to write in a manner close to that of Hopkins, Dylan Thomas, Yeats, the Jacobeans, Frost or Wilfred Owen, for the space of a poem or two, and why not? He had much to learn from all of them.

Hughes was well aware of the dangers in this respect, of 'the terrible, suffocating, maternal octopus of ancient English poetic tradition':

> The archetypes are always there waiting . . . swashbuckling Elizabethan, earthy bawdy Merrie Englander, devastatingly witty Restoration blade and so on. And some of the great poets are such powerful magnetic fields they remake us in their own image before we're aware. Shakespeare in particular of course.
> (*London Magazine*, January 1971)

But in comparison with the dangers or rather the impossibility of making poetry out of Queen's English, Shakespeare is still the greatest source of vitality. In his Introduction to *A Choice of Shakespeare's Verse* Hughes writes: 'Shakespeare's language is somehow nearer to the vital life of English, still, than anything written down since. One reason for this is that it is a virtuoso development of the poetic instincts of English dialect.' His language has

> the air of being invented in a state of crisis, for a terribly urgent job, a homely spur-of-the-moment improvisation out of whatever verbal scrap happens to be lying around, and this is exactly what real speech is. The meaning is not so much narrowly delineated as overwhelmingly suggested, by an inspired signalling and hinting of verbal heads and tails both above and below

precision, and by this weirdly expressive underswell of a musical near-gibberish, like a jostling of spirits. The idea is conveyed, but we also receive a musical and imaginative shock, and the satisfaction of that is unfathomable. (11)

At the Restoration those spirits were exorcized.

But in some respects Hughes had to get back beyond Shakespeare. One of the arms of the maternal octopus is iambic rhythm. English prose is still predominantly trochaic, true to its Germanic origins, but in verse the courtly alien iamb drove the trochee underground after Langland's last stand, into folk songs, ballads, nursery rhymes. In Hughes the old rhythms surface again (in *The Hawk in the Rain* twenty-seven of the twenty-eight two-syllable words are trochees) and we see what we had lost in weight, sinew and urgency in all those centuries of artifice and gentility.[6]

Some of the reviewers pointed to general faults such as stridency and bravado, others conceded that there were some bad poems, but most were canny enough not to specify them. In the few who did specify, there was little consensus. Some poems ('The Martyrdom of Bishop Farrar' in particular) appeared in lists of both the best and the worst poems in the book.

The only thoroughly hostile review was by Alan Brownjohn, who saw, or affected to see, nothing but 'a dismaying badness' characterized by 'a raw, sex-and-violence imagery' and 'melodramatic and slapdash hyperbole'. Others have since followed Alan Brownjohn's lead. The most extreme statement of the position is Calvin Bedient's. He claims that there is nothing admirable in *The Hawk in the Rain*, that Hughes is, in it, a mere 'voyeur of violence':

Everything – war, childbirth, the weather, laughter, love – is galvanised into the improbable: even the prodigious wears a fright wig...Occasionally the phrases are welded in a series like brass knuckles...All together, it is as if Billy the giant had chosen to speak with the lexical mincingness of an Elizabethan page. The language attempts to squeeze every thrill out of its subjects and yet to be priggishly superior to them. It turns to Shakespeare as to stilts...

It must be conceded that passages can be adduced, and are adduced by Carr, Brownjohn, Rawson and Bedient, which support these charges. All are true of some poems and parts of others. Strain as he might, Hughes cannot always disguise the staleness or crudity of some of the underlying attitudes.

The phrase 'voyeur of violence' implies that Hughes likes to imagine scenes of violence for cheap thrills. The charge relates closely to that brought by C. J. Rawson, who argues that Hughes' positives imply a facile code of suicidal heroism, a cult of the big-hearted mindless hero of legend (that his hero is still, in other words, Carson McReared). The poem most open to this charge is 'The Ancient Heroes and the Bomber Pilot' where the poet shows every sign of sharing the pilot's admiration (or perhaps 'awe' would be a fairer word) of the 'huge chested braggarts', 'their chariot-wheels tumbling the necks of screams', 'restuffing their dear fame with fresh sacks-full of heads'. All this is offered as heroism, glory and grandeur, in contrast to the activity of the pilot who only has to press a button to raze a city, or the 'timorous poet' enlarging heroisms the heroes would have got nowhere listening to. That timorous poet was indeed a voyeur of violence. In his anxiety not to be like him, Hughes occasionally writes as Bedient describes (in 'Fair Choice' and 'Complaint', for example), with the overheated imagination of his own Little Miss, who dreams of a warrior 'smashing and burning and rending towards her loin'.

No doubt it can be useful to a young poet to have his faults pointed out to him at an early stage. But in the case of Hughes his faults are very closely related to his strengths and perhaps inseparable from them, as they must be in any poet who takes so many risks. To have taken such criticism too seriously would have been to emasculate himself.

On the whole, however, the reception of *The Hawk in the Rain* did the reviewers great credit. Robin Skelton spoke for the vast majority when he wrote: 'All looking for the emergence of a major poet must buy it.'

LUPERCAL

I saw
Too far into the sea, where every maw
The greater on the less feeds evermore. –
But I saw too distinct into the core
Of an eternal fierce destruction...
The Shark at savage prey, – the Hawk at pounce, –
The gentle Robin, like a Pard or Ounce,
Ravening a worm.
(John Keats, 'Epistle to John Hamilton Reynolds')

In June of 1957 Ted and Sylvia Hughes went to live in the United States. That summer they spent in a cabin among pines on Cape Cod. They would write in the mornings, cycle to the beach in the afternoons, and read in the evenings. In the autumn Sylvia took up a teaching appointment at Smith College, Northampton, Massachusetts; but after a year decided to abandon her academic career for the sake of her writing. Hughes, meanwhile, taught for half the year at the University of Massachusetts. The next year they lived from hand to mouth in a cramped apartment on Beacon Hill in Boston. Here, in addition to much of *Lupercal*, Hughes wrote *Meet My Folks!* and most of the stories later collected in *Wodwo*. In the spring of 1959 Ted Hughes received a Guggenheim fellowship. They spent the summer camping all over the States, and the autumn at Yaddo, where Sylvia finished *The Colossus* and Ted *Lupercal* which appeared in March 1960.

There is no spectacular advance in *Lupercal*, rather a careful pruning of the luxuriance of *The Hawk in the Rain*. Gone are all the faults of the earlier book. Hardly a line in *Lupercal* is obviously derivative. The posturing has gone. The poems are no longer overloaded, forced or hectoring. A few poems ('Fourth of July', 'Historian') as a result seem threadbare, their clichés showing through. Others ('Nicholas Ferrer', 'The Good Life') are like the good poems of a minor poet. But most of the poems ('Hawk Roosting', 'View of a Pig', 'Pike', 'Crow Hill', 'Relic', 'Snowdrop', and many more) gain great strength in simplicity.

To take 'Snowdrop' as an example, this perfect poem concentrates the vision of *Lupercal* into eight lines.

> Now is the globe shrunk tight
> Round the mouse's dulled wintering heart.
> Weasel and crow, as if moulded in brass,
> Move through an outer darkness
> Not in their right minds,
> With the other deaths. She, too, pursues her ends,
> Brutal as the stars of this month,
> Her pale head heavy as metal.

It is the depth of winter and life seems to have retreated to the centre. Those creatures which hibernate are in suspended animation; those which must continue to hunt do so mechanically, like zombies or automatons, in a world given over to cold, darkness and death. It seems that mere flesh and blood could not survive, only creatures 'moulded in brass'. Yet it is now that the snowdrop blossoms. How much more hard and single-minded and irresistible as a little bulldozer the snowdrop must be to break that frozen ground with its assertion of renewal against everything, yet we know that it is also utterly frail, and a miracle.

It may be that Hughes took to heart some of the criticism of *The Hawk in The Rain*. He may have learned from the American poets he came to know in his years in America. Or this may have been his natural development in any case. Having found his voice there is no need for imitation. Having got himself a hearing there is no need for the loud-hailer. Having found his strength there is no need to flex his muscles. The style is now wholly Hughes, as he moves deeper into his chosen themes.

Many reviewers and later critics assumed that the territory Hughes was rapidly staking out was the world of animals. We have only to look down the titles of *Lupercal* to see horses, cats, a hawk, a bull, a mouse, a pig, an otter, thrushes, a bullfrog and a pike.

No poet has observed animals more accurately, never taking his eyes from the object, capturing every characteristic up to the limits of language. So vivid is his rendering, so startling and true his insights, that the way one looks at a hawk, a thrush or a pike (or, in later poems, a jaguar, a skylark or a swarm of gnats) is permanently altered. But the description generates metaphors, and the metaphors relate the creature to all other creatures and to human experiences and concepts.

In nearly all his poems Hughes strives to find metaphors for his own nature. And his own nature is of peculiar general interest not because it is unusual, but because it embodies in an unusually intense, stark form the most typical stresses and contradictions of human nature and of Nature itself. The poems are bulletins from the battleground within.

In the early poems the metaphors he found were so often animals because animals live out in such naked extremity the primary struggles, particularly that between vitality and death. They roar or bellow the evidence which men wrap in sophistry or turn a blind eye to. Their reality seems less questionable than ours.

In any discussion of Hughes as an animal poet it is not long before the name of Lawrence occurs, and rightly so. 'Bullfrog' is a particularly Lawrentian poem. There is the affectionate direct address to the bullfrog,

> But you bullfrog, you pump out
> Whole fogs full of horn – a threat
> As of a liner looming.

the easy colloquial style flexible enough to heighten instantly to

> Disgorging your gouts of darkness like a wounded god,

the unexpected, slightly comical, metaphors and exaggerations

> I expected...
> A broken-down bull up to its belly in mud,
> Sucking black swamp up, belching out black cloud
> And a squall of gudgeon and lilies

the freshness and liveliness, the touches of wit which have nothing to do with showing off but are a direct, amused, wondering and wholly serious response to a new awareness –

> all dumb silence
> In your little old woman hands.

'An Otter', too, has the creature there in a couple of perfect lines

> With webbed feet and long ruddering tail
> And a round head like an old tomcat.

So much for the appearance of an otter. Another two lines suffice for its distinctive movements:

> Gallops along land he no longer belongs to;
> Re-enters the water by melting.

Then, like Lawrence, into the little myth:

> Seeking
> Some world lost when first he dived, that he cannot come at since.

The otter is 'neither fish nor beast. . . Of neither water nor land.' He wanders in search of the long-lost world he once ruled, where he knew himself and his kingdom.

The poem is less a description of an otter than an invocation of the spirit of an otter. The subject was suggested to Hughes by an Ouija board. The Ouija spirit liked poetry (particularly Shakespeare) and one hot day wrote a poem about 'a cool little spirit that wanted to live in the bottom of icebergs'. Hughes wrote Part I with great labour over a long period and was not really satisfied with it. The second part virtually wrote itself and seemed to Hughes to be the Ouija spirit's revision of the first part – and very much better. Here the otter is not just dispossessed, but hunted. As he hides under water, his dual nature forces him to breathe the air tainted by men and dogs. 'The otter belongs'

> In double robbery and concealment –
> From water that nourishes and drowns, and from land
> That gave him his length and the mouth of the hound.

So, in exile, the water's surface ('the limpid integument') is where he thrives. If he ventures on land he must not linger:

> Yanked above hounds, reverts to nothing at all,
> To this long pelt over the back of a chair.

The otter is the opposite of the hawk who rules his element imperiously, the kingdom of daylight. The otter is also a predator, giving short shrift to the trout, but, since man arrived on the scene with his trained dogs, is also prey, dual again in this.

No analogues are offered. But the otter, crying without answer for his lost paradise, is surely, in part, an image of the duality of man, neither body nor spirit, neither beast nor angel, yearning for his Eden home where death was not.

In 'The Bull Moses', a boy leaning over the half-door of the byre can at first see nothing but a 'blaze of darkness' – a darkness which strikes the eye as rich with dangerous potencies. Though he cannot see the bull, his other senses register very strongly the bull's presence:

But the warm weight of his breathing,
The ammoniac reek of his litter, the hotly-tongued
Mash of his cud, steamed against me.

Then gradually, as if his mind's eye were giving the evidence of the other senses their appropriate embodiment, he begins to make out

The brow like masonry, the deep-keeled neck:
Something come up there onto the brink of the gulf,
Hadn't heard of the world, too deep in itself to be called to...

Moses belongs to another world beyond the world of human consciousness, a gulf between. He looms up out of that potent darkness and now stands in a bovine twilight at the brink, the meeting point of the two worlds.

There was a time when bulls were undominated. Now

Each dusk the farmer led him
Down to the pond to drink and smell the air,
And he took no pace but the farmer
Led him to take it, as if he knew nothing
Of the ages and continents of his fathers,
Shut, while he wombed, to a dark shed
And steps between his door and the duckpond;
The weight of the sun and the moon and the world hammered
To a ring of brass through his nostrils.

The bull meekly submits to servitude. The boy is vaguely aware of what sleeps within the bull – 'the locked black of his powers' which no bolt or ring of brass could hold in check should he revolt. And why doesn't he? Has he forgotten his wild ancestors who roamed continents? Of the jaguar in *The Hawk in the Rain* we were told:

His stride is wildernesses of freedom:
The world rolls under the long thrust of his heel.
Over the cage floor the horizons come.

Moses, too, is like a visionary in his cell:

Some beheld future
Founding in his quiet.

The animal lives in a world without time or death. The consciousness of Moses is a racial consciousness. What redeems his servitude is that he 'wombs', that is, he fills the wombs of many cows with his progeny, passing on what Lawrence, also writing of a bull, called the 'massive Providence of hot blood'. He is but a link in the unbroken continuity from his wild ancestors to his wild descendants, when man has ceased to rule. He is progenitor, Patriarch, and, like the other Moses, he beholds the Promised Land he will never himself enter, satisfied that simply by ensuring the continuity of the race, he has played his part. His descendants will escape from captivity and inherit the earth. Providence will see to that – the powers which inhabit the darkness of his dream.

The blackness beyond the gulf is not only the other world of the bull, it is also 'depth beyond star', the outer darkness surrounding the small area lit by the lamp of human consciousness, the source of those imperatives by which non-human creatures live. There is a corresponding darkness within ourselves, for the look into the blackness of the byre is also 'a sudden shut-eyed look Backwards into the head'. The gulf between man and animal is also the gulf between civilized man and his animal self, which is also his angelic self – the only self capable of recognizing a divinity in the darkness and being at one with it.

'Pike' is another fine poem, with Lawrentian passages which are yet pure Hughes:

> silhouette
> Of submarine delicacy and horror.
> A hundred feet long in their world.

The horror is in the pitch of specialization this fish has reached as killer:

> The jaws' hooked clamp and fangs
> Not to be changed at this date;
> A life subdued to its instrument;

as though the whole creature existed purely to enable its jaws to go about their business. Two marvellously economical anecdotes substantiate the claim:

> Three we kept behind glass,
> Jungled in weed: three inches, four,
> And four and a half: fed fry to them –
> Suddenly there were two. Finally one
>
> With a sag belly and the grin it was born with.
> And indeed they spare nobody.
> Two, six pounds each, over two feet long,
> High and dry and dead in the willow-herb –
>
> One jammed past its gills down the other's gullet:
> The outside eye stared: as a vice locks –

The same iron in this eye
Though its film shrank in death.

When, at the end, the narrator fishes in terror at night

For what might move, for what eye might move

he is no longer fishing for pike, but for the nameless horror which night's darkness frees to rise up from the legendary depth of his dream, his unconscious.

Prehistoric bedragonned times
Crawl that darkness with Latin names...

These lines are from 'To Paint a Water Lily' where again there are two worlds, that above and that below the surface, a world of daylight and a world of living darkness:

Now paint the long-necked lily-flower

Which, deep in both worlds, can be still
As a painting, trembling hardly at all

Though the dragonfly alight,
Whatever horror nudge her root.

In 'Fish' Lawrence has a passage about a pike:

But watching closer
That motionless deadly motion,
That unnatural barrel body, that long ghoul nose,...
I left off hailing him.

I had made a mistake, I didn't know him,
This grey, monotonous soul in the water,
This intense individual in shadow,
Fish-alive.

I didn't know his God.
I didn't know his God.

But the thought of that unknown God does not make his hair freeze on his head with terror. Lawrence has not noticed 'the malevolent aged grin'. The other, smaller fish know fear, when the pike comes, but it is

gay fear, that turns the tail sprightly, from a shadow.

None are eaten, and what their own bellies gulp we are not told.

Food, and fear, and joie de vivre,
Without love.

The other way about:
Joie de vivre, and fear, and food,
All without love.

In Hughes' pond there is little room for joie de vivre. Lawrence not only insists on its presence, he insists on its primacy. It is essential to his metaphysic.

In his poems Lawrence seldom writes of predators (his mountain lion is seen as victim rather than killer) and shows little interest in the eating habits of the beasts he does describe. Yet in his prose he shows a full awareness:

Food, food, how strangely it relates man with the animal and vegetable world. How important it is! And how fierce is the fight that goes on around it. The same when one skins a rabbit, and takes out the inside, one realizes what an enormous part of the animal, comparatively, is intestinal, what a big part of him is just for food-apparatus; for *living on* other organisms. ('Reflections on the Death of a Porcupine')

This is also the main theme of Hughes' 'Mayday on Holderness':

What a length of gut is growing and breathing –
This mute eater, biting through the mind's
Nursery floor, with eel and hyena and vulture,
With creepy-crawly and the root,
With the sea-worm, entering its birthright.

Hughes muses on Holderness as Joyce's Stephen Dedalus mused among the seawrack on Sandymount strand: 'A misbirth with a trailing navelcord, hushed in ruddy wool. The cords of all link back, strandentwining cable of all flesh....' And the links are alimentary as well as navel: 'God becomes man becomes fish becomes barnacle goose becomes featherbed mountain. Dead breaths I living breathe, tread dead dust, devour a urinous offal from all dead' (*Ulysses*, 'Proteus').

Hughes evokes the same continuity. As the Humber feeds the North Sea with its dregs and refuse, including dung, corpses and misbirths, so his body, he feels, is a mere sheath for that 'mute eater' the intestine, designed, like an incinerator, like any scavenger, to receive all remains.

The same pattern is endlessly repeated.

There are eye-guarded eggs in these hedgerows,
Hot haynests under the roots in burrows.
Couples at their pursuits are laughing in the lanes.

The North Sea lies soundless. Beneath it
Smoulder the wars: to heart-beats, bomb, bayonet.
'Mother, Mother!' cries the pierced helmet.

The eggs, so carefully watched over by the parent birds, are to produce new prey, if they are not sucked dry before they hatch. The laughing couples produce cannon-fodder for the next war. It is all like a madness, a frenzy. When Hughes writes of

> The expressionless gaze of the leopard,
> The coils of the sleeping anaconda,
> The nightlong frenzy of shrews...

he is writing not out of wonder and admiration, but out of horror, a horror he can evoke in a single line:

> The crow sleeps glutted and the stoat begins.

To call this pattern unredeemable would imply a concept of redemption. To call it mad would imply a concept of sanity. But here

> The stars make pietas. The owl announces its sanity.

There is nothing outside the pattern from which any other standard of holiness or sanity could be drawn.

When Lawrence was sickened by the war, he wrote: 'It isn't my disordered imagination. There is a wagtail sitting on the gate-post. I see how sweet and swift heaven is. But hell is slow and creeping and viscous and insect-teeming; as is this Europe now, this England' (*Collected Letters*, 338). The sanity announced by Lawrence's wagtail is 'sweet and swift' having nothing whatever in common with the madness and obscenity of men marching to war. But the 'sanity' of Hughes' owl is indistinguishable from its 'nightlong frenzy'. If the natural is the sane, then killing is sane. Wagtails also kill to live. Of course men need not kill each other to live. But slaughter is slaughter. If it is mad and obscene in men, why is it sweet and swift in a wagtail? In fact, one realizes, it is not the killing Lawrence finds mad and obscene so much as the regimentation. Killing as such he does not seem to mind: 'Leave me my tigers, leave me spangled leopards, leave me bright cobra snakes, and I wish I had poison fangs and talons as good. I *believe* in wrath and gnashing of teeth and crunching of cowards' bones. I believe in fear and pain and in oh, such a lot of sorrow' (*Collected Letters*, 651). Or again: 'The tiger, the hawk, the weasel, are beautiful things to me; and as they strike the dove and the hare, that is the will of God, it is a consummation, a bringing together of two extremes, a making perfect one from the duality' ('The

Crown'). This is very close to the position Hughes comes through to in 'Crow's Table Talk': 'The tiger blesses with a fang.'

But Hughes earns the right to this hard-won position as Lawrence does not, by confronting and living through in his work the fear and pain and sorrow. He hears the inaudible

> battle-shouts
> And death-cries everywhere hereabouts
> ('To Paint a Water Lily')

He shares the terror of the mouse 'staring out the chance it dared not take' and knows that a man stands in God's eye no better than the mouse in the cat's. When Lawrence's cat torments a chipmunk 'it is a game, and it is pretty'.

Lawrence is not only callous in comparison with Hughes, he is also, in his animal poems, frequently sentimental. In 'A Living' for example:

> A bird
> picks up its seeds or little snails
> between heedless earth and heaven
> in heedlessness.
>
> But, the plucky little sport, it gives to life
> Song, and chirruping, gay feathers, fluff-shadowed warmth
>
> and all the unspeakable charm of birds hopping and fluttering and being birds.
> – And we, we get it all from them for nothing.

Hughes sees nothing heedless or sporting or charming about a bird eating snails:

> Terrifying are the attent sleek thrushes on the lawn,
> More coiled steel than living – a poised
> Dark deadly eye, those delicate legs
> Triggered to stirrings beyond sense – with a start, a bounce, a stab
> Overtake the instant and drag out some writhing thing.
> ('Thrushes')

The thrushes are terrifying not only for their ravening of writhing things, but for the too streamlined efficiency with which they pursue their unwavering purpose – the efficiency of a bullet (whose one path is direct through the bones of the living). Whitman thought he could 'turn and live with animals':

> They do not lie awake in the dark and weep for their sins.
> ('Song of Myself', 32)

Hughes draws the same distinction, but does not choose the animals or even admire them. Their efficiency is too horribly automatic, like

> The shark's mouth
> That hungers down the blood-smell even to a leak of its own
> Side and devouring of itself...

What a man does neither defines nor deifies him, nor can he, unless he is that hardly human thing, a genius, crash straight through doubts, obstructions, temptations, sin, guilt and despair:

> how loud and above what
> Furious spaces of fire do the distracting devils
> Orgy and hosannah, under what wilderness
> Of black silent waters weep.

Beyond the little area lit by his consciousness, his desk-lamp, is a vast darkness peopled by demons. The distracting devils which sin, praise, or despair are those suppressed powers within any man which will not let him be satisfied with the heroisms he invents at his desk, or with any enclosed self-worshipping activity. A man totally given over to those powers, genius or hero, is a madman or automaton. A man totally cut off from them denies, trivializes or perverts the life that is in him, drops out of the divine circuit from which alone come the energies to destroy or create.

Several of the poems in *Lupercal* derived from an abandoned long poem about England, for which 'Mayday on Holderness' was to have been a sort of overture, announcing all the main themes. The central figure was a river, the bloodstream of England, and this image was related to that of the adder, the buried, denied and feared elemental life of England. Within this larger framework was a technical exercise in writing about animals, an exploration of several modes, moving from the completely external, objective, materialistic, at the beginning of 'View of a Pig':

> Just so much
> A poundage of lard and pork.

– a mode suitable only for dead animals:

> They were going to scald it,
> Scald it and scour it like a doorstep.

– through the more sensitive, anecdotal, but still essentially human mode of 'Pike', a mode which allows the speaker to only hint at the connection between the pike, the legendary past of England, and his own dark dreams; through the almost occult summoning of the spirit of the otter; to the completely internal mode of 'Hawk Roosting', where the voice, the very consciousness, is the hawk's.

The whole poem is in the first person – a hawk's eye view of the world. The hawk, taking himself to be the exact centre, assumes that trees, air, sun and earth are there for his convenience; that the purpose of creation has been solely to produce him; that the world revolves at his bidding; that all other creatures exist only as prey; that his eye is stronger than change or death:

> It took the whole of Creation
> To produce my foot, my each feather:
> Now I hold Creation in my foot
>
> Or fly up, and revolve it all slowly –
>
> ...
>
> The sun is behind me.
> Nothing has changed since I began.
> My eye has permitted no change.
> I am going to keep things like this.

At a deeper level the hawk becomes a spokesman for Nature herself and speaks in accents close to those of Whitman when he permits Nature ('without check, with original energy') to speak through him:

> I know I am solid and sound,
> To me the converging objects of the universe perpetually flow...
> I know I am deathless...
> I see that the elementary laws never apologize...
> I exist as I am, that is enough...
> My foothold is tenon'd and mortis'd in granite...
>
> ('Song of Myself', 20)
>
> All forces have been steadily employ'd to complete and delight me,
> Now on this spot I stand with my robust soul
>
> (*Ibid.*, 44)

Nature speaks through Tennyson too, a Nature 'red in tooth and claw', a loveless, careless, ravenous Nature:

> She cries 'A thousand types are gone:
> I care for nothing, all shall go.
>
> Thou makest thine appeal to me:
> I bring to life, I bring to death:
> The spirit does but mean the breath:
> I know no more.'
>
> ('In Memoriam', LV)

Tennyson had built his faith on the assumption that love was Creation's final law. When Nature undeceived him he could only cry

Are God and Nature then at strife?

In Hughes we find neither the admiration of Whitman nor the anguish of Tennyson. All these animal and nature poems get their characteristic tension from the attempt to fuse into a unified response both admiration and horror. The reconciling spirit might be described as one of awe. This was certainly the spirit in which the ancient Egyptians saw the hawk:

Under the name Hor – which in Egyptian sounds like a word meaning 'sky' – the Egyptians referred to the falcon which they saw soaring high above their heads, and many thought of the sky as a divine falcon whose two eyes were the sun and the moon. The worshippers of this bird must have been numerous and powerful; for it was carried as a totem on prehistoric standards and from the earliest times was considered the pre-eminent divine being. The hieroglyph which represents the idea of 'god' was a falcon on its perch. (Larousse *Encyclopaedia of Mythology*, 21)

In other words, a hawk roosting was 'god'. In his *London Magazine* interview (January 1971) Hughes said of his hawk:

That bird is accused of being a fascist...the symbol of some horrible totalitarian genocidal dictator. Actually what I had in mind was that in this hawk Nature is thinking. Simply Nature. It's not so simple maybe because Nature is no longer so simple. I intended some Creator like the Jehovah in Job but more feminine. When Christianity kicked the devil out of Job what they actually kicked out was Nature...and Nature became the devil. He doesn't sound like Isis, mother of the gods, which he is. He sounds like *Hitler's familiar spirit*. There is a line in the poem almost verbatim from Job. (8)

Indeed Job's god is the god of hawks:

Doth the hawk fly by thy wisdom, and stretch her wings
toward the south?
Doth the eagle mount up at thy command, and make her nest
on high?
She dwelleth and abideth on the rock, upon the crag of the
rock, and the strong place.
From thence she seeketh the prey, and her eyes behold afar off,
Her young ones also suck up blood: and where the slain are,
there is she.

(Job 39: 26–30)

And Job's God speaks like Hughes' hawk:

> Whatsoever is under the whole heaven is mine.
> (Job 41: 11)
>
> I kill where I please because it is all mine.
> ('Hawk Roosting')

That was before Jehovah became the God of Love; before he became Jehovah, for Job called him such primitive names as El, Eloah and Shaddai.

In Job we find God still acknowledges as his own the most crude and savage powers of nature – behemoth and leviathan. Behemoth is clearly phallic:

> Lo now, his strength is in his loins, and
> his force is in the navel of his belly.
> He moveth his tail like a cedar: the
> sinews of his stones are wrapped together.
> He is the chief of the ways of God.
> (Job 40: 16ff)

Leviathan represents the unkillable, untameable dragon (libido) of the sea (unconscious):

> Behold, the hope of him is in vain:
> shall not one be cast down even at the
> sight of him?
> (Job 41: 9)

Later the Hebrews, to accommodate their God to human morality, handed Nature over to the devil. For in terms of the Christian ethic, or of any sort of human morality, the hawk is evil or mad. An example the poem more directly evokes than Hitler is Shakespeare's Richard of Gloucester:

> For the one path of my flight is direct
> Through the bones of the living

is a paraphrase of Richard's

> For many lives stand between me and home.
> (3 *Henry VI*, III, iii, 173)

The hawk's solipsism is also Richard's:

> I am myself alone. (V, vi, 83)

By attributing to the hawk a consciousness which can express itself in our language and concepts, the poem also invites us, though we envy the hawk his centrality, his freedom from the falsifying dreams, sophistries and arguments which distract and deflect men, to count the cost of letting such energies loose in a man.

Speaking of Job 38–41, the Voice out of the Whirlwind, I. A. Richards, says: 'It is not well to reflect whether more than two thousand years' adoration of this utterance (however magnificent its phrases) might not have something to do with the sad state of the world and with the mad and abominable tyrannies which have so mercilessly infected it?' (*Beyond*, 73) Perhaps Job himself was suppressing similar doubts when he put his hand over his mouth.

> Though he slay me, yet will I trust in him:
> but I will maintain mine own ways before him.
> (Job 13: 15)

The chief of the ways of Job is his sense of justice. How can he hope to maintain that against a god of whom he has already said

> For he is not a man, as I am, that I should answer him,
> and we should come together in judgment.
> (Job 9: 32)

This god is not interested in justice or morality. When Job tries to negotiate, God shouts him down, smashing straight through his arguments with sheer brute force. What is left for him? A choice of capitulation, futile rebellion, or putting his hand over his mouth?

(The same choice confronts Crow, who is both Job and hawk, and Prometheus on his crag whose unjust God daily sends his vulture out of the sun to torment him – a bird whose manners are tearing out livers.)

All efforts to understand Nature in terms of human morality are as doomed as Job's effort to understand his God. His successors decided to remake God in their own image, separating out and exalting the Logos, leaving the dark side of God, unacknowledged, marauding destructively as Satan, serpent, dragon, Gog, unredeemable Nature and the ghosts of all the Pagan gods and goddesses. And it is this process which Hughes sees as having more to do with the sad state of the world than the adoration of Job's savage God which Richards strangely imagines to have characterized the last two thousand years.

In *Lupercal* Hughes gives us a few figures who escape the destructive extremes. There is Dick Straightup 'strong as the earth', a living legend because impervious to those forces to which Hughes feels himself most vulnerable:

> But this one,
> With no more application than sitting,
> And drinking, and singing, fell in the sleet, late,
> Dammed the pouring gutter; and slept there; and, throughout
> A night searched by shouts and lamps, froze,
> Grew to the road with welts of ice. He was chipped out at dawn
> Warm as a pie and snoring.

The tramp in 'November' also withstands the worst that weather can do. Then there are the 'Acrobats'. It is gravity they defy as they fling

> Out onto nothing, snap, jerk
> Fulcrumed without fail
> On axes immaterial as
> Only geometry should use.

Hughes wonderfully mimes their 'hurtle and arc'

> somersaulting
> (As might hardly be dared in the head)
> Bodily out on space,
> Gibboning, bird-vaulting . . .

The verbs themselves launch out into space with their heavily stressed first syllables. And that parenthesis achingly arrests the somersault in mid-air. Such defiance of natural laws is 'unearthly', miraculous. But the watching crowd have no share in it. It makes them only the more conscious of their insecurity and vulnerability and mortality

> bearing
> Plunge of that high risk without
> That flight; with only a dread
> Crouching to get away from these
> On its hands and knees.

The acrobats are the exception which proves the rule. The world of nonchalant ease, freedom and grace which they inhabit ('a hundred feet above ground') is as remote from ordinary men as heaven itself. Ordinary men can but dream of such a world, or strive by means of vigil, ordeal, prayer and spiritual disciplines at the body's expense, towards it. But

The acrobats flashed
Above earth's ancient inertia,
Faltering of the will,
And the dullness of flesh –
In the dream's orbit; shone, soared,
Mocking vigil and ordeal,
And the prayer of long attempting
Body had endured
To break from a hard-held trembling seat
And soar at that height.

When Hughes was a boy, his brother told him the story of a tramp sleeping in the heather, who stirred at an unlucky moment and was shot dead for a fox by an alert farmer. Already the tramp, in his imagination, was associated with those creatures we call vermin, shoot at will and hang on gibbets 'pour encourager les autres'. Other meanings of the tramp figure emerge in *Lupercal.* In 'Things Present' the tramp in his sodden ditch is defined by what he lacks – fire, cat, bread, shoes, honour and hope. His ancestors who gradually acquired these appurtenances of civilized living 'honed their bodies away' in the effort, that is, lost the stability and centrality that goes with a sense of the bulk and weight, the instant and heat, of one's own body. Most significantly he lacks 'a roof treed to deflect death'. Imagine those characters in 'Wind' deprived of their roof and fire.

In 'November' we learn why the tramp is willing to forego these things. The speaker is the same speaker as in 'The Hawk in the Rain', desperately conscious of his own exposure, vulnerability and mortality, running for shelter from the 'drilling rain'. The tramp embodies a less spectacular, more passive form of the same mastery of the elements which characterizes the hawk in the earlier poem.

In a let of the ditch a tramp was bundled asleep:
Face tucked down into beard, drawn in
Under its hair like a hedgehog's. I took him for dead,

But his stillness separated from the death
Of the rotting grass and the ground. A wind chilled,
And a fresh comfort tightened through him,
Each hand stuffed deeper into the other sleeve.

His secret is his 'strong trust'.

I thought what strong trust

Slept in him – as the trickling furrows slept,
And the thorn-roots in their grip on darkness;

And the buried stones, taking the weight of winter;
The hill where the hare crouched with clenched teeth.

What, exactly, does the tramp trust? That Nature will look after him, like the Babes in the Wood? That spring cannot be far behind, and better days? The speaker runs into a wood for shelter and there finds himself confronted by a gibbet:

The keeper's gibbet had owls and hawks
By the neck, weasels, a gang of cats, crows:
Some, stiff, weightless, twirled like dry bark bits

In the drilling rain. Some still had their shape,
Had their pride with it; hung, chins on chests,
Patient to outwait these worst days that beat
Their crowns bare and dripped from their feet.

These creatures share the patience of the tramp, even his posture 'chins on chests'. Is their patience misplaced, since they are not, like the tramp, the furrows and the thorn-roots, merely asleep? Nature has no spring or better days in store for them.

The tramp, like them outcast, dispropertied, unaccommodated, has nothing to lose. He is willing to forego even a roof, because being without hope he is not prepared to devote his life to the doomed attempt to deflect death. His trust is in all life's purposes or processes, including death.

In 'Crag Jack's Apostasy' Crag Jack is another tramp or outsider. His name implies his toughness, the qualities he shares with Heathcliff: 'an unreclaimed creature, without refinement, without cultivation'. Apostasy is the abandonment of religious faith. The opening lines –

The churches, lord, all the dark churches
Stooped over my cradle once:

evoke an image of witches suffocating the new born child with sterile blessings, obscuring the light; also, perhaps of the Calder Valley, the cradle of a Methodism which often took an extremely repressive Calvinistic form. (Joseph and the Reverend Jabes Branderham in *Wuthering Heights* are caricatures of this.) Crag Jack has come clear of the world (power, wealth, comfort, security) and the churches with their dogmas, theologies and traditional imagery.

I came clear, but my god's down
Under the weight of all that stone:
Both my power and my luck since
Have kicked at the world and slept in ditches.

Though he has no desire to be reclaimed, Crag Jack fears to become, like Heathcliff, a 'wolfish man'. He has retained a deep need to worship, but not the god of the churches.

I do not desire to change my ways,
But now call continually
On you, god or not god, who
Come to my sleeping body through
The world under the world; pray
That I may see more than your eyes
In an animal's dreamed head...

Exposed as he is to life at its most severe, his imagination can find no appropriate image for the forces which control life other than that of a wolf's head or eagle's feet. Crag Jack is like The Toughest in *Recklings* who also survives the collapse of church-towers and hears 'the laughter of great outer darkness' threatening 'to close its teeth on the skull'. The Great Outer Darkness is a name for God. It is also, in 'The Toughest', 'the same as the small inner darkness'. The images of organized religion do not match those of the violent world Crag Jack inhabits. They are supplanted by his dream images. The only god who reveals himself to Crag Jack is the god of predators, the god of ruthless killing; or, if this god has other aspects, it is only in this aspect that he ever reveals himself. 'Plum Blossom' III in *Recklings* might be one of Jack's dreams:

Inside the head of a cat
Under the bones, the brains, the blood-tissue,
Bone of the bone and brain of the brain,
Blood of the blood and tissue of the tissue,
Is God's head, with eyes open.
And under that my own head, with wide eyes.
And under that the head of a cat, with eyes
Smiling and closed.

These images, wolf's head, eagle's claws, shark's mouth, the curved jawbone which did not laugh

But gripped, gripped and is now a cenotaph
('Relic')

dominate *Lupercal*. Crag Jack's god is the god of death, of the underworld. If we must name him he is Pluto or Dis, or Februus, to whom the month of February was sacred. In 'February' the dominant image is again the wolf – winter gripping the world with vice-like jaws. The word 'wolf' throws up several images in the poet's mind – the wolves he remembers from those horrific nursery stories *Red Riding Hood* and *The Wolf and the Seven Little Kids*, the wolves of Norse legends, 'gibbet-hung wolves' he has seen in engravings, or the caged wolves he has seen at the zoo. But none of these images suffices to personify the spirit of February, none captures the pure spirit of wolf as it is captured in

> A photograph: the hairless, knuckled feet
> Of the last wolf killed in Britain. . .

These feet run and run in the darkness of his dream, and

> By day, too, pursue, siege all thought. . .

There are no wolves in Britain, no large predators at all to make the nights dangerous. And we like to think that we have got rid of the wolfishness in our own natures. But these feet run

> Through and throughout the true world

disdaining the storied, pictured or tamed world, searching

> For their vanished head, for the world
> Vanished with the head, the teeth, the quick eyes –

the world in which wolves roamed at will before man rifled the forests. And man, meanwhile, is terrified that these disembodied feet will choose his head, will occupy the brain they lay siege to, driving out his 'reasonable ways'.

> Now, lest they choose his head,
> Under severe moons he sits making
> Wolf-masks, mouths clamped well onto the world.

Making wolf-masks is the attempt to divert the wolf-spirit into the false world of art or fiction, where it can be dealt with. But that final image of the world held between the teeth of a wolf-mask through whose eye-holes the quick eyes of the savage god might look out is far from reassuring.

'Fire-Eater' is yet another variant on 'Egg-Head' (in *The Hawk in the Rain*). The poem falls into two halves (the second a mirror-image of the first). The first half is about the stars as fire-eaters, the second about the speaker's claim to be himself a fire-eater on a much vaster scale.

> Those stars are the fleshed forebears
> Of these dark hills, bowed like labourers,
>
> And of my blood.
>
> The death of a gnat is a star's mouth: its skin,
> Like Mary's or Semele's, thin
>
> As the skin of fire:
> A star fell on her, a sun devoured her.

The stars are like materialized fires, the gods making themselves visible to men. We give them the names of gods. These gods gave life, and they snuff it out as easily as swallowing the tiny spark which is the life of a gnat. Mere skin is no protection. Both Mary and Semele were pierced by stars, that is by gods. When Semele rashly persuaded Zeus to let her see him in all his glory, the vision killed her. But from her body Zeus took the unborn child and fostered him in his own body until he was born as Dionysus. Semele is a counterpart of Persephone, a virgin seduced by Pluto in the form of a snake and possibly with the aid of an apple. She also 'died' but gave birth in fire to a divine son, Dionysus again, who brought the gift of wine, as Demeter, mother and counterpart of Persephone, brought the gift of grain. Thus, in the pagan myth, the Fall, the crucifixion of the god and the birth of the god are one divine event. To be pierced by the god may be death, but it is also the guarantee of immortality. And in Jerusalem two thousand years after Christ as at Eleusis a thousand years before, the miracle is celebrated by the leaping of fire from the Holy Sepulchre.

There is a legend that the sacred fire at Eleusis once restored a blind man's sight, as Orion restored his by gazing at the sun. To expose oneself to 'the whelm of the sun' is to risk death, but also to let in restoration and fertility.

However, the speaker in the poem, far from showing a due reverence and humility before these powers, claims to be himself a fire-eater capable of managing whole constellations:

> My appetite is good
> Now to manage both Orion and Dog
>
> With a mouthful of earth, my staple.
> Worm-sort, root-sort, going where it is profitable.
>
> A star pierces the slug,

> The tree is caught up in the constellations.
> My skull burrows among antennae and fronds.

This is Faustus again, whose first request to Mephistophilis was for knowledge of astronomy. But before he can swallow stars, this man must eat earth as staple, burrowing downwards like any worm or root into inert matter. (We think of Blake's Newton at the bottom of the sea of materialism, his back to the sun and stars, putting the universe on paper.)

Even the slug is 'pierced' by the divine fire. Even the trees are 'caught up in the constellations', even the insects reach up their antennae, the plants their fronds towards the vivifying stars. But the last we see of our hero he is still underground, still eating earth not fire, and now a skull emptied of what fire it ever had. So much for his arrogant appetite to contain the universe.

'Fire-Eater', like 'Urn Burial', seems to me a bad poem, though Sylvia Plath thought it the best poem in *Lupercal.* These poems are so cryptic and oblique that they can only be read as puzzles to be solved. The images are clues which send us groping far from the poem. There is insufficient continuity, coherence or realization for us to have much faith in any answers we might ultimately come up with. It would not surprise me to learn that my interpretation of 'Fire-Eater' is completely wide of Hughes' intention. It would not much trouble me either, since I believe a poet has the obligation to give his intentions rather more flesh and bone than this.

A specific example of a failed fire-eater is given in 'Strawberry Hill'. Strawberry Hill was the name of the house which Horace Walpole bought in 1747 and converted into a monument to the Gothic tastes of the time. He added battlements, pinnacles and all the other vulgarities which were supposed to suggest wild Nature, the supernatural, and the romantic, heroic past. The forces such writers as Walpole trivialized and sought to tame in their architecture and 'Gothick' novels, in that same age when the last wolf was killed in England, are here represented by a stoat which they expected to dance to their tune.

> A stoat danced on the lawns here
> To the music of the maskers;
> Drinking the staring hare dry, bit
> Through grammar and corset.

Blood, skulls, horror, death, the supernatural were all treated as mere playthings easily contained by artificial stylistic devices.

They nailed to a door
The stoat with the sun in its belly,
But its red unmanageable life
Has licked the stylist out of their skulls,
Has sucked that age like an egg and gone off. . .

That life is unkillable. It killed them and their age. It 'got into some grave', returned to the underworld, but

Emerges, thirsting, in far Asia, in Brixton.

Emerges, that is, wherever and whenever violence breaks out, for all our assurance that we are highly civilized and that civilization means having it well under control.

The god of the underworld may be the god of death, and February the month of the dead, but Persephone in the underworld is fertilized by Pluto and gives birth to Dionysus, who is Pluto himself in his creative, life-giving aspect. The wolf and the stoat cannot be exorcised from the human world, and if they could, along with the goat and all the other beasts of our being, there would be an end to the race.

One way to negotiate with these powers is through ritual. We call the animals fauna. Fauna was, in Roman mythology, the wife or daughter of Faunus, the fertility god, who corresponds closely to Pan or Dionysus. Under the name of Lupercus he was worshipped in Rome at a temple on the Palatine called the Lupercal. This temple was so called (*lupus* being Latin for wolf) because it was believed to be on the site of the cave where the she-wolf (which is the symbol of Rome) suckled Romulus and Remus, founders of the city. The rituals, the Lupercalia, were celebrated on the 15th of February. The purpose of the rituals was to restore fertility to barren women. Goats and dogs were sacrificed. Young men, athletes, were touched with blood and milk by the priests, then raced through the streets striking the waiting women as they passed with whips of goat-skin. Calphurnia, wife of Julius Caesar, once stood there, and one of the runners was Mark Anthony:

Forget not, in your speed, Antonius,
To touch Calphurnia; for our elders say,

> The barren, touched in this holy chase,
> Shake off their sterile curse.
> (*Julius Caesar*, I, ii)

The athletes run not to distinguish themselves but to snatch the lowliest, the barren women 'flung from the wheel of the living', back into that wheel, into 'the figure of the racers'.

'Lupercalia' fittingly ends the volume, for it offers to resolve in ritual the dilemma of Crag Jack and the horrors evoked in so many of the poems. It is made up of four short poems, each describing one of the participants – the dog, the barren woman, the goats and the racers.

The dog, though its blood is declined from the days when it was wolf, still 'held man's reasonable ways between its teeth'. There is still the 'old spark of the blood-heat' in him. And it is this, 'the brute's quick' which will be tinder, it is hoped, the touch of life on the woman's barren body. What gave the bull Moses his foothold in life, his sense of the continuity of his race, both heir and progenitor, is what she lacks, what makes her a hostage to death:

> The past killed in her, the future plucked out.

The dog dies that she might live again.

The goat has always been thought of as an embodiment of libidinousness, the lower half of the satyr, and of Pan the goat-god, and of the devil.

> Goats, black, not angels, but
> Bellies round as filled wine-skins
> Slung under carcase bones.

That marvellous image is so right purely as a visual image, descriptive, yet also suggests prodigality and licence, Dionysus and the Bacchic rites. The god is even more evident in the goat's eyes:

> Yet that's no brute light
>
> And no merely mountain light –
> Their eyes' golden element.

The goat is also characterized by the 'stink of a rank thriving'. All these are to pass to the women through the goat-skin thongs.

In 'Acrobats' the performers are

> Fulcrummed without fail
> On axes immaterial as
> Only geometry should use.

The racers in their blessed fury achieve an unearthly access of power and become

> A theorem of flung effort, blades:
> Nothing mortal falters their poise.

But where the circus crowd were merely spectators excluded from the 'grace' of the acrobats, here the crowd are all participants as they urge on the athletes, their representatives. The racers become conductors of energy between earth and sky:

> The earth's crammed full,
> Its baked red bellying to the sky's
> Electric blue.

Through the ritual they are blessed by dog and goat, caught up in the intercourse of earth and sky, and as they strike a woman they draw her into their pattern, the divine circuit:

> And deliberate welts have snatched her in
> To the figure of racers.

So the poem and the book end with a prayer for life, for the miraculous fertilizing touch of the god:

> Maker of the world,
> Hurrying the lit ghost of man
> Age to age while the body hold,
> Touch this frozen one.

WODWO

The roaring of lions, the howling of wolves, the raging of the stormy sea, and the destructive sword, are portions of eternity, too great for the eye of man.
(William Blake, 'Proverbs of Hell')

In December 1959 Ted and Sylvia Hughes returned to England for good, and, after a few weeks at Heptonstall, settled in February in a small flat near Primrose Hill where their first child Frieda was born in April. It was impossible to work in the flat, but the W. S. Merwins lent them a room in theirs. Sylvia would use it in the morning while her husband looked after Frieda. His turn would come in the afternoon. Sylvia worked mainly on *The Bell Jar*; Hughes wrote poems, some of which later appeared in *Recklings* and some in *Wodwo*, several radio plays, and a grand oratorio of the *Bardo Thodol* for the Chinese composer Chou Wen Chung, which was never used.

The following summer they moved to the thatched cottage in Devon where Hughes still lives, with an orchard on one side and a churchyard on the other. There Nicholas Farrar Hughes was born in January 1962. Hughes wrote rapidly – poems, stories, plays, reviews for the *New Statesman*. Sylvia Plath entered upon the phase of her *Ariel* poems. Their creative partnership was flowering, but their marriage was under strain. In August Hughes left her for another woman, and she began divorce proceedings. Sylvia was exhausted and could not face another winter in Devon. She found a flat at Primrose Hill and took a five-year lease. It was the coldest winter for half a century. She was ill and depressed. On 11 February 1963 she committed suicide.

Later that month Hughes wrote 'The Howling of Wolves' and in March 'Song of a Rat', then nothing (except a long play from which 'Ghost Crabs', 'Waking' and Part III of 'Gog' were salvaged) until 1966, when he went to Ireland and started with 'Gnat Psalm' and 'Skylarks'.

Recklings are the smallest and weakest animals in a litter – runts, wasters. Perhaps Hughes thought of these poems as throwouts and failed experiments, but hadn't the heart to burn them. Many of them give the impression of being exercises in new styles, not quite brought off. And some are opaque in their dense symbolism – private poems. Almost all are very different from anything we have had before, stripped-down, skeletal poems, with little rhetoric and few animals. Some have a moving simplicity and understatement like the compassionate 'Small Events'; some, like 'Poltergeist', an epigrammatic wit; some a terse colloquial vigour. Ideas are now being handled as confidently as experiences. The most powerful poem, 'Logos', was carried over into *Wodwo*; 'A Match', 'On the Slope' and 'To be a Girl's Diary', all fine, went into the American *Wodwo* as 'Root, Stem, Leaf'. But there were several other poems well worth saving in *Recklings* – 'Memory', 'Thaw', 'Plum Blossom', 'Unknown Soldier'.

But to compare *Recklings* with *Wodwo* is to recognize that Hughes is a good judge of his own work. Here we have ample justification for those experiments, and for calling those thin years fallow, not sterile. Here Hughes comes into his own as a poet with a great range of themes and styles, and, if he must be labelled, a 'metaphysical' poet.

The reviewers of *Wodwo* were again (with very few exceptions) impressed, though several admitted their bafflement. It was not a reviewable book. These poems need to be lived with for years, not days, before it becomes possible to see *Wodwo* whole, not just as a collection of marvellous though often enigmatic poems.

The unenthusiastic reviewers wanted Hughes to be a different kind of poet, with different themes. They entirely missed the point that an inspirational poet like Hughes (or any great poet) does not choose what to write or how to write. He writes what he must. And they missed what some other reviewers tried to point to: 'He comes face to face with those forces in the physical world which are outside the range of moral choice or rational control, forces we have to live with or die with' (Norman Nicholson). 'Often pieces read like the tales of the stranger from beyond normal bournes, returning with a renewed clarity of vision, sharp as toothache, as uninvited as Lazarus' (Barbara Lloyd-Evans).

From the first poem, 'Thistles', on, we meet poetic utterance perfectly at one with its subject:

Every one a revengeful burst
Of resurrection, a grasped fistful
Of splintered weapons and Icelandic frost thrust up
From the underground stain of a decayed Viking.

Look at those spiky clusters of consonants, 'sp', 'spl' and, especially, 'st'. It is impossible to read the lines other than spitefully.

Or the subject may be a harebell and the language fragile and tender:

That trembles, as under threats of death,
In the summer turf's heat-rise,
And in which – filling veins
Any known name of blue would bruise
Out of existence – sleeps, recovering,
The maker of the sea.
('Still Life')

This is the voice of a man who speaks poetry as his first language. Despite the absence of rhyme or regular rhythms it never approaches prose. In the whole of *Wodwo* I can find only one stanza which could have been written by a bad poet – the conclusion of 'Ludwig's Death Mask':

. . .
Caused himself flee seventeen feet down
Through the church-floor into dumb earth touched
His ears dead to continue complete
In union with the communion of angels.

Within the unity of his vision of life, presented most starkly in such poems as 'Pibroch', there are many different kinds of poem. There are poems about landscapes (owing much in their powerful simplicity and brevity to Eliot's 'Landscapes'); about specific animals and plants and people; about what Lawrence calls 'the animal, in all its animal difference and potency, its hinterland consciousness which circles round the isolated consciousness of man' (*Apocalypse*, 41); about the two worlds, the natural and the supernatural, a gulf between; about the first and last things, sometimes handled in the abstract, sometimes in agonizingly concrete images, sometimes in myths. The myths are, I think, the most impressive. The best description of them is Hughes' own, though he is speaking of Vasko Popa's ability to make miniature myths out of two bones or a quartz pebble:

It is in this favourite device of his, the little fable of visionary anecdote, that we see most clearly his shift from literary surrealism to the far older and deeper thing, the surrealism of folklore. Folktale surrealism is always urgently connected with the business of trying to manage practical difficulties so great that they have forced the sufferer temporarily out of the dimension of coherent reality into that depth of imagination where understanding has its roots and stores its X-rays. (Introduction to Vasko Popa's *Selected Poetry*, 14–15)

There is also a great deal of variety in style and technique, and in tone. Nearly every poem is witty, as the Metaphysicals were witty, in perceiving new connections. Description generates metaphor. Then the metaphor takes over and becomes the meaning. From the thistle as 'a grasped fistful of splintered weapons' we move to:

> Then they grow grey, like men.
> Mown down, it is a feud. Their sons appear,
> Stiff with weapons, fighting back over the same ground.
> ('Thistles')

The wit is usually a means of deepening the seriousness of a poem. Occasionally it conveys a savage irony:

> Desertion in the face of a bullet!
> ('Bowled Over')

or a metaphysical dilemma:

> He is a man in hopeless feathers
> ('Kafka Writes')

or it can be epigrammatic, gnomic, as in 'The Bear' or 'Theology'. At other times it is frankly humorous without the humour in any way compromising the seriousness, as in 'Gnat Psalm'.

Some poems are expansive and free, in the Lawrence manner ('Skylarks'), others extremely concentrated, with regular stanzas. Some progress by narrative, some by argument, some by what looks like the spontaneous generation of images ('Cadenza') or sound patterns. Hughes is trying to recapture 'Some sort of language or set of sounds I can hear going on in the bottom of my mind, that's not quite English and not quite music. It's probably some sort of forgotten inherited language' (*The Poet Speaks*, 88). Perhaps a language better fitted to express the deepest rhythms and tensions of experience.

The tension, in *Wodwo*, is in the struggle for meanings, not for effects, the struggle to part meanings from their bedrock in the physical world. The eye strains to focus further, but the voice now has the calm assurance of the man who says what he must say, whether or not anyone listens or understands or applauds. If the men in the public bar fail to comprehend the hazy diminished images which flicker on the TV screen, the reality those images derive from is not diminished and must be witnessed afresh by the poet:

> On a flaked ridge of the desert
>
> Outriders have found foul water. They say nothing;
> With the cactus and the petrified tree
> Crouch numbed by a wind howling all
> Visible horizons equally empty.
>
> The wind brings dust and nothing
> Of the wives, the children, the grandmothers
> With the ancestral bones, who months ago
> Left the last river,
>
> Coming at the pace of oxen.
>
> ('Public Bar TV')

Ted Hughes is, of course, no philosopher. Few of his ideas are original. He takes what he can from diverse sources. (The same could be said of Shakespeare, Donne, Eliot, Beckett...) What we are primarily interested in is not the meanings themselves, as they can be paraphrased, but the new relationship between these perennial meanings and the raw materials – the world, experience, language. It is symbolism which most potently makes these new connections. The symbol has a foot in each world, one in the world of experience, one in the world of meanings.

In our efforts to extract meanings we must guard against the assumption that whatever meanings we extract are in some way the equivalent of the poem, or replace it, or the equally dangerous assumption that the best poems are those which elicit the lengthiest explication. These may be poems where the meaning is too near the surface, so that one is invited to discuss the meaning almost independently of the poem, or too far from it, so that one is obliged to tease it out.

Some of the poems in *Wodwo* are perfectly transparent, others perfectly solid – so much of a piece, so self-sufficient that there is no point at which the probe can enter. 'The Green Wolf', for example, is a good poem, but 'The Bear' is much finer. The symbols here are not pointing towards meanings outside themselves. They are the meanings and they resist translation into any other terms. Yet the poem is in no way obscure. We don't feel that meanings are being deliberately withheld or hidden, or that something is being said obliquely which could just as well be said directly. The poem derives from a much longer narrative poem called 'The Brother's Dream'. It is, presumably, the dream of a Christian brother, who goes, of his own will, in search of the embodiment of his terror. In an eternal mountain landscape with blasted bristling pine-trees, the savage spirit of that place manifests itself as a huge bear which the frail brother calls out of its cave, and, transformed into 'a steel madman', stabs to the heart. George MacBeth describes this poem (in *Poetry 1900 to 1965*, p. 332) as 'a reworking of the legend of St George and the Dragon in modern psychological terms. The bear is perhaps an image for our animal nature, or more precisely the emotion of fear, which can only be controlled by the ruthless cruelty of the will.'[1]

In 'The Bear' all the externals and particulars fall away. The bear is no longer seen, it is seen through – to the spirit and essence of bears and of the world which created them. If a mountain cave is the pupil in the sleeping eye of the mountain, the cave-bear is 'the gleam in the pupil', the spirit of the mountain. The oldest chapels on earth are those of Neanderthal man in high mountain caves, filled with cave-bear skulls and sacred to the bear as mountain god. Part of the initiatory ordeal of the Eskimo shaman is the acquisition of a mystical faculty for contemplating his own skeleton, and in this he needs the help of a bear to devour his flesh. 'The Bear' is part of Hughes' initiation into the secrets of the earth, a confrontation with that which seems capable of swallowing all we are.

Wodwo differs from the earlier books most obviously in its much bleaker vision, a vision now much closer to Beckett's than to Lawrence's:

> Within seconds the new born baby is lamenting
> That it ever lived.
>
> ('Logos')

In 'Lines To A Newborn Baby', written shortly after the birth of Frieda, Hughes tells her:

> You will find a world tossed into shape
> Like a hatful of twisted lots; locked in shape
> As if grown in iron: a stalagmite
> Of history under the blood-drip.

The child will cry all its life in vain

for milk
From the breast
Of the mother
Of the God
Of the world
Made of Blood.
('Karma')

The evidence is everywhere. In 'The Green Wolf' your neighbour lies paralysed

While somewhere through a dark heaven
The dark bloodclot moves in

like a predator. 'The Green Wolf' is a strange title for a poem in which no wolf appears, and in which there is nothing to explain how a wolf can be green.[2] The wolf, as we saw in discussing *Lupercal*, is one of Hughes' primary symbols of savage, destructive nature. But green is the colour of vegetation and growth. The oxymoron corresponds closely to Dylan Thomas's 'green age':

The force that through the green fuse drives the flower
Drives my green age.

'The Green Wolf' continues:

The punctual evening star,
Worse, the warm hawthorn blossoms, their foam,
Their palls of deathly perfume,
Worst of all the beanflower
Badged with jet like the ear of the tiger
Unmake and remake you.

The White Goddess is both Queen of May, when the hawthorn, a tree sacred to her, blossoms, and Queen of Death, both Demeter and Persephone. The scent of the hawthorn blossom is simultaneously deathly (it is still called 'mother-die blossom' in some parts of the country) and erotic. The association of beans with the White Goddess is even closer:

The Pythagorean mystics were bound by a strong taboo against the eating of beans and quoted a verse attributed to Orpheus, to the effect that to eat beans was to eat one's parents' heads. The flower of the bean is white and it blooms at the same season as the hawthorn. The bean is the White Goddess's... The reason for the Orphic taboo was that the bean grows spirally up its prop, portending resurrection, and that ghosts contrived to be reborn as humans by entering into beans and being eaten by women. (*The White Goddess*, 69)

Hughes would not call it resurrection; simply unmaking and remaking in a pointless cycle:

> The lips of time leech to the fountainhead
> ('The Force That Through the Green Fuse')

Hughes believes with Heraclitus that everything is born out of the death of something else. Heraclitus wrote: 'Mortals are immortals, and immortals are mortals, the one living the other's death and dying the other's life.' Hughes quotes him in 'Ghost Crabs':

> They are the powers of this world.
> We are their bacteria,
> Dying their lives and living their deaths.

Heraclitus also believed that Nature was a perpetual flux: 'This world was ever, is now, and ever shall be an ever-living Fire, with measures kindling and measures going out.' In 'That Nature is a Heraclitian Fire and of the Comfort of the Resurrection' Hopkins wrote:

> Million-fueled, nature's bonfire burns on.

No doubt he knew that 'bonfire' originally meant 'bone-fire':

> Flesh fade, and mortal trash
> Fall to the residuary worm; world's wildfire, leave but ash.

He trusted the Resurrection to lift him out of the fire transformed into immortal diamond. Hughes can find no such comfort:

> all
> One smouldering annihilation.

'Still Life' might seem to be a more hopeful, even a religious poem. Here Hughes takes stone as the most perfect, most self-sufficient of substances, giving nothing of itself, eternal, itself the measure of the transience of all other things.

> It expects to be in at the finish.
> Being ignorant of this other, this harebell...

But stone is poverty-stricken, 'hoarding its nothings'. In fact it is

> imprisoned
> Like nothing in the Universe.
> ('Pibroch')

There is no such thing as still life. Life 'trembles, as under threats of death'. There is nothing in stone to answer to the blueness of a harebell, which, for all its frailty, is a manifestation of energy, not matter; that is to say, a miracle:

this harebell,
That trembles, as under threats of death,
In the summer turf's heat-rise,
And in which – filling veins
Any known name of blue would bruise
Out of existence – sleeps, recovering,
The maker of the sea.

The power which sleeps in the veins of the harebell is the power which made the sea, which made the stone, and will ultimately use the roots of the harebell to break the stone. In this cycle of making and unmaking what significance can we attach to beauty?

A companion-piece to 'Still Life' is 'Pibroch', perhaps the ultimate expression of Hughes' vision of the world in *Wodwo*. A pibroch is, in Hughes' words, 'a piece of music for bagpipes, part elegiac, part martial'. The power of this poem derives from its witty but deadly serious anthropomorphism, the attempt to find adequate human terms in which to describe the life of an archetypal landscape of sea, stone, wind and a tree. The sea is 'meaningless', 'bored', 'without purpose'. The stone is 'imprisoned', 'created for black sleep', 'blind'. The wind rushes senselessly over and round, incapable of any relationship.

Drinking the sea and eating the rock
A tree struggles to make leaves –
An old woman fallen from space
Unprepared for these conditions.
She hangs on, because her mind's gone completely.

We are challenged, all the time, to reverse these metaphors, to see this landscape as an image of the human condition. If the tree is like a crazy old woman, isn't any person hanging on to barren life as tenaciously as the tree, as crazy as the old woman?

Minute after minute, aeon after aeon,
Nothing lets up or develops.
And this is neither a bad variant nor a tryout.
This is where the staring angels go through.
This is where all the stars bow down.

This also is a miracle. The only angels are the forces which, staring without seeing, mad in human terms, pass this way unknowing, intent on other, unknowable purposes or on none, their one path direct through the bones of the living.

If we could see, in imagination or nightmare, these invisible powers, what would they look like? In 'Ghost Crabs' (a poem of great urgency and excitement) Hughes imagines, each nightfall, the sea uncovering

> Giant crabs, under flat skulls, staring inland
> Like a packed trench of helmets.
> Ghosts, they are ghost-crabs.

The comparison of the crabs with flat skulls and helmets suggests helmet crabs, which are not true crabs at all, but extremely primitive creatures of the spider family. Fossils have been found 400 million years old, little different from the living species. The same image reminds us also of the ending of 'Mayday on Holderness':

> The North Sea lies soundless. Beneath it
> Smoulder the wars: to heart-beats, bomb, bayonet,
> 'Mother, Mother!' cries the pierced helmet.
> Cordite oozings of Gallipoli,
>
> Curded to beastings, broached my palate,
> The expressionless gaze of the leopard,
> The coils of the sleeping anaconda,
> The nightlong frenzy of shrews.

Taken together, the two associations suggest the sea as cradle of primitive life-forms, permanent battleground where jaws

> Eat and are finished and the jawbone comes to the beach:
> ...and is now a cenotaph
>
> ('Relic')

and grave of all things. The sea, through all its 'accumulations and changes' ('The Voyage') simply continues the beginning:

> Time in the sea eats its tail, thrives, casts these
> Indigestibles, the spars of purposes
> That failed far from the surface.
>
> ('Relic')

Perhaps the pierced helmets, the broken shells, pursue their frenzied murderous purposes as ghosts, ghost crabs. They can be seen only with the mind's eye:

> Their bubbling mouths, their eyes
> In a slow mineral fury
> Press through our nothingness where we sprawl on our beds,
> Or sit in rooms.

They invade our dreams and nightmares.

> These crabs own this world.
> All night, around us or through us,
> They stalk each other, they fasten on to each other,
> They mount each other, they tear each other to pieces,
> They utterly exhaust each other.
> They are the powers of this world.
> We are their bacteria,
> Dying their lives and living their deaths.

Hughes here vividly dramatizes his sense that there are forces working in us and through us for which we are not ultimately responsible, historical forces, genetic forces:

> They are the moil of history, the convulsion
> In the roots of blood, in the cycles of concurrence.

The horror of the poem is not only in what the crabs are and do, but in the fact that they are so totally oblivious of the devastating effect they have on the human effort to live in this world:

> Their hungers are homing elsewhere.

Crabs are peculiarly apt since they appear to be machines specialized for stalking, fastening, mounting, tearing, kept, in the daytime, at the bottom of the sea, which is also the unconscious. When Eliot's Prufrock cried out to be freed from his disabling self-consciousness so that he could simply grab what he wanted from life, he cried:

> I should have been a pair of ragged claws
> Scuttling across the floors of silent seas.
> ('The Love Song of J. Alfred Prufrock')

Though the crabs seem wholly destructive and demonic, they stare and 'go through' like the 'staring angels' of 'Pibroch'. If they are 'God's only toys', it follows that we are not God's toys. God is as unaware of us as the crabs are. For his toy soldiers the world is 'empty battleground'; for him it is empty playground as he childishly, pointlessly, unleashes these murderous toys.

Did God create them? Has he any control over them? A rather

different version of his role is offered in 'Logos'. The Logos, according to Robert Graves, is the secret name of God, the God who existed before creation. Graves suggests that this God was enthroned in place of the White Goddess as a result of a religious revolution initiated by Ezekiel:

> The result of envisaging this god of pure meditation, the Universal Mind still premised by the most reputable modern philosophers, and enthroning him above Nature as essential Truth and Goodness was not an altogether happy one. The new God claimed to be dominant as Alpha and Omega, the Beginning and the End, pure Holiness, pure Good, pure Logic, able to exist without the aid of woman; but it was natural to identify him with one of the original rivals of the Theme and to ally the woman and the other rival permanently against him. The outcome was philosophical dualism with all the tragi-comic woes attendant on spiritual dichotomy. If the True God, the God of the Logos, was pure thought, pure good, whence came evil and error. (*The White Goddess*, 465)

The first two stanzas are about this God, the God of perfect strength who is in control of creation. But they contain many suggestions that his creation of man 'was not an altogether happy one'. Creation is seen as the moulding of flesh and blood onto a radiant star, a mystical endless knot (Donne's 'subtil knot which makes us man'), a godly pattern of spiritual perfection (Yeats' 'ghostly paradigm of things'), onto, that is, the Logos itself. But the pentagram is 'blinding' and the body 'frail' – too frail to be able to look upon the radiance within. Far from sharing God's perfect strength, the odds are that the baby will not survive long enough to become a person. God gives us the freedom to have babies, but if our purpose in doing so is to assert a claim to everlasting life, then it is doomed from the start.

> Creation convulses in nightmare. And awaking
> Suddenly tastes the nightmare moving
> Still in its mouth
> And spits it kicking out, with a swinish cry – which is God's first cry.

We are now moving toward the universe of *Crow*, where a whole creation myth is generated by that question: 'whence came evil and error?' This third stanza gives us a version of the birth of God, where in the beginning was creation and nightmare. Even in creation's primeval sleep the nightmare is within it, and the beginning of everything, the first birth, is the spitting out of the nightmare, whose birth cry – gross and degraded – is the first cry of the now incarnate God, appropriately 'swinish' since his mother, creation, is none other than the White Goddess or Sow Goddess who eats her own young.

As soon as 'ancient law' and all the 'truths' of the well-meaning God of the Logos descend into matter, they are broken down by the still more ancient powers of nature which are inimical to all laws and truths and whose highest purpose is to streamline its killers so as to destroy the more efficiently everything it creates – creates, apparently, for the purpose of destroying.

> God is a good fellow, but his Mother's against him.

God has the best of intentions, but he is at odds with a goddess older and still stronger than himself.

'Reveille' is a rude awakening of Adam and Eve to sexuality and death.

> No, the serpent was not
> One of God's ordinary creatures.

God had never intended there to be this creature in the world, and its purpose was not God's. Eden was God's dream. The reality was the nightmare to which Adam and Eve awoke. The serpent is also the great dragon which holds the world in its coils, poisoning, crushing, burning, the principle of corruption in all things:

> The black, thickening river of his body
> Glittered in giant loops
> Around desert mountains and away
> Over the ashes of the future.

In 'Endgame' Hamm tells of a madman, a painter, who thought the end of the world had come:

> I'd take him by the hand and drag him to the window. Look! There! All that rising corn! And there! Look! The sails of the herring fleet! All that loveliness! He'd snatch away his hand and go back into his corner. Appalled. All he had seen was ashes.

All the loveliness is in fact a mere dream, an illusion, to the artist or prophet, the man who is aware of the skull beneath the skin and the vanity of everything under the sun. The end of the world is always with us, since the principle of self-destruction was within it from the beginning, the worm in the bud, the serpent in Eden.

In 'Theology' (inspired by Popa's 'The heart of the quartz pebble') Hughes goes further. The serpent did not simply corrupt humanity, he swallowed it:

Adam ate the apple.
Eve ate Adam.
The serpent ate Eve.
This is the dark intestine.

'This', of course, is the world as we know it. God, it seems, cannot kill the serpent to release his prime creation from sin and death. He can only call, peevishly, 'Adam, where art thou?'

'Gog' is the fullest (and most difficult) exploration in *Wodwo* of the relationship between God, man and the serpent, here called Gog, who is identified with the Dragon of the Book of Revelation:

It ended by being about the dragon in Revelations that's waiting under the woman in heaven, between the sun and moon, waiting for her to deliver the child with its mouth open. (*The Poet Speaks*, 90)

I awoke to a shout: 'I am Alpha and Omega'.

In *Revelation* Gog is awoken by Satan, but here it is God's claim to be the first and the last which wakes him. If God, the God of the Logos, is all, what is Gog? It is God's claim to be everything and yet to exclude the World, the Flesh and the Devil, which provokes into wakefulness and destructive activity the sleeping dragon, which is all that is not Logos.

The dog's god is a scrap dropped from the table.
The mouse's saviour is a ripe wheat grain.
Hearing the Messiah cry
My mouth widens in adoration.

Gog does not worship Holiness and Truth and Logic; he worships food, like all the creatures of earth. When he hears the birth-cry of Christ, 'the dragon stood before the woman which was ready to be delivered, for to devour her child as soon as it was born' (Book of Revelation, 12: 4). Lichens, air and dust have no mouths to fill. But Gog has no choice. He is not responsible for his massive bones, his teeth, his terrible appearance and jarring song, nor for the trail of destruction he leaves behind him.

The implication is that if God had not made his claim to be the Logos, Alpha and Omega, thus denying the existence of Gog, Gog would have slept on. His awakening is therefore like that of Yeats' 'rough beast' in 'The Second Coming':

The darkness drops again; but now I know
That twenty centuries of stony sleep
Were vexed to nightmare by a rocking cradle,

And what rough beast, its hour come round at last,
Slouches towards Bethlehem to be born?

Part I of 'Gog' first appeared in 1961, Part III as 'The Knight' in 1966, and Part II not until *Wodwo* itself in 1967. The three parts are very difficult to relate. In Part II we have a vision of a world which belongs to death, dust and nothingness.

Then whose
Are these
Eyes,
eyes and
Dance of wants,
Of offering?

The clue comes in the last line when we are told that all created things are 'her mirrors'. Who, then, is 'she'? The only woman in the poem so far is the weeping mother who has lost her son to Gog. She was neither dancing nor offering. Only Gog was dancing. Part III gives us some help. The Knight's enemy is woman and dragon, woman and dragon, it comes slowly clear, in alliance against him, virtually indistinguishable from one another. The woman's weeping turns into a secret laughter, a smile, a seductive glance, a 'ribboned gift', a kiss:

Shield him from the dipped glance, flying in half light, that tangles the heels,
The grooved kiss that swamps the eyes with darkness.

The Knight is fighting to come clear of woman, whose smile is in her belly, whose womb is a 'tireless mouth', a 'fanged grail', an 'octopus maw', whose womb, in other words, is the mouth of Gog.

Bring him clear of the flung web and the coil that vaults from the dust.

The flung web is love, the coil is 'this mortal coil' (the body encircling and entangling the soul) and also the serpent or dragon reared up waiting to swallow the new-born child. The dragon is incarnation and therefore death and therefore reincarnation to keep the cycle going – Karma.

Death is not failure and cease
But clean back to a fresh start
Laying the original wide open
Like a bitch on heat
a secret laughter
('As Woman's Weeping')

The Knight, like Crow after him, is taking the 'Examination at the Womb Door' the purpose of which is to close the womb door, to avoid reincarnation, to break out of the greedy dream, the illusion of the life of the senses, the dance, and try to reach the light, the Logos.

The main obstacle is Woman, woman as mother, as fallen Eve, as Whore of Babylon, as spurned Venus, as revengeful White Goddess, as Gog waking within her every Spring:

> My mouth is the despair of God
> Formed only for men.
>
> The serpent remains earthen, brutishly-veined,
> Rooted in crevices, living on flies and men –
>
> The serpent that should have strangled me
> And then eaten itself.
>
> I sing, stamping the gruelling drum-beat
> To renew fallen men.
>
> Love is weak to protect as webs.
>
> In April my body begins to frighten me
> And my sleep fills with weeping –
>
> Again and again the forced grave of men.
>
> ('Fallen Eve')

Thus the poem is a battle between Gog and woman on the one side, God and man on the other, exactly the battle described by Graves in *The White Goddess*.

The Messiah who is born in the New Testament Revelation is to 'rule with a rod of iron', (or in Moffat's translation 'shepherd with an iron flail'). He grows up to be the horseman of iron:

> And I saw heaven opened, and behold a white horse; and he that sat upon him was called Faithful and True, and in righteousness he doth judge and make war.
>
> And he was clothed with a vesture dipped in blood: and his name is called The Word of God.
>
> And out of his mouth goeth a sharp sword, that with it he should smite the nations: and he shall rule them with a rod of iron. (Book of Revelation, 19: 11, 13, 15)

The lance and the grail were the great male and female sexual symbols of the pagan fertility religions. As the serpent, another phallic symbol, was degraded and denied and thrown out of heaven as Lucifer, so in the new religion of the dead body, the lance and grail became mere relics of the crucifixion. Here the grail is restored to its original meaning, but becomes the enemy the Knight rides against. His phallus is transformed into a destructive lance-blade or gunsight. No doubt, like Calvin, he has iron arteries too. Like Blake's visionless crazed God, Urizen, this Messiah seeks to live by and impose on others

> the ruled slab, the octaves of order,
> The law and mercy of number.

As in Blake, as in Lawrence, the energies he denies rear up against him:

> The sun erupts. The moon is deader than a skull.
> ('Gog')

> My heavens are brass my earth is iron my moon a clod of clay
> My sun a pestilence burning at noon and vapour of death in night
> (Blake, *The Four Zoas*)

If we get out of contact and harmony with the sun and moon, then both turn into great dragons of destruction against us. (Lawrence, *Apocalypse*)[3]

He finds he cannot destroy the dragon without destroying life itself. Since the serpent's coil is 'under his ribs' the horseman is seeking to destroy an essential part of himself:

And the vital twist, the mysterious chemical change that converts the resisting high-minded puritan to the being of murder and madness, is that occult crossover of Nature's maddened force – like a demon – into the brain that had rejected her...

Coriolanus, looking at his wife and mother, sees the Roman mob who want to tear him to pieces, and begins to act like a madman...(*A Choice of Shakespeare's Verse*, 192–3)

> He will need to be strong
> To follow his weapons towards the light.
> Unlike Coriolanus, follow the blades right through Rome...
> ('Gog')

This Hughes sees as the basic psychology of Fascism (which is what 'Gog' began by being about). He will need to be strong to overcome

> The whorish dragon of the dark ages
> Helmed with a modern capital and devouring
> Virginal St George as a flower.
> ('Humanities')

She is 'the real deity of Medieval England, the Celtic pre-Christian goddess, with her tail wound round those still very much alive pre-Christian and non-Christian worlds'. She is 'the old Mediterranean serpent goddess, the Anathema of the Old Testament'. This 'Queen of Heaven who was the goddess of natural law and of love, who was the goddess of all sensation and organic life – this overwhelmingly powerful, multiple, primaeval being, was dragged into court by the young Puritan Jehovah' (*A Choice of Shakespeare's Verse*, 186–7). The trial of strength continues. But in the Queen's armoury there are many 'empty armours, at attention, loyal St Georges surviving the worm and the virgin, faces open for inspection' ('The Wound').

Despite the fact that it contains five stories and a play in addition to the poems, *Wodwo* is a far more unified work than its predecessors, as Hughes himself claims in his prefatory note:

> The stories and the play in this book may be read as notes, appendix and unversified episodes of the events behind the poems, or as chapters of a single adventure to which the poems are commentary and amplification. Either way, the verse and the prose are intended to be read together, as parts of a single work.

I propose to look now at the stories and the play, to try to determine what they have in common, and then to see to what extent the poems relate to the same 'single adventure'.

The earliest of these stories is 'The Rain Horse'. It is an exercise in the Lawrence manner, drawing heavily on Ursula's encounter with the horses at the end of *The Rainbow*.[4] Nevertheless it is distinctively Hughes. A young man returns nostalgically to a once familiar landscape. But he has changed a lot in twelve years. The land no longer recognizes him. He feels an outcast. He loses his way, ruins his shoes in mud, fears for his new suit as it begins to rain. – 'He had come too far' – too far from the comfort and familiarity of his ordinary urban life. He finds himself, like the protagonists of 'The Hawk in the Rain', and 'November', exposed to the elements. He can find some shelter from the rain, but none from the rain-horse, the malevolent spirit of this non-human world into which he has wandered. The horse murderously attacks him, again and again, with an occult foreknowledge of his movements.

The man insists on bringing his rational intelligence to bear, trying to account for the horse's malice, predict its movements and outwit it, while the horse obviously inhabits a reality not subject to such reasoning. 'Its whinnying snort and the spattering whack of its hooves seemed to be actually inside his head...' He is running from and fighting against something he carries within him, which he can only escape from by damaging his heart and cutting out an important part of his brain. In a sense he had already done that, and this is what provokes these powers to such malevolence against him. He is tame. He has taken it for granted that horses are tame, either working or making their contribution to the picturesque landscape. This landscape refuses to gratify him by being picturesque. It is part of his own life he has denied which turns against him.[5]

In 'The Harvesting' Grooby has waited far too long in the sweltering heat for the hare to break from the dwindling square of wheat. He has ignored all the signs of sunstroke and has already fallen almost under the blades of the cutter. At last the hare breaks and it is a race between Grooby and the colliers' dogs. He fires and falls, struck by blackness:

> One need possessed him. It drove him to struggle up the hill. None of his limbs belonged to him any more, and he wondered if he still lay in the wheat and whether the cutter blades had indeed gone over him. But loudest of all he heard the dogs. The dogs were behind him with their inane yapping. He began to shout at them and shouted louder than ever when he heard the sound that twisted from his throat, the unearthly thin scream. Then the enormous white dog's head opened beside him, and he felt as if he had been picked up and flung and lost awareness of everything save the vague, pummelling sensations far off in the blankness and silence of his body.

The epigraph:

> And I shall go into a hare
> With sorrow and sighs and mickle care

is a witch spell for turning oneself into a hare. The next stanza begins:

> Hare, take heed of a bitch greyhound
> Will harry thee all these fells around.

Grooby, as his human consciousness blacks out with sunstroke and the blow of his gun's recoil, finds himself gone into the hare that moment caught by the dogs.

'Sunday' begins with an evocation of a stifling scrubbed Sunday morning in Mytholmroyd, the church-going slopes spotless and harmless, forbidden grass in the Memorial Gardens, even the pavements 'untouchably proper'. The men wear 'tight blue pin-stripe suits' and Michael wears his 'detestable blue blazer'. Sitting in chapel is the situation of greatest constraint he knows, and he shuts his eyes, letting his imagination fill his mind (as it always does on such occasions) with the image of a wolf which 'urged itself with all its strength through a land empty of everything but trees and snow'. The wolf is that in him which refuses to be constrained, tamed, disciplined, like those Vikings, 'the snow's stupefied anvils', who spent themselves in 'beforehand revenge'.

> For the gruelling relapse and prolongueur of their blood
> Into the iron arteries of Calvin,
> ('The Warriors of the North')

that which draws him away from chapel and the Sunday routine and respectability towards Top Wharf Pub, where, his father has told him, a man called Billy Red will kill rats in his teeth like a terrier. The thought of that savagery, that closeness of the human to the animal world, obsesses the boy and reduces everything else in his consciousness to unreality. When he hears the rat scream 'his stomach began to twist and flex like a thick muscle'. After its death 'he put his hand to his scalp and pressed the scorch down into his skull, but that didn't seem to connect with the dull, thick pain'. He runs, speechless, through a land empty of everything but that pain.

Michael's problem is partly sexual. He cannot relate the wolf which roams in his imagination or the killing of the rat to the Sunday world of respectability and demure girls in floral dresses. Billy Red's fascination for the watchers is the fascination of someone who is too close to the animal world for those who are too far from it. His counterpart is the girl who ignored Michael, 'perched on the last ten inches of the bench, arranged her wide-skirted, summery, blue-flowered frock over her knees, and busied herself with her mirror'. She cannot remain in Billy Red's world even as spectator. Michael cannot run away from it. He carries it within him.

'The Suitor' is about a boy, perhaps Michael a few years later, in the grip of an infatuation for a girl. Instinct has dragged him miles in the rain, late at night, to her street, in the hope of merely glimpsing her. But another man is also waiting in the rain for her.

Both stealthily, separately, enter her garden. As he crouches straining every sense, suddenly the boy hears, not a yard behind him, the sound of a flute: 'I express my amazement by pulling a slow, skin-stretching grimace, a contorting leopard-mask, in the pitch darkness. I hold it, as the flute-notes play over my brain.' We remember that the rain horse first appeared to the man 'like a nightmarish leopard'. Hughes wrote of a jaguar: 'He is an ancient symbol of Dionysus, since he is a leopard raised to the ninth power' (*London Magazine*, January 1971, 8). To the Greeks the panther was a mythical beast, half leopard, half lion, sacred to Dionysus. Etymologically, 'panther' means, in Greek, 'all-beast'. Its name also associates it with Pan, whose flute here plays over the brain of his leopard-masked initiate.[6]

The poem 'Heatwave' in *Recklings* describes the uncharted silence of sunstruck London and continues:

> Men can't penetrate it. Till sundown
> Releases its leopard
>
> Over the roofs, and women are suddenly
> Everywhere, and the walker's bones
>
> Melt in the coughing of great cats.

In 'The Wound'[7] the walker is a young soldier with a bullet hole right through his head, accompanied by his sergeant who is dead. The path crosses a black icy river. As they cross and approach a ruined château they are watched by women who laugh. The laughter turns to a wail, then a yap, a barking, which passes between them disembodied. As the Queen ushers them in to the banquet, there is the baying and snarling and howling of dogs and the screeching and squealing of pigs. The uproar turns into the shrieking laughter of the women. The Queen offers them 'peacock, snipe, woodcock, quail, black-cock, game-cock and cock starlings. Dogfish, catfish and assorted shellfish. Cod and conger, gudgeon and sturgeon...eels...duck, a hare, a boar and a roebuck.' Most of these are either aphrodisiacs or creatures sacred to fertility deities, or both. The quail, for example, was associated with lust. Graves tells us 'that the Phoenician Hercules, Melkarth, died yearly and that the quail was his bird of resurrection' (*White Goddess*, 133). The hare was sacred 'because it is very swift, very prolific – even conceives when already pregnant – and mates openly without embarrassment' (*White Goddess*, 293). Pigs were particularly sacred to the Moon-goddess because they 'vary between white, reddish and black, feed on corpse-flesh, are prolific but eat their own young, and their tusks are crescent-shaped' (*White Goddess*, 222). The roebuck was the guardian of the secret (the name of the deity) in the sacred grove. In the reaction away from the worship of the Moon-goddess many of these creatures became taboo foods in many cultures.

Ripley refuses the burnt offerings ('birds gone black, fish curling their ends up, fumigants not food'). He refuses red meat also: 'I get nightmares being eaten by bulls.'[8]

He is a vegetarian:

> Fearful of the hare with the manners of a lady,
> Of the sow's loaded side and the boar's brown fang,
> Fearful of the bull's tongue snaring and rending,
> And of the sheep's jaw moving without mercy,
> Tripped on Eternity's stone threshold.
>   Staring into the emptiness,
> Unable to move, he hears the hounds of the grass.
> ('A Vegetarian')

The hounds of the grass are what Ripley also hears at the château. He, like all creatures, is doomed ultimately to be dismembered. At one point the women, like the frenzied Bacchantes in *The Bacchae*, dismember Sergeant Massey. The men have crossed the Styx. This Queen is also 'the Queen of Hell, in which aspect her wild boar is the demon of destruction and death. In that form she is also Hecate, Goddess of witchcraft, all magical operations, the underworld, spirits, the moon, darkness, hounds, etc.' (*A Choice of Shakespeare's Verse*, 189). She is the leprosy-white goddess, nightmare and incubus; her other colours are the red of shed blood and the black of the grave and nothingness. But this triple-Goddess is dual in all her colours. White is also the colour of the new shoot, red of love, and black of divination. It is a girl who leads Ripley out of the château and gets him walking again. He is found muttering 'Will you marry me.'

Unlike Sergeant Massey, Ripley has not, in fact, died. 'What are you doing here?' the Queen asks him. And the women never touch him. 'I came back without a hand, but my comrade was devoured' says the epigraph. Ripley comes back with his terrible wound, leaving Massey and all his other comrades to be devoured by the women, their partners in the Dance of Death. 'He must have walked over nine miles with that lot, straight towards us. That's animal instinct for you.'

'The Wound' moves into and out of a surrealistic world. 'Snow' is wholly surrealistic and calls in question the very existence of a normal world to return to. The protagonist is an even worse case than Ripley. He has been wandering through a perpetual snowstorm for five months without food. He has no memory of a time when he was not walking through a twilight of snow. He seems to have 'dropped out of nothing casually' as Wodwo puts it. But, unlike Wodwo, he has a highly developed mind which he seeks to anchor in his 'reasonable hopes', his 'system of confidence' based on the facts which he takes to be on his side. The facts are that there is something firm enough to support him under his feet from which he deduces that he is on a planet and not in the gulf. The atmosphere is breathable, from which he deduces that he is on Earth. His physical shape is what he feels it ought to be – it corresponds to the images of his dreams. And then there is his excellent clothing and his chair, from which he deduces another world than this world of snow, a world of civilization, of purposive human activities and relationships. This is the world he dreams about and is obliged to think of as 'the world as it is' – reality, because if the world of snow were the real world 'I could have known no purpose in continuing the ordeal. I could only have looked, breathed and died, like a nestling fallen from the nest.' But in 'the world as it is' nestlings do fall from the nest:

> So this year a swift's embryo, cracked too early from its fallen egg –
> There, among mineral fragments,
> The blind blood stirred,
> Freed,
> And, mystified, sank into hopeful sleep.
>
> ('Small Events')

Mystified is what this man refuses to be. Logic is his lifeline. The chair testifies to the reality of the world it comes from, predicates the entire Universe. How can there be a chair without a carpenter? How can there be consciousness without identity? At this point the story becomes a Kafkaesque satire on rationalism. In *Metamorphosis* Gregor Samsa, having woken up to find himself turned into a beetle, says to himself: 'I'd better get up, since my train goes at five.'

Hughes' hero, having described his hands and feet as 'so black and shrunken on the bone' that 'one could believe I was several hundred years old, or even dead', goes on 'I have my job to get back to, and my mother and father will be in despair'. Yet he realizes that he must not trust logic too far:

If I were to take this drift of thoughts to the logical extreme there is no absolute proof that my job, my parents, Helen and the whole world are not simply my own invention, fantasies my imagination has improvized on the simple themes of my own form, my clothes, my chair, and the properties of my present environment.

He falls back on 'conviction, faith', his last defence against 'a huge futility' which threatens to grip him. He has reached, in Nietzsche's words in *The Birth of Tragedy*, 'those outer limits where the optimism implicit in logic must collapse. When the inquirer, having pushed to the circumference, realizes how logic in that place curls about itself and bites its own tail, he is struck with a new kind of perception.' He is on the brink of the Absurd.

'Cogito ergo sum' proves nothing, since the 'I' which is to be proved is already present in the proposition 'I think'. The argument is circular. Descartes nowhere proves that thought requires a thinker. That Hughes should use the phrase 'this drift of thoughts' surely leads us to relate the man's thoughts to the snowflakes (which he begins to call to and give the names of people). The snowflakes are thoughts, words, people, experiences, moments. In Beckett's *Endgame* they are the millet grains of Zeno's paradox, which can never be completely transferred from one pile to another, half the pile at a time, since, there being no highest number, there can be no smallest fraction:

Then babble, babble, words, like the solitary child who turns himself into children, two, three, so as to be together, and whisper together, in the dark. Moment upon moment, pattering down, like the millet grains of... that old Greek, and all life long you wait for that to mount up to a life. (*Endgame*)

And that life is 'a vast grey dissolution' and a patter of small events half of which are deaths. Hamm calls, as though to the man in the snow: 'Use your head, can't you, use your head, you're on earth, there's no cure for that' (*Endgame*). Pozzo calls to him: 'One day like any other day, one day he went dumb, one day I went blind, one day will go deaf, one day we were born, one day will die, the same day, the same second, is that not enough for you?

(*Waiting for Godot*). Hughes calls to him: 'Where are you heading? Everything is already here' ('You Drive in a Circle').

The 'single adventure' in these prose pieces is clear. In each case the protagonist, in a moment of crisis or state of extremity, loses his hold on habit, on the day-to-day 'reality' of work and play, peaceful Sundays, chapel, pin-stripe suits, suburban streets; loses his hold on the mind which insists on the reality of this world. Thus diminished and defenceless, another reality invades the vacuum of his brain. The man in 'The Rain Horse' only escapes when he submits to the 'superior guidance' of his most primitive instinct. Afterwards he 'just sat staring at the ground, as if some important part had been cut out of his brain'.

In 'The Harvesting' the brain is blacked out by the sun, then supplanted by the consciousness of a hunted hare. In 'Sunday' the screeching of the rat is not in the same world as the pleasant Sunday scene:

> supplanting every human brain inside its skull with a rat-body that knots and unknots.
>
> ('Song of a Rat')

In 'The Suitor' Pan himself fills the boy's brain with an 'inane ecstasy'. In 'The Wound', Ripley's brain is supplanted first by a bullet, then by 'animal instinct', then by images of the powers of the Great Outer Darkness, ('which is the same as the small inner darkness'). And in 'Snow' the protagonist's brain hangs on, madly refusing to acknowledge the void.

The boy Michael in 'Sunday' grew up to write 'Song of a Rat'. The rat in extremity, in the grip of death, stands on the threshold between two worlds, the world of dogs, traps, and a vulnerable body, meaning living and dying, and the world of disembodied spirits and powers which know nothing of space and time, life and consciousness. Here

> The rat is in the trap...
>
> Iron jaws, strong as the whole earth
> Are stealing its backbone.

The rat cannot reconcile itself to suffering as man has tried to do, by inventing some larger purpose in terms of which suffering, even one's own, can be accepted, by inventing such evasive sophistries as:

'This has no face, it must be God'

or

'No answer is also an answer'.

The rat can only confront the horror, which is all pain and death. For him there can be no distinction between understanding and experience. He can understand death only by dying.

The rat understands suddenly. It bows and is still,
With a little beseeching of blood on its nose-end.

Section II, 'The Rat's Vision', expands on that understanding. What the rat sees at that moment is the earth as a vast design of dereliction, like a no-man's-land, in mourning for its losses, anticipating nothing but further losses. The land is 'widowed'. The old barbed wire and 'trenched' gateway complete the suggestion of a deserted battlefield given over to wind and snow.

The rat screeches
And 'Do not go' cry the dandelions, from their heads of folly
And 'Do not go' cry the yard cinders, who have no future, only their
 infernal aftermath
And 'Do not go' cries the cracked trough by the gate, fatalist of star-
 light and zero
'Stay' says the arrangement of stars
Forcing the rat's head down into godhead.

The dandelions are finished, mere clocks now caught in the one-way process, the trap. The cinders are already burned out. The trough holds no water and so is doomed to futility and emptiness. They cry, 'do not go' to the rat, but they have gone themselves, for going is the system. The Universe is so arranged that life, in saying 'stay', opens its iron jaws for the kill.

The final section 'The Rat's Flight', follows the rat beyond death into his godhead. 'The horned Shadow of the Rat' crosses into power, leaving the rat's body as

A bloody gift for the dogs
While it supplants Hell.

It needs the whole weight of universal law to force his head down. He puts up such resistance that when he does let go, his soul catapults from him across the gulf with such velocity that it jolts the stars in their sockets and consumes the flames of hell. The fires of hell are continually recharged thus with the flames of Nature's bonfire.

Gnats are living sparks of that bonfire. 'Gnat-Psalm' is one of the most successful poems in *Wodwo*. At one level it is a marvellous evocation of a swarm of gnats:

> Scribbling on the air, sparring sparely,
> Scrambling their crazy lexicon.

The very words of the title, 'gnat' and 'psalm', with their clusters of surplus consonants, are a joy to players of Lexicon or Scrabble. Half the letters are quite without substance and seem to have come together by a process of shuffling. The dance is interpreted as the writing of illegible ephemeral messages on the air, then as

> Immense magnets fighting around a centre

but finally not as dancing or writing or fighting but as singing the song of themselves and of 'all the suns', the song of themselves as suns, as sources of brimming energy not to be blotted out by the earth's sun.

Their vision is very like the rat's vision, a vision of a world emptied of life, through which the wind howls and dances its death dance. But their song is quite unlike the rat's song. The rat's body anchors him in that world; the separation from it is an agony and a violation. The gnat-god, like every other, has been crucified, nailed to the cross of the physical world, which holds the body while the soul is torn from it. But it is so almost-bodiless ('its skin thin as the skin of fire' as 'Fire-Eater' put it), its connection with the solid world so tenuous that the cross is but air. It is nailed to nothing and the nails in its hands and feet do not stop them from dancing.

Gnats are nailed to their own dancing bodies, which with their mummy faces and the dangling legs of victims are already ridden to death. Their dance is not a violation or an agony. It is what they live for – to burn themselves up, to ride their own bodies to death. The vegetarian

> Tripped on Eternity's stone threshold

and heard 'the hounds of the grass'. But the gnats, living on air, are so insubstantial and weightless

> their agility
> Has outleaped that threshold
> And hangs them a little above the claws of the grass...

The rat had to cross into power over that terrible threshold of death. The gnats' hold on life is so tenuous that death is no matter. They are spirits already

> You are the angels of the only heaven!
> And God is an Almighty Gnat!

In Ionesco's *The Chairs*, the orator arrives to bring to a world whose cities 'faded right away' four hundred thousand years ago the secret of life, the occult doctrine, the key to the mystery. He turns out to be dumb, but chalks on a blackboard the word ANGEPAIN, Angelbread, then, as if equally significant, NNAA NNM NWNWNW V. Then, rubbing all this out, he writes ΛADIEU ΛDIEU ΛPΛ. Getting no reaction, since the room is empty, he leaves, disgruntled.

The gnats shuffle their 'dumb Cabala' (an oxymoron, since the Cabala was a purely oral tradition), rub out everything they write, jerk their letters into knots and tangles. Thus God reveals himself and his secrets, in the paradoxes of angels and pain, angels and bread, spirit and substance, power and helplessness, godhead and absence. What can human hands, tongue, brain accomplish in the face of such a God.

The poem ends with these vivid and expressive images and freely mimetic rhythms:

> My hands fly in the air, they are follies
> My tongue hangs up in the leaves
> My thoughts have crept into crannies
>
> Your dancing
>
> Your dancing
> Rolls my staring skull slowly away into outer space.

'Skylarks' is the most assured and accomplished of the larger poems in *Wodwo*. It is one of the great poems of the language. Quickly the poem is into its striking descriptive metaphors:

> Barrel-chested for heights,
> Like an Indian of the high Andes,
>
> A whippet head, barbed like a hunting arrow...

But before it can generate any rhythmic impetus and really launch the skylark, the rhythm drags it down again with struggling, leaden lines:

But leaden
With muscle
For the struggle
Against
Earth's centre.

Shelley, assuming the skylark's song to be an expression of careless rapture, and feeling that no creature of earth could know such pure delight and 'ignorance of pain', is driven to call his skylark an 'unbodied joy', a 'blithe Spirit'. Hughes, on the contrary, starts from the bird of muscle, blood and bone, feathers thrashing, lungs gasping, heart 'drumming like a motor', voicebox grinding like a concrete-mixer, and cannot believe that such climbing and singing can be done for joy.

> And singing still dost soar, and soaring ever singest

wrote Shelley. Why, and at what cost, Hughes asks.

Lead is the heaviest of the earth's substances, the most inimical to flight. But in its struggle against gravity the lark needs substantial muscles; it needs ballast if it is not to be wrecked by the storms of its own breath as the gaspings 'rip in and out':

Leaden
Like a bullet
To supplant
Life from its centre.

Life's centre, its only home, is the earth. Insubstantial ephemeral creatures such as gnats seem almost independent of it, but most creatures hang on, with mindless grip. The rat, try as it might, cannot uproot itself into its screeching. When its grip is broken by death, it rockets away from the earth. But the skylark can, without dying, launch off from earth in the body, uproot itself into its song, then fling that song like a sacrifice to the sun. But life's centre is also within, and to supplant that with a bullet is suicidal. Skylarks are 'crueller than owl or eagle' because their 'one path is direct through the bones of the living' ('Hawk Roosting') but, unlike a predator, the bones are their own. And what

> Gives their days this bullet and automatic
> Purpose? ('Thrushes')

The image of the head 'barbed like a hunting arrow' now generates the deeper image 'shot through the crested head'. The barb is what fixes there the command

Not die
But climb
Climb
Sing
Obedient as to death a dead thing.

Why should the command begin 'Not die', as though the command to die might have been expected? The earth is sending the skylarks to be 'burned out', 'sucked empty' by the sun. In 'The Crown', Lawrence describes it thus: 'It is a leap taken into the beyond, as a lark leaps into the sky, a fragment of earth which travels to be fused out, sublimated, in the shining of the heavens' (*Phoenix* II, 374). 'Fused out', 'sublimated', 'burned out' – what Lawrence and Hughes are both here trying to convey is surely a process of separating out the physical and the spiritual, body and soul, the soul to be taken up into the heavens, the body flung back to earth ('a gift for the dogs'), a process of breaking down

Like a breaker of ocean milling the shingle,

of total abandonment:

I suppose you just gape and let your gaspings
Rip in and out through your voice box

of giving up the ghost. But the skylark is commanded to do this *without dying*, and to live at that pitch is agony, self-immolation, crucifixion. By the time we come to the song itself

Joy! Help! Joy! Help!

it is 'Joy!' not 'Help!' which needs explaining.[9]

The watching poet loses sight and sound of the lark, now given over to the sun. It is as though the lark has crossed, for a moment, the threshold, the impossible gulf, leaving the earth also 'fused out' to its dross, irredeemably mere dust and clay, and the poet, wingless, enfolded by it:

The lark is evaporating
Till my eye's gossamer snaps
and my hearing floats back widely to earth

After which the sky lies blank open
Without wings, and the earth is a folded clod.

Is it fanciful to hear an echo in these lines of Keats' 'Ode to a Nightingale':

> Now more than ever seems it rich to die,
>   To cease upon the midnight with no pain
>   While thou art pouring forth thy soul abroad
>   In such an ecstasy!
>   Still wouldst thou sing, and I have ears in vain –
>   To thy high requiem become a sod.

The word 'folded' has several layers of suggestion: the earth folded in its time-bound geological strata; the earth with folded arms, ignoring the lark's cries for help with a foolish smile; but primarily, the earth with folded wings, pretending that flight is impossible, that there are no such things as skylarks. Is the earth hoping that its little missionaries will convert heaven to its own pointless processes?

At last the earth recalls them

> and they stoop
>
> And maybe the whole agony was for this
>
> The plummeting dead drop
>
> With long cutting screams buckling like razors

These lines describe quite literally the most spectacular but least familiar phase of the lark's flight. But the language takes us also beyond the literal. 'Stoop' is normally used of birds of prey stooping for the kill. The primary meaning of the word, in any case, is 'to bow down'. Razors would normally be folded or closed like wings. Here they are cutting to kill. What is being described here is a suicide-dive. 'The earth gives them the O.K.' means that they need no longer climb and sing but may now die and end their agony. But as their singing itself was, in its total self-abandonment, a little death, a miming of death, so too the suicide-dive is a mime, stopping just short of mixing their heart's blood with the mire of the land, able to stop short only perhaps, because they are now 'weightless', already sucked empty by the bloodthirsty sun.

I have deliberately ignored so far the poem's wit and humour, never more evident than in section VII. It is a sign of Hughes' new assurance that he feels he can afford not to be portentous or bullying, that he can be assumed to be taking himself seriously without having to be seen to be doing so. The poem itself is 'folded' in that it can be read simply as the record and rendering of the experience of watching and listening to larks 'all the dreary Sunday morning', or as a little myth as I have read it. And the two are not kept apart. Hughes weaves in and out. At the end, for example, he suddenly flares and glides off from the suicide-dive to witty, accurate observation of the skylarks in a tone of affectionate anthropomorphic banter.

> But just before they plunge into the earth
>
> They flare and glide off low over grass, then up
> To land on a wall-top, crest up,
>
> Weightless,
> Paid-up,
> Alert,
>
> Conscience perfect.

If the agony was not for suicide, then it was for *this*, for just being skylarks at one with the world. Hughes exploits the disparity between the real birds and the symbolic drama he has cast them in for comic purposes. But the disparity is there outside the poem and won't go away. What does it mean to be a skylark? Are they mad or are we?

So evocative and lucid and accessible is this poem at one level that many reviewers and critics have been betrayed into praising it for its charm. Possibly in order to make this response impossible Hughes added two new sections in *Selected Poems*. The new section IV describes the lark at the top of his flight as

> Like a mouse with drowning fur
> Bobbing and bobbing at the well-wall
>
> Lamenting, mounting a little –

stressing again the death theme. The other new section, section VIII, transforms the poem by giving it a new ending which, instead of returning us reassuringly to the self-satisfied larks, opens out the myth to relate directly to Celtic mythology in the figure of Cuchulain.

> Manacled with blood,
> Cuchulain listened bowed,
> Strapped to his pillar (not to die prone)
> Hearing the far crow
> Guiding the near lark nearer
> With its blind song
>
> *'That some sorry little wight more feeble and misguided than thyself*
> *Take thy head*
> *Thine ear*
> *And thy life's career from thee.'*

Cuchulain is the type of the hero, blinded by honour, who uses his superhuman strength to resist death. Though he is doomed from the start, his death foreknown, he believes that his courage will win him undying fame. He is invincible, but not invulnerable. He can only be overcome by magic or treachery. Even when he is strapped to a pillar and bleeding his life away, his enemies dare not approach to finish him (by beheading him) until Morrigu, the crow-headed Goddess of War, perches on his shoulder.

Cuchulain is like 'The Contender' in *Crow*:

> There was this man and he was the strongest
> Of the strong.
> He gritted his teeth like a cliff.
> Though his body was sweeling away like a torrent on a cliff
> Smoking towards dark gorges
> There he nailed himself with nails of nothing
>
> ('The Contender')

It is a 'senseless trial of strength'. He is as mad as the old woman in 'Pibroch' who 'hangs on because her mind's gone completely'.

The skylarks have also been 'sucked empty', have battered out their last sparks at the limit, but not for fame, not in resistance to life's imperatives, but in blind obedience and self-abandonment. Their song tells Cuchulain that, though he is 'the strongest of the strong' he is feeble in relation to the non-human powers he resists and totally misguided in that resistance. The lark blinded by the sun and guided by the bird of death, the crow, curses him with the curse he most dreads – that his death shall not be glorious, but humiliating.[10] The lark's words are a translation of part of a Gaelic charm.

This new closing section seems to be a Crow poem, or even a Prometheus poem (Prometheus and Cuchulain having much in common) arbitrarily tacked on to the ending of 'Skylarks' and different from it not only in subject matter but also in style and tone.

Perhaps Hughes wanted to guard against the possibility of a sentimental reading of 'Skylarks' or a reading which takes it to be no more than a very fine descriptive poem. The whole poem must be read differently with this ending. Much more weight must be given to the skylarks as living sacrifices and to their 'agony'.

But I feel that in trying to redress the balance Hughes has gone too far in the opposite direction and violated the unity of the poem with an ending quite lacking the wit which plays in the rest of the poem in the space between the vivid description and the symbolic significance.

Wings, as we saw in 'Skylarks', are for leaping off from earth towards the sun. They are for escaping from the weight of mortality. They are for gnats, birds and angels. Perhaps man flew once

> With unearthly access of grace,
> Of ease: freer firmer world found
> A hundred feet above ground.
> ('Acrobats')

Then came the fall. The only vestige of flight is the shadow of a huge broken wing man now trails behind him. The fall was from the grace of total self-abandonment into self-consciousness and blind rationality. As Blake chose real men, Newton and Locke, as exemplars of fallen man in his age, so Hughes chooses, in 'Wings', Sartre, Kafka and Einstein as exemplars in ours.

The pre-Christian prototype of fallen man was Icarus, who strained the resources of intellect and science to reach the sun on artificial wings. Hughes is concerned with the spiritual wings the soul miserably flaps in its cage, and with the blindness of men who substitute knowledge for vision.

All these parts of 'Wings' are marvellous purely physical descriptions of their subjects, Sartre's globular head and 'extinct eyeball', Kafka's big-eyed owlishness, like a pallid night-creature exposed to the glare of the photographer's lights, and Einstein's

> tired mask of folds, the eyes in mourning,
> The sadness of the monkeys in their cage—

In 'M. Sartre Considers Current Affairs', having fallen from that true vision which enables you

> To see a World in a Grain of Sand
> And a Heaven in a Wild Flower,
> Hold Infinity in the palm of your hand
> And Eternity in an hour
> (Blake, 'Auguries of Innocence')

Sartre regrows the world inside his skull, like the spectre of a flower. 'Spectre' is a term used by Blake in a very special sense which fits 'Wings' perfectly and adds greatly to its coherence.

(The half-quotation from Blake in 'single sandgrain' invites us to make the connection.) John Beer explains Blake's terms as clearly as they allow:

> The unified personality is unified by the vision which is allowed to shine through it; self-love is equivalent to the setting up of an inward barrier. It creates a new force, the selfhood, which stands between the vision and its free expression.
>
> As the selfhood begins to assume a life of its own, appropriating to its own use the energies of the individual, it becomes, in Blake's terminology, the 'spectre'; the imagination which remains is called the 'emanation'.
>
> The terms may perhaps be associated with Blake's critique of eighteenth-century mathematical thought as a way of thinking which divided the forces of the universe into two distinct phenomena – the 'spectre' sun, the spherical body which provides a focus for laws of gravitation, and the 'emanation' of vivifying light, which is mysteriously produced by this apparently dead body. If men saw even the sun as a divided image it was not surprising that they should conform to the same pattern, becoming what they beheld: each man became centre of his own mechanically organized little universe, disregarding his imagination as a meaningless accessory except in moments when he wished to relax from the serious clockwork of life. Blake felt, evidently, that if men saw the sun as he saw it, a form which is imposed on that infinite energy of the universe which shouts 'Holy, holy, holy is the Lord God Almighty, – and necessarily imposed if human life is to survive at all – they would see their own humanity in the same light. Spectre and emanation would disappear, their functions being integrated back into a human nature which acted no longer as a moonlit mechanism but as an expressive unity of vision and desire, seeing every thing that lives as holy.
>
> Until such an awakening, the spectre retains power in the individual, permitting his vision to linger on as impotent emanation. In representing the two split forces pictorially, Blake usually gives them both wings: the spectre has the dark sinister wings of the bat, the emanation the coloured irridescent wings of the butterfly. (*Blake's Visionary Universe*, 39–40)

The intellectual defines the world as the contents of his own brain, which has no miracles to reveal:

> Angels, it whispers, are metaphors, in man's image,
> For the amoeba's exhilarations.

His 'extinct eyeball' can see only facts, all of which are subsumed by the fact of mortality:

> His eyes are imprisoned in the fact
> That his hands have sunk to the status of flies.
>
> With skull-grins, the earth's populations
> Drift off over graves...

The only wings he sees are those of carrion-eaters, flies and skate.

His spirit, imprisoned in rationalism, denies Heaven, Infinity, Eternity. He sinks, like Blake's Newton, to the bottom of the sea of materialism.

> Pondering on the carrion-eating skate.
>
> And on its wings, lifted, white, like an angel's,
> And on those cupid lips in its deathly belly,
> And on the sea, this tongue in his ear, licking the last of pages.[11]

Kafka, for Hughes,

> is an owl, 'Man' tattooed in his armpit
> Under the broken wing...

The tattoo can only be seen when the wing is lifted in flight, but the broken wing cannot be lifted. Similarly the owl's large eyes are for peering into the darkness, but Kafka is condemned by his flightlessness to live in the stunning glare, under the arc-lamp of man's rational consciousness.

> He is a man in hopeless feathers

given the need to fly, commanded by his own nature to fly, without the means to fly. It is the predicament of the artist as described by Beckett in his *Dialogues with Georges Duthuit* 'The expression that there is nothing to express, nothing with which to express, nothing from which to express, no power to express, no desire to express, together with the obligation to express.' It is the predicament Kafka expressed in his diaries, his aphorisms, his fiction:

There is a goal, but no way. (*Reflections*)

Writing is a form of prayer. (*Reflections*)

Sometimes I think I understand the Fall of Man better than anyone else. (*Letters to Milena*)

Still unborn and already compelled to walk around the streets and speak to people. (*Diaries*)

The Castle in particular expresses the futility of the attempt to approach grace by the experience of reason. There may be a way from God to man, but there is no way from man to God. Yet Kafka felt the obligation to keep up his hopeless 'assault on the last earthly frontier' (*Diaries*).

Man has no other equipment for this assault but logic, language and mathematics. Perhaps Einstein flew highest of all, far into space, but without ever escaping from the prison of his own intellect:

Star peering at star through the walls
Of a cage full of nothing.[12]

He saw no miracles in space such as had sustained his ancestors in the desert:

And no quails tumbling
From the cloud. And no manna
For angels.
Only the pillar of fire contracting its strength into a star-mote.

Indeed he sought not the miracle of sweet water, but salt, stagnant knowledge:

Now the sargasso of a single sandgrain
Would come sweeter than the brook from the rock
To a mouth
Blasted with star-vapour.

The nearest he gets to prayer is in his playing of Bach. But music is also mathematics:

But it is the cauldron of the atom.
And it is the Eye of God in the whirlwind.
It is a furnace, storming with flames.

We are back to the Heraclitian fire of the material world, and to mortality, and the human consequences of mathematics in our time:

It is a burned-out bottomless eye-socket
Crawling with flies
In fugues...

His prayer for motherly love is answered not by angels but by a rising cloud of flies, not by the pillar of cloud by day, but by the mushroom cloud of nuclear explosion.

The inability to weep or love is symptomatic of a shifting of the centre of gravity away from 'man's sense of himself,...his body and his essential human subjectivity' and a surrender of his individuality to an 'impersonal abstraction'. For a physicist 'the centre of gravity is...within some postulate deep in space, or leaking away down the drill-shaft of mathematics'. (Introduction to Vasko Popa's *Selected Poetry*, 10–11.)

The poet and the physicist are concerned to explore 'the same gulf of unknowable laws and unknowable particles', but the poet must do it very differently. Hughes' metaphor for the poet's way is 'Wodwo'.

Sir Gawayn, in his journey through the Wirrall, fought with, among other creatures of that remote region, wodwos:

> Sumwhile with wormes he werres, and with wolves als
> Sumwhile with wodwos, that woned in the knarres,
> Bothe with bulles and beres, and bores otherwhile,
> And etaines, that him anelede of the heghe felle.
>
> (*Sir Gawayne and the Grene Knight*, 720–4)
>
> (Sometimes with serpents he fought, and with wolves also
> Sometimes with wodwos, that lived in the rocks,
> Both with bulls and bears, and at other times with boars,
> And giants that pursued him on the high fells.)

'Wodwos' is sometimes translated 'trolls', sometimes 'satyrs', sometimes 'wildmen of the woods'. It is this uncertainty of status – man or beast or monster or goblin – which attracts Hughes. Introducing a reading of the poem Hughes described his wodwo as 'some sort of satyr or half-man or half-animal, half all kinds of elemental little things, just a little larval being without shape or qualities who suddenly finds himself alive in this world at any time'.

In 'Wodwo' the speaker is himself a wodwo finding himself at large in a world inhabited by other creatures whose relation to himself he does not in the least understand, without roots ('dropped out of nothing casually'), not knowing why his nose leads him to water or his hands pick bark off a rotten stump, not knowing who he is or what he is doing there, supposing himself to be the exact centre of 'all this' and seeking to discover the circumference of himself. 'Very queer', he concludes, 'but I'll go on looking.'

Hughes is a wodwo in all his poems, asking these same questions of the world in which he finds himself, looking at that world and its creatures to discover where he ends and the other begins, and what relationship exists between the naked self and 'the endless without-world of the other'.

That Hughes is here expressing the activity of the poet, or of any man 'trying to find out what does exist, and what the conditions really are' is evident if we compare the poem with this prose passage:

> ...the living suffering spirit, capable of happiness, much deluded, too frail, with doubtful and provisional senses, so undefinable as to be almost silly, but palpably existing, and wanting to go on existing...homing in tentatively on vital scarcely perceptible signals, making no mistakes, but with no hope of finality, countinuing to explore.

It could be a paraphrase of 'Wodwo' but it is not. It is from Hughes' Introduction to Vasko Popa's *Selected Poetry* and it describes the efforts of a generation of East European poets to come to terms through poetry with the hostile world in which they are obliged to live and to salvage their humanity and self-respect.

The poet is also a child, for the world of children is very like the wodwo's world:

Theirs is not just a miniature world of naive novelties and limited reality – it is also still very much the naked process of apprehension, far less conditioned than ours, far more fluid and alert, far closer to the real laws of its real nature. It is a new beginning, coming to circumstances afresh. It is still lost in the honest amoebic struggle to fit itself to the mysteries. It is still wide open to information, still anxious to get things right, still wanting to know exactly how things are, still under the primeval dread of misunderstanding the situation. Preconceptions are already pressing, but they have not yet closed down, like a space helmet, over the entire head and face, with the proved, established adjustments of security. Losing that sort of exposed nakedness, we gain in confidence and in mechanical efficiency on our chosen front, but we lose in real intelligence. We lose in attractiveness to change, in curiosity, in perception, in the original, wild, no-holds-barred approach to problems. In other words, we start the drift away from the flux of reality and so from any true adaptation. We begin to lose validity as witnesses and participants in the business of living in this universe. (*Children as Writers* 2, v)

We have just been given, in the penultimate poem in the book, an example of such valid witnessing and participation. In 'Full Moon and Little Frieda', for the first time, there is a moment of harmony:

A cool small evening shrunk to a dog bark and the clank of a bucket –

And you listening.
A spider's web, tense for the dew's touch.
A pail lifted, still and brimming – mirror
To tempt a first star to a tremor.

Cows are going home in the lane there, looping the hedges with their
warm wreaths of breath –
A dark river of blood, many boulders,
Balancing unspilled milk.

'Moon!' you cry suddenly, 'Moon! Moon!'

The moon has stepped back like an artist gazing amazed at a work
That points at him amazed.

The poem testifies in its delicacy of utterance, its utterly fresh sense of wonder, to the possibility of knowing 'the redeemed life of joy' in normal daily experience, when, with an unspectacular access of grace, the elements of a scene – human, animal, domestic, rural, cosmic – suddenly cohere to express a plenitude, all the 'malicious negatives' miraculously melted away.

The evening has shrunk not only because the light is failing but also because, as it does so, time seems to slow down, as it approaches that crucial moment of nightfall, dewfall, the first tremor of the first star. And the poet is aware that his daughter is the hand pointing to that moment because she is utterly open, without defences, without distracting consciousness of past and future, to the scene, her fine web of senses perfectly tuned to it, tense as a spider's web, brimming as a lifted pail.

The cows, too, are part of the scene, the condensation from their 'warm wreaths of breath' falling like dew on the hedges, their udders brimming like the pail of water, their blood like a river flowing darkly through, bringing fertility, their bony haunches like boulders ballasting the moment, balancing its fragility and delicacy with permanence and solidity.

Perhaps it needs the child to register and hold all this because the poet cannot open himself, cannot jettison his knowledge of past and future, his knowledge that blood can be spilled as easily as milk and run in rivers outside the body, that boulders in a river are dangerous, that darkness is dangerous, that the moon is a fickle murderous goddess, that, as an earlier version ended:

> Any minute
> A bat will fly out of a cat's ear.

The poem as we have it holds all this at bay, submerges all darker knowledge which might disturb the perfect harmony of man and nature the child experiences.

With no self-consciousness to close her, she points at the moon with an amazement the moon can only reciprocate, like an artist whose work has come to life or perfectly reflects the life of its creator. Sylvia Plath said of her poem 'Nick and the Candlestick': 'A mother nurses her baby son by candlelight and finds in him a beauty which, while it may not ward off the world's ill, does redeem her share of it' (*The Art of Sylvia Plath*, 171). 'Full Moon and Little Frieda' is without irony because, through his child, Hughes is able to see the world with the eyes of unfallen vision. It is the first of his *Songs of Innocence*.

CROW

The man of theory, having begun to dread the consequences of his views, no longer dares commit himself freely to the icy flood of existence but runs nervously up and down the bank. He no longer wants to have anything entire with all the natural cruelty of things: to such an extent has the habit of optimism softened him. Wisdom, unmoved by the pleasant distractions of the sciences, fixes its gaze on the total constellation of the universe and tries to comprehend sympathetically the suffering of that universe as its own.

(Friedrich Nietzsche, *The Birth of Tragedy*)

In 1957 Ted Hughes met the American sculptor, engraver and publisher Leonard Baskin. Baskin was obsessed by corpses, and a variety of other things attended this obsession, including crows (which he engraved with disturbingly anthropoid characteristics). A later invitation from Baskin to Hughes to write a few little poems to accompany his engravings was the cause of the first Crow poems. Up to 1964 Hughes had never written about crows, though he was familiar with the prominent and rather grim part they play in so much of the world's folklore.

The first appearance of a crow was in a dialogue from *Eat Crow* (written in 1964):

SHE: A crow is a sign of life. Even though it sits motionless.

MORGAN: And a man, lying alone, among stones, with a rifle, lying limply, in a waterless land, in a grey desert of tumbled stone, with one bullet, a man dryer than a lizard, is a sign of life. Even though he does not move.

SHE: The crow watches the man.

MORGAN: Between the crow and the man, across three hundred yards of primaeval stone, a horrible connection has found its way. Now these two can never separate. The stones are in their usual trance, rapt to the circles of galactic dust. They hear nothing of the song of silence these two sing together, these two silent living ones, alone with each other in the stone land...The furnace roars in the silent man, and the crow glitters, in the early grey light, molten bronze and phosphors settling in his darkness, set out to cool, fresh from the furnace. The crow ruffles.

SHE: The crow is composed of terrible black voice. He is neither stone nor light. But voice that can hardly utter. He looks this way and that. The forms of the stones, the fractures of heavenly accident, the resolute quality of light, hold the crow anaesthetized, every hour in more skilled patience, resigned to the superior stamina of the empty horizon, limber and watchful.

MORGAN: The laws are still with the living.

SHE: The crow arrived before dawn, smelling the man, and settling to watch at extreme range.

MORGAN: And when he saw the crow, in the blue thinning light, the man gave thanks to the studded, baleful pallor of the heavens, and to this strange-faced company of stones. His prayer has produced not quails and not manna. A crow has come up from the maker of the world.

SHE: The crow watches the man.

Crow and man are signs of life because life is neither stone nor light, neither matter nor spirit; it is that which must struggle to preserve itself at the expense of others. The man must eat. He cannot eat stone nor drink light; he cannot become other than he is, needing to kill some other living thing to survive. So he waits with his rifle and one bullet for the crow to come within range. The crow too must eat, and cannot kill a man; but he can outwait him. This is the horrible connection between creature and creature: kill to live. Is it a god of love who has thus answered the man's prayer for food?

Several poems in *Wodwo* clearly announce the coming of Crow. In 'Logos', 'Reveille' and 'Theology' all the main characters of *Crow* except Crow himself are assembled – God, Adam, Eve and the Serpent. And all the conditions for his annunciation, the conviction that this cannot be the world God sought to create, perhaps not even the world he did create ('this is the dark intestine'), that there must be something outside God, prior to him, unimpressionable, inimical to his purposes, perhaps itself the creator of God or a precondition of his existence, or his necessary incarnation:

Creation convulses in nightmare. And awaking
Suddenly tastes the nightmare moving
Still in its mouth
And spits it kicking out, with a swinish cry – which is God's first cry.

. . .

God is a good fellow, but His mother's against Him.

('Logos')

The blackbird in 'Stations' III is almost Crow. And Crow has something in common with the wodwo, who asks:

Why do I find
this frog so interesting as I inspect its most secret
interior and make it my own?

Crow

plucked grass-heads and gazed into them
Waiting for first instructions.
He studied a stone from the stream.
He found a dead mole and slowly he took it apart,
Then stared at the gobbets, feeling helpless.
He walked, he walked
Letting the translucent starry spaces
Blow in his ear cluelessly.
('Crow Hears Fate Knock on the Door')

'Dawn's Rose' is, in its way, a perfect poem, a distillation of the spirit of *Crow*, as 'Pibroch' is of *Wodwo* or 'Snowdrop' of *Lupercal*. It has a mood of quiet thrilling loneliness:

Dawn's Rose

Is melting an old frost moon.

Agony under agony, the quiet of dust,
And a crow talking to stony skylines.

Desolate is the crow's puckered cry
As an old woman's mouth
When the eyelids have finished
And the hills continue.

A cry
Wordless
As the newborn baby's grieving
On the steely scales.

As the dull gunshot and its after-râle
Among conifers, in rainy twilight.

Or the suddenly dropped, heavily dropped
Star of blood on the fat leaf.

The crow's 'puckered cry' is equally like an old woman's death-rattle or a new-born baby's 'grieving' as its body is first brought into contact with cold steel. The cry is like the gunshot which perhaps wounded the crow and caused the cry.

So real is that sudden spattering of red on green in the last lines that we forget it is 'only' a metaphor for the wordlessness of the crow's cry, itself 'only' a giving voice to the general desolation. The poem itself is laminated, 'agony under agony', the dust quickly settling on yesterday's millionth layer.

But the language of 'Dawn's Rose' is too musical, its imagery too traditional to be typical of *Crow*. It is recognizably in the same tradition as, for example:

The woods decay, the woods decay and fall,
The vapours weep their burthen to the ground,
Man comes and tills the field and lies beneath,
And after many a summer dies the swan.
(Tennyson, 'Tithonus')

Hughes is well aware of the power and beauty which are at his command in the more traditional modes, but the overriding consideration is the necessity to 'Sing one's own tune':

I think it's true that formal patterning of the actual movement of verse somehow includes a mathematical and a musically deeper world than free verse can easily hope to enter...and the very sound of metre calls up the ghosts of the past and it is difficult to sing one's own tune against that choir. It is easier to speak a language that raises no ghosts. (*London Magazine*, January 1971, 20)

The rejection of musical language and traditional imagery which Hughes feels his theme demands is evident in 'Crow and the Birds'.

In 'Cape Ann' Eliot lists for ten lines the appropriate responses to all the 'delectable' birds seen and heard at that place. All are easy to appreciate, empathize with, anthropomorphize –

But resign this land at the end, resign it
To its true owner, the tough one, the sea-gull.
The palaver is finished.

Only the seagull does not pretend to be 'sweet' or to be concerned with anything but his own survival and that of his species. 'Crow and the Birds' opens with fourteen lines in which the distinctive sounds and movements of many birds are inscaped, and it is claimed for them that they are able, by being so wholly themselves, to get clear of the complexities and ugliness which characterize human life in an age of technology and pollution. They do not share man's smudge and smell. The images they generate are all of purity and naturalness. The reader who is despairing of finding beauty at this point in *Crow* will come with pleasure upon the opening lines of this poem:

When the eagle soared clear through a dawn distilling of emerald
When the curlew trawled in seadusk through a chime of wine-
    glasses
When the swallow swooped through a woman's song in a cavern
And the swift flicked through the breath of a violet

But it is all 'palaver'. They are not doing these things to gratify man's aesthetic sensibilities. The eagle soars to scan the earth for prey, and the swift, as we know from 'Crow Tyrannosaurus', is

> Pulsating
> With insects
> And their anguish...

Crow, the tough one, does not hide behind a disguise of beauty:

> Crow spraddled head-down in the beach-garbage,
> guzzling a dropped ice-cream.

The rejection of the palaver is also a crucial stylistic decision, like Eliot's

> The poetry does not matter
> ('East Coker').

The first idea of *Crow* was really an idea of a style. In folktales the prince going on the adventure comes to the stable full of beautiful horses and he needs a horse for the next stage and the king's daughter advises him to take none of the beautiful horses that he'll be offered but to choose the dirty, scabby little foal. You see, I throw out the eagles and choose the Crow. The idea was originally just to write his songs, the songs that Crow would sing. In other words, songs with no music whatsoever, in a super-simple and a super-ugly language which would in a way shed everything except just what he wanted to say without any other consideration and that's the basis of the style of the whole thing. I get near it in a few poems. There I really begin to get what I was after. (*London Magazine*, January 1971, 20)

Why does Hughes choose a crow as his protagonist? The prevalence of ravens and crows in folklore derives largely from the real bird's characteristics. The crow is the most intelligent of birds, the most widely distributed (being common on every continent), and the most omnivorous ('no carrion will kill a crow'). Crows are, of course, black all over, solitary, almost indestructible, and the largest and least musical of songbirds. It is to be expected that the Songs of the Crow will be harsh and grating. He kills a little himself, and, as carrion eater, is dependent on the killing of others and first on the scene at many disasters.

Eskimo legend tells that in the beginning the raven was the only creature and the world was, like him, black. Then came the owl and the world became white like him, with the whiteness of unending snow. Hughes' mythology of Crow is deeply rooted in such legends. Within it are several little contradictory apocryphal accounts of the creation of Crow. The most central goes like this:

God, having created the world, has a recurring nightmare. A huge hand comes from deep space, takes him by the throat, half-throttles him, drags him through space, ploughs the earth with him then throws him back into heaven in a cold sweat. Meanwhile man sits at the gates of heaven waiting for God to grant him audience. He has come to ask God to take life back. God is furious and sends him packing. The nightmare appears to be independent of the creation, and God cannot understand it. The nightmare is full of mockery of the creation, especially of man. God challenges the nightmare to do better. This is just what the nightmare has been waiting for. It plunges down into matter and creates Crow. God tests Crow by putting him through a series of trials and ordeals which sometimes result in Crow being dismembered, transformed or obliterated, but Crow survives them all, little changed. Meanwhile Crow interferes in God's activities, sometimes trying to learn or help, sometimes in mischief, sometimes in open rebellion. It is, perhaps, his ambition to become a man, but he never quite makes it.[1]

The whole myth is to be told as an epic folk-tale in prose with songs by and about Crow interspersed. A great deal of unpublished material exists, but the project is still incomplete. Few of the poems in *Crow* demand a knowledge of the mythic framework, some of which can, in any case, be deduced from the poems themselves.[2]

Crow has a distinguished lineage in mythology. The God of healing known variously as Cronos, Saturn, Aesculapius and Apollo, was a Crow-god. A Celtic name for him was Bran. Crow is a totem of England because Bran, when he knew himself to be dying, ordered his head to be severed and buried on 'The White Hill' (now Tower Hill) as a charm to protect England from invasion. This tradition has persisted to such an extent that when, during the Second World War, the Tower ravens died out, new ones were immediately supplied and their wings clipped to prevent them escaping.

The Celtic death-goddess, the Morrigu, was, as we have seen, a crow. She is the underground form of the original life-goddess. The crow is prominent in many other mythologies from America to China, and in alchemy. All these are ancestors of Hughes' Crow. *Crow* could easily have been as overtly syncretic as *The Waste Land*, a history of religion and ideology from Babylonian creation myth, through Middle Eastern religions to the collision of Judaism and its neighbours, the Manichees, the early Christians and the Roman Empire, the Reformation and its impact in England, Puritanism, down to the sickness of England now. It is not syncretic because

My main concern was to produce something with the minimum cultural accretions of the museum sort – something autochthonous and complete in itself, as it might be invented after the holocaust and demolition of all libraries, where essential things spring again – if at all – only from their seeds in nature – and are not lugged around or hoarded as preserved harvests from the past. So the comparative religion/mythology background was irrelevant to me, except as I could forget it. If I couldn't find it again original in Crow, I wasn't interested to make a trophy of it.

This method makes life very difficult for the reader, who, in the less successful poems, is confronted with something which, in the absence of clues to its antecedents, looks merely random and slapdash. For example, the beginning of 'A Kill':

Flogged lame with legs
Shot through the head with balled brains
Shot blind with eyes
Nailed down by his own ribs
Strangled just short of his last gasp
By his own windpipe
Clubbed unconscious by his own heart

look like nothing more than a lame attempt to revamp Marvell's splendid lines:

O who shall, from this Dungeon, raise
A Soul inslav'd so many wayes?
With bolts of Bones, that fetter'd stands
In feet; and manacled in Hands.
Here blinded with an Eye; and there
Deaf with the drumming of an Ear.
A Soul hung up, as 'twere, in Chains
Of Nerves, and Arteries, and Veins.
('A Dialogue between the Soul and Body')

Not many readers will be reminded by the phrase 'balled brains' of Conchubar, who was sling-shot in the head by a missile made of the dried brains of an enemy (an ancient Celtic missile). To keep the wound closed, the missile was allowed to stay in. Eventually, hearing of the crucifixion, Conchubar went mad with rage against Christ's crucifiers, and attacked a forest. The brain-ball then burst from his skull, his brains followed it, and he died. The lines also contain references or parallels to Norse sacrificial executions ('Nailed down by his own ribs'), folk-tales, and a Manichean text. In all these sources the physical mutilations involve psychic positives, but little sense of this gets into the poem. A rather more successful handling of the same subject (with the Celtic source actually quoted at some length) is 'Crow's Battle Fury'.

But when the method works well, as in many of the poems I shall later discuss, the resultant concentration and nakedness evokes a response in the reader very similar to that which Raymond Williams noted in reading Blake's *Songs of Experience*: 'Very quickly, if not always overtly, inquiry breaks beyond the texts, and it is easy to feel that there is no stopping-point short of the history of the world.' (*Guardian*, 29 November 1973)

The absence of 'music' and 'poetry' of the kind we are familiar with in English verse since the sixteenth century does not involve any lack of rhetorical force and vitality. The language and poetic technique is more varied than before. And there is much more use than ever before of the oldest poetic devices (such as survive in nursery rhymes and ballads, folksongs and charms) – repetitions and refrains, parallelism, catalogues and catechisms, incantations and invocations.

Crow opens with a statement of the book's basic dichotomy, that between blackness and light; and an introduction, as in an overture, to several of the primary themes:

Black was the without eye
Black the within tongue
Black was the heart
Black the liver, black the lungs
Unable to suck in light
Black the blood in its loud tunnel
Black the bowels packed in furnace
Black too the muscles
Striving to pull out into the light
Black the nerves, black the brain
With its tombed visions
Black also the soul, the huge stammer
Of the cry that, swelling, could not
Pronounce its sun.

('Two Legends' 1)

The eye at least we would expect to reflect some light from the world about him or, as the window of the soul, show some spark from within. But Crow is not yet born, and birth is not a release from the tunnel, the furnace, the tomb, into light; rather it is when everything goes black. For the tunnel is the circulatory system, the furnace the alimentary system, the tomb the skull, and death owns them all.

The fire within Crow is heat without light. The lungs strive to suck in light, the muscles to pull out into the light, the brain to release its visions from the body's tomb, the cry to pronounce such words as light and love. Light is enlightenment, freedom, joy, fulfilment, atonement. Life is the incarnation of the spirit, which is the absolute need for light, within the physical universe which totally excludes it.

> Black is the earth-globe, one inch under,
> An egg of blackness
> Where sun and moon alternate their weathers
>
> To hatch a crow, a black rainbow
> Bent in emptiness
> over emptiness
>
> But flying
>
> ('Two Legends' II)

A rainbow is a sign of creative interchange between heaven and earth, of fertility, of all the varied colours of experience. It is the token of the covenant between God and every living creature of all flesh, for perpetual generations. But Crow flies over a universe empty of God, given over entirely to Death. Crow bends over the world, under the weight of the world, like an unholy ghost. The poem is an inversion of the ending of Hopkins' 'God's Grandeur':

> The Holy Ghost over the bent
> World broods with warm breast and with ah! bright wings.

But Crow's flying is at least a sign of life and selfhood ('flying the black flag of himself'). Crow cannot be crushed whatever is done to him. He is the unkillable urge to keep trying in spite of everything. He is energy itself, infinitely corruptible, infinitely educable and transformable. In that sense he is stronger than death.

In the beginning was not the Word, God, the light that shineth in darkness. In the beginning was nightmare and chaos. Fear was the mainspring of the evolutionary process which produced man.

Man created God, who, like King Lear, handed his kingdom over to death, who is stronger than hope, the will, love and life:

Adam
begat Mary
Who begat God
Who begat Nothing
Who begat Never
Never Never Never
Who begat Crow
Screaming for Blood
Grubs, crusts
Anything
Trembling featherless elbows in the nest's filth
('Lineage')

God's first cry, when he is born into such a world, is a 'swinish cry' ('Logos'). Life, in such a world, becomes 'that pushing, self-protective, malodorous, carnivorous, lecherous fever which is the very nature of the organic cell' (Campbell, *The Hero with a Thousand Faces*, 121). Only the belief that mere existence, on any terms, however brief, is a triumph of self over death, could enable Crow to pass the 'Examination at the Womb Door' and enter once more the cycle of physical life.

The Tibetan Book of the Dead teaches techniques for closing the Womb Door. The whole point of all the disciplines of Buddhism is to 'become the light', to avoid reincarnation into the illusory world of desires and appearances. To pass through the Womb Door is to fail the examination. Crow's attachment to self is so total that he strives to open the Womb Door through which he can enter the blackness, the blindness of physical vision.

The next poem 'A Kill' is, in fact, the birth of Crow (or anyone), as he is delivered into the waiting hands of the gravedigger.

Crow is a developing character. Starting from 'nothing', his quest is to learn how to live according to the laws of creation. He confronts the evidence without evasion or sophistry, (he has a bird's eye view of it), and draws the obvious conclusions. In 'Crow Alights'

Crow saw the herded mountains, steaming in the morning.
And he saw the sea
Dark-spined, with the whole earth in its coils.
He saw the stars, fuming away into the black, mushrooms of the
nothing forest, clouding their spores, the virus of God.

And he shivered with the horror of Creation.

As he approaches from deep space Crow sees the earth to be composed entirely of living things – mountains pushing up to each other and steaming like cows on a chilly morning, the sea like a sea-serpent wound about the continents, the stars sowing their baleful influences upon the world like mushrooms broadcasting their invisible spores upon the air, sparks from the fire of God or viruses from his diseased body. It all seems horrible to Crow; so horrible that it must be a hallucination. But at least it is all vividly alive and interrelated, if only as predator and prey or virus and victim are related. But when Crow alights and sees what man has done to himself and the living body of the earth he sees something less dramatic and nightmarish, something so stark and commonplace and unchanging and unmistakably there that it must be reality, but something more horrible because utterly drained of life, utterly disconnected from the source, rootless, solitary, alienated.

He saw this shoe, with no sole, rain-sodden,
Lying on a moor.
And there was this garbage can, bottom rusted away,
A playing place for the wind, in a waste of puddles.
There was this coat, in the dark cupboard, in the silent room, in the
    silent house.
There was this face, smoking its cigarette between the dusk window
    and the fire's embers.
Near the face, this hand, motionless.
Near the hand, this cup.
Crow blinked. He blinked. Nothing faded.
He stared at the evidence.

The light fails at the window, heat fails in the hearth. Life burns away like a smoking cigarette. Nothing is in a vital relationship with anything else. Motionless hand cannot connect with blank face even by lifting a cup to it. Without relatedness the human being cannot function any more than a disconnected electrical machine. He is as absurd as and redundant as a shoe with no sole or a can with no bottom. But his garbage covers the earth and his cigarettes pollute the atmosphere.

But for all that Hughes is compassionate. The man is an image of loneliness and despair. The verse is moving in its bare scrupulousness and objectivity, like Beckett's prose.

Crow's response is to blink and stare. He cannot believe his eyes. He is not moved to sympathy. Even in 'That Moment', a poem to which the poet's own compassion gives great poignancy, Crow has the more important matter of his next meal to think of.

His first sign of conscience appears in the next poem 'Crow Tyrannosaurus':

> Crow thought 'Alas
> Alas ought I
> To stop eating
> And try to become the light?'
>
> But his eye saw a grub. And his head, trapsprung, stabbed.
> And he listened
> And he heard
> Weeping
>
> Grubs grubs He stabbed he stabbed
> Weeping
> Weeping
>
> Weeping he walked and stabbed
>
> Thus came the eye's
> roundness
> the ear's
> deafness.

Crow is not free to become a vegetarian. Stabbing grubs is what it is to be a crow. He has evolved a round eye the better to see grubs and an ear deaf to the universal weeping. But for the first time he has used the word 'ought' and wept for his own victims.

In 'Crow's Account of the Battle' reality gives Crow another lesson. 'Its mishmash of scripture and physics' (heaven and earth nailed together) results in a pattern of recurring war (scripture providing the motive and physics the means) for which no one seems responsible, since 'everything took the blame' and which comes to be accepted as inevitable, normal.[3] If this is really Crow's account, then Crow is coming to feel a genuine outrage:

> And when the smoke cleared it became clear
> This had happened too often before
> And was going to happen too often in future
> And happened too easily
> Bones were too like lath and twigs
> Blood was too like water
> Cries were too like silence
> The most terrible grimaces too like footprints in mud
> And shooting somebody through the midriff

Was too like striking a match
Too like potting a snooker ball
Too like tearing up a bill
Blasting the whole world to bits
Was too like slamming a door
Too like dropping in a chair
Exhausted with rage
Too like being blown to bits yourself
Which happened too easily
With too like no consequences.

Crow's outrage finds its outlet in the superstition that there is some external evil being responsible for all this, who can be hunted down and killed, like the Beast in *Lord of the Flies* (who is not only in the evil Jack, but in the thoroughly decent and civilized boys, Ralph and Piggy), like the killer in Ionesco's *Tuer Sans Gages* who, while the idealist Berenger dashes about the city in search of him, sits in Berenger's own chair in his own locked room.

Where is the Black Beast?
Crow sat in its chair, telling loud lies against the Black Beast.

The Beast must be inside your enemy. Or inside your brother (Abel). In his pursuit of the Black Beast Crow destroys everything he wanted to save from the Beast and looks everywhere but within himself. This is Crow as Trickster:

The so-called civilized man has forgotten the trickster. He remembers him only figuratively and metaphorically, when, irritated by his own ineptitude, he speaks of fate playing tricks on him or of things being bewitched. He never suspects that his own hidden and apparently harmless shadow has qualities whose dangerousness exceeds his wildest dreams. As soon as people get together in masses and submerge the individual, the shadow is mobilized, and, as history shows, may even be personified and incarnated. (C. G. Jung, 'On the Psychology of the Trickster Figure', Radin, *The Trickster*, 206)

It was also Jung who suggested, in *Answer to Job*, that God hid the devil from his own consciousness in his own bosom.

Crow's progress continues through 'Crow on the Beach':

He knew he grasped
Something fleeting
Of the sea's ogreish outcry and convulsion.
He knew he was the wrong listener unwanted
To understand or help –
His utmost gaping of brain in his tiny skull
Was just enough to wonder, about the sea,
What could be hurting so much?

until, in 'Crow's Nerve Fails', he finally recognizes himself as the Black Beast.

The strange combination of roles we find in Crow – all-suffering Everyman, culture-hero, clown-devil – links him unmistakably with one of the oldest figures in all mythology, Trickster: 'a clown figure working in continuous opposition to the well-wishing creator. . . as accounting for the ills and difficulties of existence this side of the veil.' (Campbell, *The Hero With a Thousand Faces*, 292). Paul Radin, in *The Trickster*, tells us about the Winnebago Trickster, Wakdjunkaga. After Earthmaker has created the universe and all its inhabitants, he discovers that evil beings, led by the Satan figure Hereshguina, not created by Earthmaker and existing since the beginning of time, are about to exterminate man, and sends Wakdjunkaga to teach man how to survive. But Wakdjunkaga is completely incompetent and selfish: 'He was like a small child crawling about. He accomplished no good and in fact injured Earthmaker's creation.' Because of him men die and steal and abuse women and lie and are lazy and unreliable. Sometimes he is even equated with Hereshguina. 'He does not at first accept responsibility for his actions, holding the world outside of himself as compelling him to behave as he does.' But later he shows signs of 'an awaking consciousness and sense of reality, indeed, the beginning of a conscience'.

All this could be describing Crow. In fact on the north-west coast of America the Trickster is Raven, who differs from Wakdjunkaga primarily in his insatiable appetite. The Eskimo of Bering Strait also have a Raven as trickster-hero.

Joseph Campbell records the following Trickster myth:

> The black Tatars of Siberia say that when the demiurge Pajana fashioned the first human beings, he found that he was unable to produce a life-giving spirit for them. So he had to go up to heaven and procure souls from Kudai, the High God, leaving meanwhile a naked dog to guard the figures of his manufacture. The devil, Erlik, arrived while he was away. And Erlik said to the dog: 'Thou hast no hair. I will give thee golden hair if thou wilt give into my hands these soulless people.' The proposal pleased the dog, and he gave the people he was guarding to the tempter. Erlik defiled them with his spittle, but took flight the moment he saw God approaching to give them life. God saw what had been done, and so he turned the human bodies inside out. That is why we have spittle and impurity in our intestines. (Campbell, *op. cit.* 294)

In 'A Childish Prank', God, having created Adam and Eve without souls, is beaten by the problem of how to invest them with any kind of purpose or stimulate them to any activity. Crow steps in and invents sexuality which has kept the race in perpetual motion ever since.

Christianity, for Hughes, is 'just another provisional myth of man's relationship with the creator' (*London Magazine*, January 1971, 16). Its inadequacies, as such, give rise to much of the comedy in *Crow*, where the God of Genesis often figures as something of a well-meaning booby. 'Apple Tragedy', for example, is also apple farce. Hughes here interprets the connection between the apple and original sin as cider, invented by God, drunk by Adam, Eve and the Serpent, and responsible for all our subsequent transgressions. If we imagine the Genesis story having derived from the interpretation or, more likely, the misinterpretation of an ancient icon on which the dumb images of God, serpent, man, woman, apple, hanged man, crucified man or God appeared, this reinterpretation is as good as any.

Sometimes, however, Crow's pranks or ineptitudes have consequences of full tragic proportions. In 'Crow's First Lesson', God tries to teach Crow to say Love, but the word is not in him:

> Crow gaped, and the white shark crashed into the sea

The incident is straight out of trickster mythology:

> To Karvuvu admired the Thum-fish and wanted to make one, but when he was taught how, he carved a shark instead. This shark ate the Malivaran-fish instead of driving them ashore. To Karvuvu, crying, went to his brother and said: 'I wish I had not made that fish; he does nothing but eat up all the others.' 'What sort of fish is it?' he was asked. 'Well,' he answered, 'I made a shark.' 'You really are a disgusting fellow,' his brother said. 'Now you have fixed it so that our mortal descendants shall suffer. That fish of yours will eat up all the others, and people too. (Campbell, *op. cit.*, 293)

Love is the first word God tries to teach Crow because God wishes all creation to be founded on it. But Crow can only express the principle of his own being, which is 'entire with all the natural cruelty of things'. God curses and weeps, for the effect of a world of sharks, blueflies, tsetses, mosquitos and stifling sexuality upon man

> Who trusted God was love indeed
> And love Creation's final law –
> Though Nature, red in tooth and claw

With ravine, shrieked against his creed.
(Tennyson, 'In Memoriam')

An even more serious intervention occurs in 'Crow Blacker Than Ever':

When God, disgusted with man,
Turned towards heaven.
And man, disgusted with God,
Turned towards Eve,
Things looked like falling apart.

But Crow   Crow
Crow nailed them together,
Nailing Heaven and earth together –

So man cried, but with God's voice.
And God bled, but with man's blood.

Then heaven and earth creaked at the joint
Which became gangrenous and stank –
A horror beyond redemption.

Man cannot be man, cannot live in this world, because his spirit strains towards heaven (a world without darkness, suffering and death). God cannot be God, for he must share the sufferings of this world. But Crow can be Crow

Flying the black flag of himself.

His intervention, perhaps misguided, is nevertheless an effort towards wholeness, an effort to live simultaneously on earth and in all the heavens and hells rather than allow things to fall apart and life to be polarized into irreconcilable extremes. Here is an example of the ease with which Hughes can move from comedy to deepest seriousness, of how Crow's wildly improbable escapades can dramatize the biggest theological issues. The incongruity is already there in the gap between the world as it is and the world as a loving God must have intended it. What has this earth to do with that heaven, that men must strain to become light and God be nailed to a cross in a vain attempt to teach man to pronounce the word 'love'?

'Crow Communes', one of the most tightly organized poems in *Crow*, is another variation on the same theme.

'Well,' said Crow, 'What first?'
God, exhausted with Creation, snored.
'Which way?' said Crow, 'Which way first?'

God's shoulder was the mountain on which Crow sat.
'Come,' said Crow, 'Let's discuss the situation.'
God lay, agape, a great carcase.

Crow is willing to accept instruction from God, but God's silence obliges him to let his own instincts point the way.

Crow tore off a mouthful and swallowed.
'Will this cipher divulge itself to digestion
Under hearing beyond understanding?'

The title implies not only that Crow attempts to converse with God and is reduced to talking to himself, but also that he participates in the rite of Holy Communion, or an unholy parody of it. In the Eucharist man becomes God by eating his body and drinking his blood. But if the body of God is merely this world, there can be nothing redemptive about eating it:

The dripping blood our only drink,
The bloody flesh our only food:
In spite of which we like to think
That we are sound, substantial flesh and blood...
(T. S. Eliot, 'East Coker')

The great carcase of God from which Crow tears off a mouthful is not only the unredeemed world. It is also the corpse of that redemptive love – 'agape' – which was also the name of a love-feast held by the early Christians in connection with the Lord's Supper. Crow feels much stronger for his meal. That is his only illumination, his only claim to be 'the hierophant', the expounder of sacred rites and mysteries.

Crow, the hierophant, humped, impenetrable.
Half-illumined. Speechless.
(Appalled.)

Crow is so appalled by the secret he has half-perceived that he is struck dumb. Humped like a stone, impenetrable as stone, silent as stone, covered with the pall of his own blackness, he stands at the end more like a gravestone than a priest.

The God Crow has to deal with is neither God the Creator nor the God who spoke to Job out of the whirlwind. That God, who incorporated Satan and serpent, hawk and shark, could easily have coped with Crow.

Finding the right speech for Crow involved me in inventing a longish series of episodes, beginning in traditional fashion, in heaven, where Crow is created, as part of a wager, by the mysterious, powerful, invisible prisoner of the being men called God. This particular God, of course, is the man-created, broken down, corrupt despot of a ramshackle religion, who bears about the same relationship to the Creator as, say, ordinary English does to reality. He accompanies Crow through the world in many guises, mis-teaching, deluding, tempting, opposing and at every point trying to discourage or destroy him. Crow's whole quest aims to locate and release his own creator, God's nameless hidden prisoner, whom he encounters repeatedly but always in some unrecognisable form. (*Crow*, Claddagh Records CCT 9–10, 1973)

The form in which Crow most frequently encounters his own creator is the serpent, which is God's prisoner only in the sense that it is imprisoned within its serpent form in which it cannot be seen by man or Crow as other than ugly and destructive. In 'A Horrible Religious Error' Crow blames the serpent for the deplorable condition of fallen man and woman, and thinks he has saved them by eating it. He thinks he is swallowing death, but he is swallowing something much bigger (creation itself, mother of all), as in the archetypal religious error, the slaughter of Tiamat by the upstart god Marduk.[4]

In Hughes' adaptation of Seneca's *Oedipus* Jocasta says:

I carried him for disease
for rottenness and dropping to pieces
I carried him for death bones dust   I knew
but I carried him not only for this I carried him to be king of this
and my blood didn't pause
didn't hesitate in my womb
considering the futility
It didn't falter reckoning the odds

...

and what was I   what cauldron was I
what doorway was I   what cavemouth

Her womb is the cave of the sphinx in 'her nest of smashed skulls and bones'. She is like the woman in 'Fleeing from Eternity' who, 'lying among the bones on the cemetery earth', sang out of her belly. The song is the hope that the mother invests, that the gods and the whole earth invest in every new birth. The new-born baby Jocasta delivered into the blackness of the sphinx's maw was 'a bag of blood a bag of death a screaming mouth', but also

he was a king's son   he was a man's shape
he was perfect

...

he was the warrant of the gods
he was their latest attempt
to walk on the earth and to live
he only had to live.

But Oedipus cannot live without solving the sphinx's riddle –

Four legs three legs two legs one leg
Who goes on them all.

The correct answer – 'Man' – would imply an acceptance of a definition of man's life in terms of its stages within time towards death, and that would be to admit that we are already inside the sphinx – 'as if we were living inside her carcase'.

'Song for a Phallus' is a savagely comic rendering of the Oedipus story. Oedipus here pits himself against his mother, his fate, the facts of life. He seeks to counter the riddle of the sphinx (the serpent is 'the sphinx of the final fact') with sheer brutality:

Oedipus took an axe and split
  The Sphinx from top to bottom
The answers aren't in me, he cried
  Maybe your guts have got 'em.

The answer indeed emerges in the form of his own mother. But Oedipus is ruthless, crazed, in his determination to smash his way out of the darkness, the cycle of birth and death and replacement represented by the mother:

He split his Mammy like a melon
  He was drenched with gore
He found himself curled up inside
  As if he had never been bore.
                    Mamma   Mamma

This symbolic violation of the mother, and the infantile 'Mamma Mamma' at the end of every stanza, suggest that his fury is a transference of the repressed incest-wish. Jung gives an interpretation of the sphinx which exactly fits the use Hughes makes of it and enables us to relate it to many of his other theriomorphic images:

In consciousness we are attached by all sacred bonds to the mother; in the dream she pursues us as a terrible animal. The Sphinx, mythologically considered, is actually a fear animal, which reveals distinct traits of a mother derivate. In the Oedipus legend the Sphinx is sent by Hera, who hates Thebes on account of the birth of Bacchus; because Oedipus conquers the Sphinx, which is nothing but fear of the mother, he must marry Jocasta, his mother, for the throne and the hand of the widowed queen of Thebes belonged to him who freed the land from the plague of the Sphinx. The genealogy of the Sphinx is rich in allusions to the problem touched upon here. She is a daughter of Echnida, a mixed being; a beautiful maiden above, a hideous serpent below.

In this she is all women:

Above – the well-known lips, delicately downed.
Below – beard between thighs.

Above – her brow, the notable casket of gems.
Below – the belly with its blood-knot.

Above – many a painful frown.
Below – the ticking bomb of the future.

Above – her perfect teeth, with the hint of a fang at the corner.
Below – the millstones of two worlds.

Above – a word and a sigh.
Below – gouts of blood and babies.

Above – the face, shaped like a perfect heart.
Below – the heart's torn face.

('Fragment of an Ancient Tablet')[5]

Jung continues:

This double creature corresponds to the picture of the mother; above, the human, lovely and attractive half; below, the horrible animal half, converted into a fear animal through the incest prohibition. Echnida is derived from the All-mother, the mother Earth, Gaea, who, with Tartaros, the personified underworld (the place of horrors), brought her forth. Echnida herself is the mother of all terrors, of the Chimaera, Scylla, Gorgo, of the horrible Cerberus, of the Nemean Lion, and of the eagle who devoured the liver of Prometheus; besides this she gave birth to a number of dragons. One of her sons is Orthrus, the dog of the monstrous Geryon, who was killed by Hercules. With this dog, her son, Echnida, in incestuous intercourse, produced the Sphinx. (*Psychology of the Unconscious*, 112–13)

Several other poems link Crow with Oedipus. In 'Oedipus Crow', Crow in his pride wants to deny his own mortality, to cut himself off from all mortal things, to measure time by his own pulse. Oedipus too regarded himself as the measure of all things and sought to evade his fate. But every step brought him closer to it, until, mutilated, he served as a living warning to mankind.

In 'Revenge Fable'

> There was a person
> Could not get rid of his mother
> As if he were her topmost twig.
> So he pounded and hacked at her
> With numbers and equations and laws
> Which he invented and called truth.
> He investigated, incriminated
> And penalized her, like Tolstoy,
> Forbidding, screaming and condemning,
> Going for her with a knife,
> Obliterating her with disgusts
> Bulldozers and detergents
> Requisitions and central heating
> Rifles and whisky and bored sleep.
>
> With all her babes in her arms, in ghostly weepings,
> She died.
>
> His head fell off like a leaf.

This poem is about the desecration of nature – 'the great civilised crime of intelligence that like the half-imbecile, omnipotent, spoiled brat Nero has turned on its mother' (*The Art of Sylvia Plath*, 190).

In 'Crow and Mama' also Hughes sees all our frenzied intellectual and technological activity as an attempt to get rid of the mother. The Rationalist pursues what he chooses to call 'truth' by means of his arbitrary systems. The idealist, the humanist, in his pursuit of improvements, turns his back on his own basic humanity, the bond of blood, the 'strandentwining cable of all flesh', as Stephen Dedalus calls it (*Ulysses*, 34), linking all back to Eden, back to that 'belly without blemish' which is also the 'womb of sin'. Crow can travel by car or plane or rocket, but he drives in a circle, arriving always at his point of origin, his consubstantiality with his mother, with his furthest ancestors, with 'all flesh'. This unbroken umbilical cord carries the doom of Oedipus or any man (nemesis in the chromosomes) but also 'the warrant of the gods'. It is the tap root, the source of vitality and creativeness as of sin and destruction. To cut it or repudiate it is suicidal.[6]

St George, in Crow's account of him, is just such a 'civilized man'. He is a mathematician, nuclear physicist, bio-chemist:

He sees everything in the Universe
Is a track of numbers racing towards an answer.
With delirious joy, with nimble balance
He rides those racing tracks. He makes a silence.
He refrigerates an emptiness,
Decreates all to outer space.

He is Einstein again

Finding the core of the heart is a nest of numbers.

But

the centre of gravity is not within some postulate deep in space, or leaking away down the drill-shaft of mathematics, but inside man's sense of himself, inside his body and his essential human subjectivity, his refusal to surrender his individuality to any impersonal abstraction. (Introduction to Vasko Popa's *Selected Poetry*)

When a man does surrender his individuality he turns his heart into a nest of monsters whose shapes he then projects onto those nearest to him. Believing himself to be the pure heroic St George he kills these dragons of his own creating. St George, not the dragon, is the Black Beast.

Hughes is here bringing up-to-date not only the story of St George but 'the whole repetitive history of the militant ethos... and the madness behind it – unacknowledged because it contains everything rejected and ignored'. The immediate source was a Japanese folk tale about a Samurai whose professional pride and militancy ossifies into a madness in which he kills his wife and children. The same thing happened to Hercules in that little-known part of his story Seneca deals with in *Hercules Furens*.

There are even older sources, for example the brutal slaughter of Tiamat, the mother (often represented as serpent or dragon), by Marduk: 'Tiamat was a personification of the sea and represented the feminine element which gave birth to the world. In the continuation of the story she represents the blind forces of primitive chaos against which the intelligent and organising gods struggle' (Larousse *Encyclopaedia of Mythology*, 50).

The violence of 'Crow's Account of St George' is comparable with that of the *Epic of the Creation*:

He let fly an arrow, it pierced her belly.
Her inner parts he clove, he split her heart.
He rendered her powerless and destroyed her life.
He felled her body and stood upright on it.

St George killing the dragon is the debased form in which this myth has come down to us. Hughes takes him to stand for the kind of madness, which, in the name of intelligence, seeks to destroy or at least dissociate itself from Nature on the grounds that Nature eats her own offspring (in other words includes death).

> Hero by hero they go –
> Grimly get astride
> And their hair lifts.
>
> She laughs, smelling the battle – their cry comes back.
>
> Who can live her life?
> Every effort to hold her or turn her falls off her
> Like rotten harness.
>
> Their smashed faces come back, the wallets and the watches.

This is 'Bones', the crazy pony on which they ride out, the inevitable death within their own bodies. To seek out death itself, riding on death as we ride our own skeletons, hoping to kill death, would be madness.

The journey must be, as Lawrence says, 'into the everlasting hinterland of consciousness'. The dragon we must do something about is the terror, the fear of death and everything else in nature or space which we fear because we do not understand, or understanding, cannot be reconciled with. What would it mean to kill the dragon? Nature is indivisible. Kill the red dragon of destruction and you kill the green dragon of creation. Kill the powers of the non-human world and you kill the earth-mother, the tree upon which humanity is a leaf.

Numbers create bombs and monsters. Words, too, can kill. They have an existence quite apart from anything in the real world, especially those great abstractions like 'Freedom' to which many men have sacrificed themselves and others. We think in words, yet our vocabulary comes loaded with the assumptions of our culture:

> Words are continually trying to displace our experience. And in so far as they are stronger than the raw life of our experience, and full of themselves and all the dictionaries they have digested, they do displace it. (*Poetry in the Making*, 120)

Words like 'civilization', 'science', 'progress' and 'productivity' displace an unspeakable reality

> ...burning whole lands
> To dusty char.

Such a word eats people and drains Nature until it puddles 'like a collapsing mushroom' for lack of any more to digest:

> Its era was over.
> All that remained of it a brittle desert
> Dazzling with the bones of earth's people
>
> Where Crow walked and mused.
>
> ('A Disaster')

In 'The Battle of Osfrontalis' words lay claim to determine Crow's life, responsibilities, aspirations, indulgences. But Crow, unlike man, is word-resistant. He is too firmly grounded for them in the reality of a pie, pickled onions, and a glass of water.

> Words retreated, suddenly afraid
> Into the skull of a dead jester
> Taking the whole world with them –
>
> But the world did not notice.
>
> And Crow yawned – long ago
> He had picked that skull empty.

A world given over to the pseudo-life of words might as well be inside the skull of a dead jester where ghostly words reverberate without meaning. Crow long ago learned what Hamlet so belatedly learns, the absurdity of words.

Nevertheless, in 'Crow Goes Hunting', Crow decides to try words. Surely you can catch things by simply naming them. But his words, clear-eyed, resounding and well-trained as they are, cannot pluck out the heart of the mystery of a hare:

> Crow was Crow without fail, but what is a hare?
>
> It converted itself to a concrete bunker.
> The words circled protesting, resounding.
>
> Crow turned the words into bombs – they blasted the bunker.
> The bits of bunker flew up – a flock of starlings.
>
> Crow turned the words into shotguns, they shot down the starlings.
> The falling starlings turned to a cloudburst.
>
> Crow turned the words into a reservoir, collecting the water.
> The water turned into an earthquake, swallowing the reservoir.
>
> The earthquake turned into a hare and leaped for the hill
> Having eaten Crow's words.

The elusiveness of real experience and real creatures when we try to capture them with words is cleverly conveyed here by refashioning an ancient magical formula found at its purest, perhaps, in the *Romance of Taliesin*:

And she went forth after him, running. And he saw her, and changed himself into a hare and fled. But she changed herself into a greyhound and turned him. And he ran towards a river, and became a fish. And she in the form of an otter-bitch chased him under the water, until he was fain to turn himself into a bird of the air. She, as a hawk, followed him and gave him no rest in the sky. And just as she was about to stoop upon him, and he was in fear of death, he espied a heap of winnowed wheat on the floor of a barn, and he dropped among the wheat, and turned himself into one of the grains. Then she transformed herself into a high-crested black hen, and went to the wheat and scratched it with her feet, and found him out and swallowed him. (Trans. Lady Charlotte Guest)

Thus Crow learns what Hughes tells us in *Poetry in the Making*:

The meaning of our experience is finally unfathomable, it reaches into our toes and back to before we were born and into the atom, with vague shadows and changing features, and elements that no expression of any kind can take hold of.

Crow is left at the end 'speechless with admiration'.

Proteus, the Old Man of the Sea, had the gift of prophecy, but was loth to reveal his secrets. He also had the ability to change shape at will. But if his questioner could keep a grip on him through all his changes, he would at last resume his natural shape and tell all. In 'Truth Kills Everybody' Crow finds Proteus, embodiment of all those exploding truths the sea contains ('the gulfing of the crab's last prayer'). Again the ancient formula of shape-changing offers Hughes a splendid model. Here, since the challenge is to hold on, not to change faster, and the contest is not between magicians, but between mere human tenacity and all the occult forces of the world, the appropriate model is 'Tam Lin', where Janet can only rescue her lover Tam Lin from the Queen o'Fairies by gripping him through all the changes he will undergo:

They shaped him in her arms twa
  An aske but and a snake;
But aye she grips and hau'ds him fast,
  To be her warldis make.

They shaped him in her arms twa
  A hot iron at the fire;
But aye she grips and hau'ds him fast
  To be her hearts desire.

Janet wins her lover. The ancient Greek who held Proteus won his secrets. But Crow's tenacity is rewarded with the truth to end all truths – universal disintegration:

> The ankle of a rising, fiery angel – he held it
>
> Christ's hot pounding heart – he held it
>
> The earth, shrunk to the size of a hand grenade
>
> And he held it he held it and held it and
>
> BANG!
>
> He was blasted to nothing.

It is the same truth Crow sees, when, in 'Crow's Vanity', he looks in 'the evil mirror'

> For a glimpse of the usual grinning face

but sees, with every breath, a new aeon of accomplishment or debacle appear, mist over, disappear. His allegiance to the illusory satisfaction of the temporal, physical world, is shaken again in 'Magical Dangers', where power, speed, freedom, wealth, sex, intelligence, all betray him. Finally

> Crow thought of nature's stupor –
> And an oak tree grew out of his ear.
>
> A row of his black children sat in the top.
> They flew off.
>
> Crow
> Never again moved.

Nature is no still life. The immense powers at work in, say, the growth of an oak, are not lessened because, by an arbitrary human time-scale, they work slowly. Time gives a little jolt and suddenly the oak-tree is fully grown with his own children perched aloft, superseding Crow.

Alan Watts could be summing up these poems when he writes: 'But the conduct and regulation of the whole human organism, not to mention the whole universe, is manifestly an affair so swift and so complex that no lumbering string of words can account for it.' He goes on to speak of those who believe in 'nature's stupor':

> The academic materialist who is, perhaps, a scientific empiricist or a logical positivist or a 'sound' statistical psychologist, whose real aim is to demonstrate that all nature is perfectly banal and dull. The trouble with this fellow is that no one ever mixed raven's blood with his mother's milk. He is marvelously and uncannily bereft of any sense that existence is odd. (*Beyond Theology*)

Owl in 'Owl's Song' does not make that mistake:

> He sang
> How the swan blanched forever
> How the wolf threw away its telltale heart
> And the stars dropped their pretence
> The air gave up appearances
> Water went deliberately numb
> The rock surrendered its last hope
> And cold died beyond knowledge
>
> He sang
> How everything had nothing more to lose
>
> Then sat still with fear
>
> Seeing the clawtrack of star
> Hearing the wingbeat of rock
>
> And his own singing.

The wolf is dead, but the star now leaves its clawtrack. The swan is dead, but the rock flies with its wingbeat. Magical transformations indeed, testifying to the power of life to renew itself. But though the roles may change, the pattern – clawtrack and wingbeat – is the same, horribly magnified to a cosmic scale. There is no reconciling predator and prey even among the stars. What frightens Owl as much as clawtrack of star or wing-beat of rock is the sound of his own singing. His singing seems no part of him. It is much more than the expression of his fear or despair which would express themselves in screaming or silence. You cannot *sing* that you have nothing more to lose; your song is something more. His singing does seem part of the total order, as though the universe were an infinite owl whose song was also his song.

What amazes Hughes is that so bleak a vision as his should issue in song, a song as unmelodious as Owl's or Crow's, but still a cry, an assertion of self-hood and consciousness against everything, or, it may even be, in harmony with everything.

'Crow's Undersong' is about an unspecified 'she', who is presumably the essential female, the eternal Eve, who guarantees the continuity of life through love, of suffering and death also, and of the hope which persists as long as there is life:

> She has come amorous it is all she has come for
>
> If there had been no hope she would not have come

And there would have been no crying in the city
(There would have been no city)

Perhaps Hughes was thinking of that other first woman, Pandora. Before she came to men Pandora was adorned with wreaths of flowers and in the wreath on her head many animals were portrayed. Her name means 'the all-giving', a name of the Earth itself. She gave to men all evils, including death, but she also brought hope, and, in her own person, a guarantee of the continuing of life, the means of replenishing the earth. Is she to be reviled for the one gift or worshipped for the other? For all her deficiencies and vulnerability, she seems able to bring human life into a living relationship with the richness of the natural world:

She comes dumb she cannot manage words
She brings petals in their nectar fruits in their plush
She brings a cloak of feathers an animal rainbow
She brings her favourite furs and these are her speeches

These rich lines suggest all the bounty of earth, an earth freely yielding far more than man needs. The phrase 'animal rainbow' suggests not only the amazing variety of creatures but also a harmonious and fruitful interrelationship, a reconciling of opposites (sun and rain, heaven and earth), and, together with the paradisal imagery of the context, the bow which the Creator sets in the cloud as the token of his covenant with the creatures of all flesh. Perhaps 'she' is the Creator, or Creatress, of all this, Nature. At all events she is the opposite of the St George figure, the man who comes so much further with his words and numbers and machines that he has utterly lost touch with nature.

Every fertility goddess is enigmatic, has her underworld or destructive form, as Hecate is the underground form of Aphrodite/Venus, and Persephone/Proserpina of Ceres/Demeter. Compare with Hughes' poem this prayer of Lucius:

Queen of Heaven, whether thou art the genial Ceres, the prime parent of fruits; – or whether thou art celestial Venus; – or whether thou art Proserpina, terrific with midnight howlings – with that feminine brightness of thine illuminating the walls of every city. (Apuleius, *The Golden Ass*)

Almost all mythologies have recognized the need for a female principle to balance and complete the male godhead. The Egyptians had Isis, the Assyro-Babylonians Ishtar (with her holy city Erech), the Greeks Astarte or Aphrodite, the Indians Shakti... In

Proverbs and Ecclesiasticus and the Song of Solomon we meet the figure of Sophia:

> The Lord possessed me in the beginning of his way,
> before his works of old.
> I was set up from everlasting, from the beginning,
> or ever the earth was.
> When there were no depths, I was brought forth:
> when there were no fountains abounding with water.

She claims to have been with God during the creation, helping, delighting him and rejoicing:

> Rejoicing in the habitable part of his earth;
> and my delights were with the sons of men.
> (Proverbs, 8:22–4, 31)

> He created me from the beginning before the world,
> and I shall never fail.
> In the holy tabernacle I served before him;
> and so was I established in Sion.
> Likewise in the beloved city he gave me rest,
> and in Jerusalem was my power.

She compares herself to many trees – cedar, cypress, palm-tree, rose, olive, terebinth – all from ancient times symbols of the Semitic love and mother goddess.

> As the vine brought I forth pleasant savour,
> and my flowers are the fruit of honour and riches.
> I am the mother of fair love,
> and fear, and knowledge, and holy hope:
> I therefore, being eternal, am given to all my children
> which are named of him.
> (Ecclesiasticus, 24: 9–11, 17–18)

Jung describes her as the

> hypostatized pneuma of feminine nature that existed before the Creation... the feminine numen of the 'metropolis' par excellence, of Jerusalem the mother city. She is the mother-beloved, a reflection of Ishtar, the pagan city-goddess...She realizes God's thoughts by clothing them in material form, which is the prerogative of all feminine beings. (*Answer to Job*, ch. III)

I don't want to suggest that the 'she' of 'Crow's Undersong' *is* Sophia or Ishtar, or any other mythological figure. These myths testify to deep and permanent truths which the imaginative writer may rediscover quite independently. For a man to try to understand a mother, a wife, or a daughter is to try to understand his own underself, the repressed feminine nature in all men.[7] An undersong is a subordinate song or strain, figuratively, an underlying meaning. Perhaps under all the Crow songs with their bleakness runs this undersong, this counter-song of love, hope, bounty and all the varied colours and relationships of the created world.

Given the terrifying world of *Crow*, what human orientation towards it is remotely adequate? Hughes explores several possibilities (perhaps all the possibilities). To give a sense of the range of his explorations, I must refer to several poems not yet included in any edition of *Crow* – 'Crow's Song About God', 'Existential Song', 'Song of Woe', 'Crow Wakes' and 'The New World', and two poems which were added to the English text in the second edition – 'The Contender' and 'Crow's Elephant Totem Song'.[8]

Kafka once said that there is no way from man to God, only a way from God to man. *The Castle* can be interpreted as an illustration of this. If this is true, it might seem at first that there is nothing to be done but wait, passively, for God (or Godot) to come. In *The Trial* a man waits all his life outside the doorway of the Law, forbidden by the fearsome doorkeeper to enter. He waits until he dies.

In 'Crow's Song About God'

> Somebody is sitting
>   Under the gatepost of heaven
> Under the lintel
> On which are written the words:
>   'Forbidden To the Living'.

The next forty-six lines are a description of this person, deformed and mutilated to a degree no real person could ever be. It would be easy to discuss the poem as yet another Hughes caricature of mutilation if we did not register that this 'person' is no real individual man, but an image of what a single man might be like on whom had been perpetrated all the violations men perpetrate not only upon themselves and one another but upon the body of the earth:

>   the life shape
> A rooty old oak-stump, aground in the ooze
> Of some putrid estuary
>   ...

His blood filtering between
In the coils of his body, like the leech life
In a slime and ochre pond
Under the smouldering collapse of a town dump

...

His solar plexus crimped in his gut, hard,
A plastic carnation
In a gutter puddle
Outside the registry office

...

Face gutted with shadow, like a village gutted with bombs

The man becomes the metaphor for a sick and polluted life which can neither cure itself nor die,

Clinging to the tick of his watch
Under a dream muddled as vomit
That he cannot vomit, he cannot wake up to vomit

The muddled dream is perhaps his hope that keeps him alive, his hope of being saved, admitted to heaven by God.

But God sees nothing of this person
His eyes occupied with His own terror
As he mutters
My Saviour is coming,
He is coming, who does not fear death,
He shares his skin with it,
He gives it his cigarettes,
He cuts up its food, he feeds it like a baby,
He keeps it warm he cherishes it
In the desolations of space,
He dresses it up in his best, he calls it his life –
He is coming.

God is also lost in a muddled dream, a nightmare terror of death, from which he cherishes the crazy hope that man will deliver him (the same man who lolls against his gatepost), since man, with death in his sperm, his body, his every act, must have come to terms with it. A God's-eye view of the havoc below confirms his assumption that man is in league with death. Meanwhile man waits at his last gasp for God to recognize his utter helplessness.

What else is open to man in this situation but to wait and hope? He can, if he thinks he has the strength, resist. 'The Contender' stiffens himself in absolute resistance:

He lay crucified with all his strength
On the earth
Grinning towards the sun
Through the tiny holes of his eyes
And towards the moon
And towards the whole paraphernalia of the heavens
Through the seams of his face
With the strings of his lips
Grinning through his atoms and decay
Grinning into the black
Into the ringing nothing
Through the bones of his teeth

Sometimes with eyes closed

In his senseless trial of strength.

His resistance is senseless because he makes no attempt to understand his position. He is without all knowledge of his enemy, until it seems to be life itself he is contending against. He is the prisoner of his own rigidity.

Yet rebellion, in a bid for freedom, is also doomed:

Once upon a time
There was a person
Running for his life.
This was his fate.
It was a hard fate.
But Fate is Fate.
He had to keep running.

He began to wonder about Fate
And running for dear life.
Who? Why?
And was he nothing
But some dummy hare on a racetrack?

At last he made up his mind,
He was nobody's fool.
It would take guts
But yes he could do it.
Yes yes he could stop.
Agony! Agony
Was the wrenching
Of himself from his running.
Vast! And sudden
The stillness
In the empty middle of the desert.

There he stood – stopped.
And since he couldn't see anybody

To North or to West or to East or to South
He raised his fists
Laughing in awful joy
And shook them at the Universe

And his fists fell off
And his hands fell off
He staggered and his legs fell off

It was too late for him to realize
That this was the dogs tearing him to pieces
That he was, in fact, nothing
But a dummy hare on a racetrack

And life was being lived only by the dogs.
('Existential Song')

The most fundamental tenet of Existentialism is that existence precedes essence. Therefore a man is what he freely chooses to become, and there is no such thing as fate. We have already seen Oedipus Crow trying to assert such freedom. 'Spontaneity', said Samuel Butler, 'is only a term for man's ignorance of the gods.' The dogs are merely the gods in their destructive aspect, the hounds of heaven.

The man in 'Criminal Ballad' is a man who suffers from a kind of double vision. Everything he looks at or experiences automatically tunes him to its opposite, which in normal experience is always at some other time, or happening only to someone else.

And when he walked in his garden and saw his children
Bouncing among the dogs and balls
He could not hear their silly songs and the barking
For machine guns
And a screaming and laughing in the cell
Which had got tangled in the air with his hearing
And he could not turn towards the house
Because the woman of complete pain rolling in flame
Was calling to him all the time
From the empty goldfish pond

He is like the god John Wain imagines in 'Poem', who is at every moment aware of 'the worst grief in the world':

To perceive that spirit of suffering in its raging purity
is to a god the burden of his divinity.

O then, if he exists, have pity on this god.
He is clamped to that wounded crust with its slime of blood.

He has no ignorance to hold him separate.
Everything is known to a god. The gods are desperate.

To perceive that spirit of suffering in its raging purity, to comprehend sympathetically the suffering of the universe as his own, is also the burden of the tragic artist. How is he to bear such a burden? Both poems are extraordinarily close to the feelings experienced by Jessie Watkins during a psychotic episode and recorded by Laing in *The Politics of Experience*:

'I had feelings of – er – of gods, not only God but gods as it were, of beings which are far above us capable of – er – dealing with the situation that I was incapable of dealing with, that were in charge and were running things and – um – at the end of it, everybody had to take on the job at the top. And it was this business that made it such a devastating thing to contemplate, that at some period in the existence of – er – of oneself one had to take on this job, even for only a momentary period, because you had arrived then at awareness of everything. What was beyond that I don't know. At the time I felt that – um – that God himself was a madman... because he's got this enormous load of having to be aware and governing and running things – um – and that all of us had to come up and finally get to the point where we had to experience that ourselves. (129)

It is the feeling that God himself is a madman which makes laughter a more ultimate response than tears to the absurd situation:

And now he ran from the children and ran through the house
Holding his bloody hands clear of everything
And ran along the road and into the wood
And under the leaves he sat weeping

And under the leaves he sat weeping

Till he began to laugh

'Excess of sorrow laughs' wrote Blake.[9] Hilarity and anguish become indistinguishable:

Remembering the painted masks and the looming of the balloons
Of the pinpricked dead
He rolls on the ground helpless.

('Crow's Battle Fury')

Death is too like pricking balloons. 'Crow's Battle Fury' offers yet another way of responding to the agony. Crow's helpless unbearable laughter finally drives him mad. He explodes with Cuchulain's battle fury (lines 13–18 are from *The Tain*). Cuchulain's madness was his belief that he could impose his will upon the world by sheer strength and energy such as cannot be in this world. Crow's fury, denied an object, destroys himself. Not as militant egotistical hero, but as reconstituted hair's-breadth survivor learning to walk again, he totters forward:

> (With his glared off face glued back into position
> A dead man's eyes plugged back into his sockets
>
> A dead man's heart screwed in under his ribs
> His tattered guts stitched back into position
> His shattered brains covered with a steel cowl)
>
> He comes forward a step,
> and a step,
> and a step –

The quotation from Jessie Watkins continues:

> 'The journey is there and every single one of us has got to go through it, and – um – everything – you can't dodge it. . .the purpose of everything and the whole of existence is – er – to equip you to take another step, and so on. . .'
>
> '. . .it's an experience that – um – we have at some stage to go through, but that was only one – and that – many more – a fantastic number of – um – things have got to impinge upon us until we gradually build ourselves up into an acceptance of reality, and a greater and greater acceptance of reality and what really exists.' (129–30)

The horrors encountered by the schizophrenic on his psychic journey are often identical with the archetypes of world mythology, the visions of the mystic and the images of the poet. Mythology, mysticism (or the religious tradition in general) and art are all means of understanding and controlling forces which the schizophrenic cannot cope with, alienated as he is in our culture from the universe they inhabit. Tragic art is a sort of intentional schizophrenia, giving an intelligible context to experiences otherwise chaotic and terrifying, objectifying them in images and myths, distancing, creating a space for contemplation, transforming chaos into clarity or harmony. 'Getting clear' is thus both a psychic or spiritual journey, and a stylistic discipline.

In his introduction to Popa's *Selected Poetry*, Hughes claims that, though the world of those East European poets of whom Popa is representative is as horrible as Beckett's, it is not absurd:

> It is the only precious thing, and designed in accord with the whole universe. . . .Like men come back from the dead they have an improved perception, an unerring sense of what really counts in being alive. This helplessness in the circumstances has purged them of rhetoric. With delicate manoeuvring, they precipitate out of a world of malicious negatives a happy

positive. And they have created a small ironic space, a work of lyrical art, in which their humanity can respect itself. (10–11)

The style of *Crow* is very much such a purged style, distilling at times an amazing clarity. 'My idea was to reduce my style to the simplest clear cell – then regrow a wholeness and richness organically from that point.' *Crow* was abandoned with Hughes scarcely beyond the first phase of this process.

In 'How Water Began to Play', water, having tried and failed both to live and to die, weeps itself clear of both life and death:

> It lay at the bottom of all things
> Utterly worn out utterly clear

The poem's title indicates a stage beyond its ending. Only after suffering the attempt to live and the desire to die is it possible to come through into a clarity of being in which innocence is regained and play is possible. The same journey is charted by Popa in 'Before Play'. Having jumped high to the top of oneself

> Thence one drops by one's own weight
> For days one drops deep deep deep
> To the bottom of one's abyss
>
> He who is not smashed to smithereens
> He who remains whole and gets up whole
> He plays

The theme of 'coming clear' is taken up again in 'Song of Woe':

> Once upon a time
> There was a person
> Wretched in every vein –
> His heart pumped woe.
> Trying to run it clear
> His heart pumped only more muddy woe.
> He looked at his hands, and they were woe.
> His legs there, long, bony and remote
> Like the legs of a stag in wet brambles,
> They also were woe.
> His shirt over the chair at night
> Was like a curtain over the finale
> Of all things.
>
> He walked out onto a field
> And the trees were grief –
> Cemetery non-beings.
> The clouds bore their burdens of grief
> Into non-being.

The flowers
The birds, the spiders
Staring into space like sacrifices
Clung with madman's grip
To the great wheel of woe.

So he flung them out among the stars –
Trees, toppling clouds, birds and insects,
He was rid of them.
He flung away the field and its grass,
The whole grievous funeral,
His clothes and their house,
And sat naked on the naked earth
And his mouth filled his eye filled
With the same muddy woe.

So he abandoned himself, his body, his blood –
He left it all lying on the earth
And held himself resolute
As the earth rolled slowly away
Smaller and smaller away
Into non-being.

And there at last he had it
As his woe struggled out of him
With a terrific cry
Staring after the earth
And stood out there in front of him,
His howling transfigured double.

And he was rid of it.
And he wept with relief,
With joy, laughing, he wept –

And at last, tear by tear,
Something came clear.

Again the poem describes a process of ego-destruction.

Reviewing a book on the Sufis Hughes claimed that 'Ash Wednesday' would qualify Eliot for the Shaman's magic drum. Hughes' 'Ash Wednesday' is 'Crow Wakes'. Here the speaker has exploded and entered a psychic landscape inside an atom. He sleeps in a stream of cleansing snow-water, but wakes to hear the voices of his bones chattering together. In Eliot there is no life in the bones, they 'atone to forgetfulness'. But in Hughes each bone takes on a life of its own. They glory in their vivid, but incompatible memories of life:

And the breastbone was crying:
'I begot a million and murdered a million:

I was a leopard.' And 'No, no, no, no,
We were a fine woman,' a rib cried.
'No, we were swine, we had devils, and the axe halved us,'
The pelvis was shouting. And the bones of the feet
And the bones of the hands fought: 'We were alligators,
We dragged some beauties under, we did not let go.'
And, 'We were suffering oxen,' and 'I was a surgeon,'
And 'We were a stinking clot of ectoplasm that suffocated a nun'

When they see him they pursue him, apparently intent on being reassembled, binding him once again to a world of killing and madness and obscenity.

They came howling after me and I ran.
A freezing hand caught hold of me by the hair
And lifted me off my feet and set me high
Over the whole earth on a blazing star
Called

The poem ends there. Perhaps that is the moment Crow wakes from his nightmare – or wakes to the nightmare of incarnation from which, in his dream, he had been miraculously rescued.

The fate of the elephant in 'Crow's Elephant Totem Song' is not dissimilar. This poem is a sort of Just So Story – How the Elephant got his Invulnerability. The elephant, originally, was delicate and small and beautiful, with 'aged eyes of innocence and kindliness'. He knew 'the Land of Peaceful', being a vegetarian who could afford to be kindly and bask in his own ease. But he was vulnerable and he lived among hyenas, each locked in the hell of his own carnivorous nature. They envied the elephant his grace and prayed to him:

Lift us from the furnaces
And furies of our blackened faces
Within these hells we writhe
Shut in behind the bars of our teeth
In hourly battle with a death
The size of the earth
Having the strength of the earth.

He could not 'correct' the hyenas, but they could force him to get himself corrected, to accommodate himself to their world, the world of the five senses.

In rage in madness then they lit their mouths
They tore out his entrails

They divided him among their several hells
To cry all his separate pieces
Swallowed and inflamed
Amidst paradings of infernal laughter.

At the Resurrection
The Elephant got himself together with correction
Deadfall feet and toothproof body and bulldozing bones
And completely altered brains
Behind aged eyes, that were wicked and wise.

So through the orange blaze and blue shadow
Of the afterlife, effortless and immense,
The Elephant goes his own way, a walking sixth sense,
And opposite and parallel
The sleepless Hyenas go
Along a leafless skyline trembling like an oven roof
With a whipped run
Their shame-flags tucked hard down
Over the gutsacks
Crammed with putrefying laughter
Soaked black with the leakage and seepings
And they sing: 'Ours is the land
Of loveliness and beautiful
Is the putrid mouth of the leopard
And the graves of fever
Because it is all we have – '
And they vomit their laughter.

And the Elephant sings deep in the forest-maze
About a star of deathless and painless peace
But no astronomer can find where it is.

The elephant is resurrected massive and toothproof, his innocence now, on the far side of experience, become wisdom. He has come clear of the frenzied fevered life of the five senses, by becoming sufficiently thick-skinned, insulated, against the pressures of the outside world to be able to create and live in terms of an inner world which death and pain cannot penetrate. No astronomer can find the star the elephant sings of because it exists only in inner space.

These 'coming clear' poems seem not only to be enacting a psychic death and resurrection, but also to be expressing a Manichean world-denying. If this world is 'the great wheel of woe', 'a grievous funeral', where the soul can find its peace only by creating a separate and opposite world within, and if this process involves jettisoning your own body and five senses, what is there left to be within? Once you have shed everything, said goodbye to the earth and your own body, where are you? Can there really be blazing stars and new worlds in a physical vacuum, in nothingness?

These are the questions Hughes asks in 'The New World', a sequence of six beautiful and eerie little lyrics written in 1968 to be set to music by Gordon Crosse. The six poems rock in a perfectly balanced tension between two impulses, the impulse to take off, to fling the world away and rush towards a distant star where all is light, and the impulse, once out there in emptiness and utter loneliness, unable to land on any star, to want desperately to get back.

> Where did we go?
> I cannot find us.
>
> Only a tie, draped on the sun.
> Only a shoe, dangling on the moon.
>
> We did not land on a star.
> Where did we go?
>
> I roam the corridors of space
> But the black between the stars
>
> Is like the honeymooners' door,
> Locked night and day.

Hughes' introduction to his *A Choice of Shakespeare's Verse* is a valuable commentary on two important recent poems, 'Crow's Song About Prospero and Sycorax', and 'Crow's Song About England'. In it he describes the symbolic fable Shakespeare found as a metaphor for his own nature. The fable is told in a fragmentary or oblique way in almost every play, but in the two long poems 'Venus and Adonis' and 'The Rape of Lucrece' we find 'the whole fable, beautifully intact and very precisely analysed'. The fable, which gives us Shakespeare's response to the permanent conflict between reason, control and morality on the one hand and Nature on the other, between Apollo (or Pentheus) and Dionysus, Adonis and Venus, Prospero and Sycorax, is also a metaphor for the crisis of sensibility through which England passed in Shakespeare's time. The dragon or savage bear is now the wild boar which killed Adonis:

> The boar that demolished Adonis was, in other words, his own repressed lust – crazed and bestialized by being separated from his intelligence and

denied. The Venus which he refused became a demon and supplanted his consciousness. The frigid puritan, with a single terrible click, becomes a sexual maniac – a destroyer of innocence and virtue, a violator of the heavenly soul, of the very thing he formerly served and adored. (192)

In *Measure for Measure* we see Adonis, now called Angelo, become Tarquin. And Hamlet is another product of the same crisis. The time is out of joint and his own split psyche mirrors the time:

And this is where Shakespeare's hero comes staggering in. Mother-wet, weak-legged, horrified at the task, boggling – Hamlet.

The young puritanical idealist from Wittenberg can cope neither with ghosts nor sexuality. Once disenchanted, he falls first into a suicidal cynicism, then into random cruelty and murderous madness. In giving him his task the ghost had warned Hamlet 'Taint not thy mind.' Only a balanced, untainted mind could possibly cope. But Hamlet, as Lawrence put it

is overpowered by horrible revulsion from his physical connection with his mother, which makes him recoil in similar revulsion from Ophelia and almost from his father, even as a ghost. He is horrified at the merest suggestion of physical connection, as if it were an unspeakable taint. This, no doubt, is all in the course of the growth of the 'spiritual-mental' consciousness, at the expense of the instinctive-intuitive consciousness. Man came to have his own body in horror, especially in its sexual implications and so he began to suppress with all his might his instinctive-intuitive consciousness, which is so radical, so physical, so sexual. (*Introduction to These Paintings*, 188)

In the terms of Hughes' analysis

Hamlet is Adonis, half-possessed by Venus (his black suit), refusing to become Tarquin complete. His madness is the first fear of the rip in his mind – through which the boar will enter. When Ophelia dies her flower-death, we know it has happened: Hamlet must now act out his Tarquin destiny – but in full consciousness, and resisting all the way, and never quite ceasing to be Adonis. It is the death of Adonis in very slow motion. (195)

Here is 'Crow's Song About Prospero and Sycorax':

She knows, like Ophelia,
The task has swallowed him.
She knows, like George's dragon,
Her screams have closed his helmet.

She knows, like Jocasta,
It is over.
He prefers
Blindness.

She knows, like Cordelia,
He is not himself now
And what he speaks must be discounted
Though it will be the end of them both.

She knows, like God,
He has found
Something
Easier to live with...

His death and her death.

The 'she' is Sycorax, the 'he' Prospero. Prospero's task was to create for his daughter a world without monsters, without passion or conflict or tragedy – a Brave New World indeed. To stop the screams merely close your helmet. To see no evil, put your own eyes out. Oedipus says to his mother:

> You are spoiling my comfortable darkness
> forcing me to see again   go away
> (Seneca, *Oedipus*, 53)

King Lear repeats the pattern of *Hamlet*:

> Hamlet, looking at Ophelia, sees his mother in bed with his uncle and goes mad...Lear, looking at Cordelia, sees Goneril and Regan and goes mad. (*Shakespeare's Verse*, 192)

His madness is the total repudiation of Nature, a repudiation more uncompromising even than Edmund's. What should have been a particular blessing becomes a general curse. To redeem Nature from that curse costs Cordelia her life.

Sycorax, the triple-Hecate, the life-bringing Venus, is Prospero's mother wife and daughter. She is the life of the senses which in his austere morality he tries to banish from his, or rather Caliban's, island.

In *The White Goddess* Graves claims that Shakespeare 'knew and feared' her:

> Her last appearance in the plays is as the 'damned witch Sycorax' in *The Tempest*. Shakespeare in the person of Prospero claims to have dominated her by his magic books, broken her power and enslaved her monstrous son Caliban – though not before extracting his secrets from him under colour of kindness. Yet he cannot disguise Caliban's title to the island nor the original blueness of Sycorax's eyes. (426)

Hughes goes further:

> Shakespeare's persistence has to be admired. After all his experience of the

odds against the likelihood, he did finally succeed in salvaging Lucrece from the holocaust and Adonis from the boar. He rescued the puritan abstraction from the gulf of Nature. He banished Venus, as Sycorax, the blue-eyed hag. He humbled Tarquin as Caliban, the poetry crammed half-beast. And within an impenetrable crucible of magic prohibitions, he married Lucrece (Miranda) to Adonis (Ferdinand). But what a wooden wedding! What proper little Puritan puppets! And what a ghastly expression on Prospero's cynical face. We know why he wants to drown his book in the sea (where Venus was born – the lap of Creation) – it contains the tragedies, with their evidence. (198)

It is a commonplace in hostile criticism of Hughes that his poems, in Colin Falck's words, 'tell us nothing about the urban and civilised human world'. On the contrary, having found his bearings and standards in his earlier work Hughes has come more and more to concern himself in his poems with the failure of English intelligence and sensibility in the modern world, the causes and results of that alienation from the sources of life which characterizes our civilization, and the mass neurosis of our urban society. In his Introduction to *A Choice of Shakespeare's Verse* Hughes gives his version of how England lost her soul:

A historical development that worked itself out in theology as a war over metaphysical symbols, worked itself out in the imagination and nervous systems of individuals as a war over 'the dark and vicious place', a struggle over the fallen body, and a final loss of the creative soul. When the physical presence of love has been degraded to lust, and forbidden lust has combined with every other forbidden thing to become a murderous devil, life itself has become a horror, the maiden has become a whore and a witch, and the miraculous source of creation has become the empty hole through into Nothing. (199)

That development did not end with the Civil War. Industrialism gave it a new impetus towards what Huxley, in 'To the Puritan All Things Are Impure', called the religion of Fordism:

Fordism demands that we should sacrifice the animal man (and along with the animal, large sections of the thinking, spiritual man) not indeed to God, but to the machine. There is no place in the factory, or in that larger factory which is the modern industrialised world, for animals on the one hand, or for artists, mystics, or even finally, individuals on the other. Of all the ascetic religions Fordism is that which demands the cruellest mutilations of the human psyche – demands the cruellest mutilations and offers the smallest spiritual returns. Rigorously practised for a few generations, this dreadful religion of the machine will end by destroying the human race.

Several poems show Crow moving in this world. The cruel mutilations by which the maiden is turned into whore are shown in 'Crow's Song About England', where Adonis, 'desensitized, stupefied and brutalized by his rational scepticism', not only denies Venus but savagely desecrates her.

Once upon a time there was a girl
Who tried to give her mouth
It was snatched from her and her face slapped
She tried to give her eyes
They were knocked to the floor the furniture crushed them
She tried to give her breasts
They were cut from her and canned
She tried to give her cunt
It was produced in open court she was sentenced

She stole everything back

She was mad with pain she humped into a beast
She changed sex he came back

Where he saw her mouth he stabbed with a knife
Where he saw her eyes he stabbed likewise
Where he saw her breasts her cunt he stabbed

He was sentenced

He escaped lobotomised he changed sex
Shrunk to a little girl she came back

She tried to keep her mouth
It was snatched from her and her face slapped
She tried to keep her eyes
They were knocked to the floor the furniture crushed them
She tried to keep her breasts
They were cut from her and canned
She tried to keep her cunt
It was produced in open court she was sentenced

She did life

What is here done to the girl is exactly the process of desecration and profanation of personal worlds of experience which Laing and others have described from the point of view of those who have to try to put the pieces together again: 'When our personal worlds are rediscovered and allowed to reconstitute themselves, we first discover a shambles. Bodies half-dead; genitals dissociated from heart; heart severed from head; heads dissociated from genitals' (*Politics of Experience*, 46).

The poem is about England in that it describes, among other things, what Englishmen have done and are doing to their richest inheritance, their mother-land.

Most of the criticisms which have been levelled against Hughes are, up to a point, true. That is, they are true (with reservations) of his worst poems and passages. Every poet has his characteristic faults (often closely associated with his characteristic strengths, especially in a poet who takes such risks). In any collection of sixty poems there are bound to be a few bad patches. But it is critical dishonesty of the worst kind to review a book (as Ian Hamilton did in the *The Times Literary Supplement*) entirely in terms of those passages, as though there were nothing else. There are many poems in *Crow* which are not open to any of Hamilton's criticisms; but he never mentions them, nor the strengths they exemplify. And he must be the only reader of *Crow* who found the experience 'a cosy unperplexing wallow'.

> The critic whose outlook is based on a rational scepticism...cannot distinguish between fears for his own mental security and the actions of the Universe...What he can do is judge works and deeds of rational scepticism within a closed society that agrees on the terms used. He can tell you why a poem is bad as a work of rational scepticism, but he cannot tell you why it is good as a poem. (*London Magazine*, January 1971)

Such critics want to safeguard their fragile values by dictating that all art which denies or even questions them is *ipso facto* bad art. For Hughes nothing is assumed in advance, no territory is out of bounds.

Crow was acclaimed by the great majority of reviewers. C. B. Cox called it 'a most extraordinary work of genius'. Alan Brownjohn wrote: 'It is not possible any longer to begrudge him major status among English poets of our time.' One would have thought not. Certainly there are faults. Crude, bludgeoning, portentous, fashionable, secondhand, facile, glib, self-indulgent – quotations could be found (and were found) to justify all these adjectives. I am sure that J. M. Newton is as aware of these faults as any other critic, but he generously saw that the only important job for the critic at this moment in response to a talent of this magnitude is to select the best poems and passages and try to account for the power and truth of them. As Jeremy Robson concluded: 'Although one may point to particular flaws and indulgences, they fall away within the context of the overall, heroic, tragic, achievement.'

PROMETHEUS ON HIS CRAG

From the point of view of a man alienated from his source creation arises from despair and ends in failure. But such a man has not trodden the path to the end of time, the end of space, the end of darkness, and the end of light. He does not know that where it all ends, there it all begins.

We are not able even to *think* adequately about the behaviour that is at the annihilating edge. But what we think is less than what we know: what we know is less than what we love: what we love is so much less than what there is. And to that precise extent we are so much less than what we are.

Yet if nothing else, each time a new baby is born there is a possibility of reprieve. Each child is a new being, a potential prophet, a new spiritual prince, a new spark of light, precipitated into the outer darkness. Who are we to decide that it is hopeless? (R. D. Laing, *The Politics of Experience*)

In 1971 Hughes accompanied Peter Brook and his International Centre for Theatre Research to Persia for the Fifth Shiraz Festival. There he wrote *Orghast* which is the name both of the play and of the invented language in which it is written. *Orghast* was based on several myths and folk tales, but at the centre was the story of Prometheus. At the same time Hughes wrote a number of little poems about Prometheus, twenty-one of which are collected in *Prometheus on His Crag*. The poems assume a knowledge of the basic myth.

Prometheus, a Titan (that is, an immortal, a primitive pre-Olympian god), created man according to some versions of the myth. According to all he became the self-elected champion of mankind against the injustice of Zeus, stealing fire from heaven that men might warm themselves and cook their meat and forge metal:

> And fire has proved
> For men a teacher in every art, their grand resource.
> (Aeschylus, *Prometheus Bound*)

His punishment was to be crucified upon a rock where a vulture gorged itself daily upon his liver, which grew again during the night. His name means Foresight, and his one weapon against Zeus was his foreknowledge that Zeus would be overthrown by his own son if he did not ultimately free Prometheus.

Zeus also punished mankind through Prometheus' brother Epimetheus (Hindsight) with the gift of the first woman, Pandora, beautiful, but bringing with her all the evils which have ever since beset mankind. She also brought Hope, lest man should seek to avoid these evils by suicide. Or in one version it is Prometheus who puts Hope into Pandora's jar. In Aeschylus Prometheus claims

> I caused men no longer to foresee their death.
> I planted firmly in their hearts blind hopefulness.

The poems are short, most of them of 11, 14 or 17 lines made up of single first and last lines with the rest in triplets. Many are internal monologues of Prometheus as he contemplates his own situation, the god who has condemned him to it, the vulture, and such fellow-sufferers as Io, a maiden turned by Zeus into a heifer perpetually pursued by a hornet, 'bucking the bee of the Creator'. They are poems stripped of everything but their meanings, expressed in a few stark images. They are the forged links of a chain, as hard as blue steel. The world is shrunk to the size of an icon, a water-bead, a grain of sand, an atom. Language is an instrument for probing relentlessly towards the centre. It is speech appropriate to one who says, in Aeschylus,

> Under such suffering, speech and silence are alike
> Beyond me.

When Hughes' Prometheus tries to speak

> the mouth shuts
> Savagely on a mouthful
> Of space-fright which makes the ears ring.

Ted Hughes has described *Prometheus on His Crag* as 'a limbo . . . a numb poem about numbness', but it is much more than that. It is the culmination of 'the search for liberation through knowledge' which has constituted Hughes' main creative effort for so long. In 'The Rock' Hughes wrote of the freedom of the moors and the constriction of the dark valley, his childhood home: 'That was where the division of body and soul, for me, began.' Its location is now the world's edge, the Caucasus, the needle of Elbruz, with Prometheus, a blue wedge through his breastbone into the rock, an immortal god nailed to the human world of injustice and agony.

Prometheus' first sensation when he recovers consciousness is that he has been changed into an eagle. He feels released rather than imprisoned.[1] All doubts and distractions fall from him as his 'lungs gulp huge clarity', the clarity of existence seen for the first time as it is:

> Unadjusted by vision or prayer–so.

He is utterly helpless, simplified to a wide eye taking all in.

> Nevertheless, now he exults – like an eagle
>
> In the broadening vastness, the reddening dawn
> Of the fact
>
> That cannot be otherwise
> And could not have been otherwise,
>
> And never can be otherwise.
>
> And now, for the first time
>   relaxing
>   helpless
> The Titan feels his strength.
>
> (poem 2)

It is the strength which comes from knowing the worst, and knowing that he can survive it. But worse is yet to come. His shout announcing the end of the 'world of holy, happy notions' (the freezing clarity kills it) also wakes the vulture whose every feather says

> 'Today is a fresh start
> Torn up by its roots
> As I tear the liver from your body.'
>
> (poem 4)

That too he must learn to live with. He has not foreseen the vulture. He has associated the 'reddening dawn' with his new awareness and power, but not his own blood suffusing heaven.

Poems 5 to 8 record the agony, and not just the agony of Prometheus:

>   So all that day
> The shuddering chestnut tree tore slowly open
>
> With its arms full,
> And under it – the woman again[2]
> With her brimming jar
>
> Calling to him.

The association of Prometheus with a chestnut tree (Yeats' 'great-rooted blossomer'), the tree with Pandora, and its arms full of chestnuts with her jar full of evils, suggests that the agony of Prometheus is comparable to all the birth-agonies of the world. Prometheus 'knew what was coming' only insofar as he knew now of the coming of the vulture and the pain. He did not know what was coming to birth. He did not foresee, blinded by pain, his own rebirth, with the splitting open of fig and mountain, the tearing of the shell by the vulture. The rough outer shell or husk of the chestnut must split open to release the gleaming kernel within.

In poem 6 Prometheus (who also gave men words, numbers, and the art of forecasting) bites his prophetic tongue off in his agony. Instead of a clearly articulated vision of the future, dead thoughts issue in senseless chatter, a heap of broken images, ancient proverbs mixed with fortune-telling and a dabbling in the occult, in a fragmented wasteland vision which is, if he only knew it, a true vision of our time:

> Below, among car-bumpers and shopping baskets,
> A monkey of voice, shuffling Tarot
> For corpses and embryos, quotes Ecclesiastes
> To the clock that talks backward.

In poem 8 Prometheus begins to recover his lucidity. He knows that the vulture holds the secret of his fate.

Eventually Prometheus begins to admire the vulture. Poem 9 is like a recapitulation of Hughes' career, with Prometheus envying the simple-mindedness and poised centrality of the vulture as Hughes had once of the hawk:

> It knew what it was doing
>
> It went on doing it
> Swallowing not only his liver
> But managing also to digest its guilt
>
> And hang itself again just under the sun
> Like a heavenly weighing scales
> Balancing the gift of life
>
> And the cost of the gift
> Without a tremor –
> As if both were nothing.

The gift is Prometheus' own gift of life and fire to men and the gods' balancing gift of Pandora ('All gifts'). The cost is her jar brimming with all the evils and pain and death. The gift and the cost together are everything, yet they balance as perfectly as if the scales were empty. Prometheus also hangs weighing the cost. In his case it seems there is the weight of the world in one pan and nothing in the other more substantial than the trembling swallow-tail butterfly which, in his dream, replaces the hammer-splayed head of the spike.

Poem 11 stands at the centre of the sequence. Here, for the first time, Prometheus is no longer screaming or incoherent. He is able to sing a song to his wounds even as the vulture reopens them.

> The sun signalled him red through his closed eyelids
> The vulture rustled
> And the smoulder of man rose from the cities.
>
> But he went on singing –
> A pure
> Unfaltering morphine
>
> Drugging the whole earth with bliss.

The body of Prometheus is the body of humanity, his wounds its smouldering cities. And it is no incomprehensible external evil which has caused the ruin of cities. It is the misuse of the gift of fire because the gift of knowledge was not accompanied by the gift of understanding. Prometheus has yet to win understanding from his wounds, but at least his pure unfaltering song brings to suffering mankind a blissful numbness.

Prometheus' first attempt to explain the vulture is as 'the revenge of the wombs/To show him what it was like' since

> He had invented them.
> Then stolen the holy fire, and hidden it in them.
>
> It seemed to him
> The wombs drummed like furnaces
> And that men were being fed to the wombs.
>
> And it seemed
> Babies were being dragged crying pitifully
> Out of the wombs.
>
> (poem 13)

The holy fire is the creative energy of the sun. But the sun derives its energy from nuclear processes which consume mass and convert it into energy. Various natural processes (wombs) convert the energy back into mass. But the system is circular. The scales are always balanced between creation and destruction. The whole process is speeded up in Prometheus' own body. What he grows in the night the sun takes back in the day.

In another attempt to understand the frenzy of life Prometheus sees everything whipping everything else with invisible whips. Men and women

> whip their animals and their engines
> To get them from under the whips
> . . .
> as if being were a whipping
>
> Even the earth leaping
>
> Like a great ungainly top
>
> (poem 14)

All life is a frantic effort to escape the lashes, the invisible tongues. But if being is a whipping there can be no escape in life. Escape, Freedom, is only 'his soul's sleepwalking'. Prometheus always wakes

> In a new aeon
> to the old chains
> and the old agony.

He is no exception. Rather he is the very prototype of the human condition. His body is at the centre of every aeon, like the grit at the centre of every pearl. Without the grit, which is suffering, there would be no pearl – the priceless recognition which can be won only from suffering.

Poem 18 is the first to suggest that the pearl is worth it. The whole scene with all the characters is presented as an icon. It is a scene of permanent religious significance, the characters fixed in their roles and relationships. But there is one tiny figure easily overlooked, not only because it is tiny, but because it does not seem to belong to the fixed tableau of torment, but seems quite free to come and go and quite insignificant:

> The figure overlooked in this fable
> Is the tiny trickle of lizard
>
> Listening near the ear of Prometheus,
> Whispering – at his each in-rip of breath,
> Even as the vulture buried its head –
>
> 'Lucky, you are so lucky to be human!'

The word 'trickle' has all the opposite associations from the word 'icon'. The lizard is part of the flux of life, an emanation of the earth itself. There is a Lawrence poem where being a lizard is contrasted with being human. It ends:

> If men were as much men as lizards are lizards
> they'd be worth looking at.
>
> ('Lizard')

All lizards are all lizard. And all are alike. A lizard has no understanding of its condition, or, if it suffers, of its suffering. It has no imagination and therefore no hope. It seems to be free but is in fact eternally imprisoned within its own predestined lizardness. Even as the vulture buries its head Prometheus asserts his humanity in continuing to defy Zeus and in trying to convert the pain into THE PAYMENT, redeeming his people by teaching them precisely how lucky they are, not simply in spite of pain and death but in a mysterious way *because* of them, to be human.

By poem 20 Prometheus has accumulated so many alternative hypotheses for the vulture's mystery that his mind circles like the vulture, seems to be bound on a wheel or confronted by an infinite recession of horrors. Or perhaps the vulture is all these things, the total, hardly conceivable cost, the dragon with a hundred mouths:

> Prometheus on his crag
>
> Pondered the vulture. Was this bird
> His unborn half-self, some hyena
> Afterbirth, some lump of his mother?
>
> Or was it his condemned human ballast –
> His dying and his death, torn daily
> From his immortality?
>
> Or his blowtorch godhead
> Puncturing those horrendous holes
> In his human limits?
>
> Was it his prophetic familiar?
> The Knowledge, pebble-eyed,
> Of the fates to be suffered in his image?
>
> Was it the flapping, tattered hole –
> The nothing door
> Of his entry, draughting through him?
>
> Or was it atomic law –
> Was Life his transgression?
> Was he the punished criminal aberration?
>
> Was it the fire he had stolen?
> Nowhere to go and now his pet,
> And only him to feed on?

Or the supernatural spirit itself
That he had stolen from,
Now stealing from him the natural flesh?

Or was it the earth's enlightenment –
Was he an uninitiated infant
Mutilated towards alignment?

Or was it his anti-self –
The him-shaped vacuum
In unbeing, pulling to empty him?

Or was it, after all, the Helper
Coming again to pick at the crucial knot
Of all his bonds...?

Image after image. Image after image. The vulture
Circled
Circled
Circled.

Prometheus is the locus of torment, the cross. He is a living oxymoron, a fractured unity. As his brother Atlas stands for ever at the Western extremity of the world holding heaven and earth apart, so Prometheus hangs for ever at the Eastern edge 'nailing heaven and earth together'. He has the worst of both worlds. He cannot be a god because, having elected to share man's condition, his 'condemned human ballast' drags him down. Half of him is now tied to mere matter, undifferentiated, unborn, incapable of ever coming into being, coming clear of the earth and its processes, pain, change and death. He cannot be a man because his godhead gives him not only immortality but a knowledge of light, harmony, ecstasy, which his human limits fall so short of.

But perhaps it is only by puncturing holes in human limits that they can be extended. Prometheus did not foresee the vulture; there may yet be other fates he has not foreseen. If 'a return to his earliest' is his only hope of freedom (poem 17) the door of his entry may be needed again. If his 'dissolution' is required, the fire must feed on him, his natural flesh be stolen. Mutilation may be the only way to achieve an enlightenment other than by alignment with the earth's laws, or perhaps the earth's laws may be seen very differently after enlightenment. Perhaps he needs to be emptied in order to make room for something new. The final image subsumes all these possibilities. The vulture may be the Helper after all.[3] Of the 'crucial knot' Joseph Campbell says:

In every system of theology there is an umbilical point, an Achilles tendon which the finger of mother life has touched, and where the possibility of perfect knowledge has been impaired. The problem of the hero is to pierce himself (and therewith his world) precisely through that point; to shatter and annihilate that key knot of his limited existence. (*The Hero With a Thousand Faces*, 147)

The tyrant Zeus, the 'supernatural spirit that he had stolen from', is the father. The 'filthy–gleeful' face of the vulture is the gloating face of that god.

The problem of the hero going to meet the father is to open his soul beyond terror to such a degree that he will be ripe to understand how the sickening and insane tragedies of this vast and ruthless cosmos are completely validated in the majesty of Being. The hero transcends life with its peculiar blind spot and for a moment rises to a glimpse of the source. He beholds the face of the father, understands – and the two are atoned. (*Ibid.*, p. 147)

Campbell defines atonement thus:

Atonement (at-one-ment) consists in no more than the abandonment of that self-generated double monster – the dragon thought to be God (superego) and the dragon thought to be Sin (repressed id). But this requires an abandonment of the attachment to ego itself, and that is what is difficult. One must have a faith that the father is merciful, and then a reliance on that mercy. Therewith, the centre of belief is transferred outside of the bedeviling god's tight scaly ring, and the dreadful ogres dissolve.

It is in this ordeal that the hero may derive hope and assurance from the helpful female figure, by whose magic (pollen charms or power of intercession) he is protected through all the frightening experiences of the father's ego-shattering initiation. For if it is impossible to trust the terrifying father-face, then one's faith must be centred elsewhere (Spider Woman, Blessed Mother); and with that reliance for support, one endures the crisis – only to find, in the end, that the father and mother reflect each other, and are in essence the same. (*Ibid.*, 130)

We are taken from the mother, chewed into fragments and assimilated to the world-annihilating body of the ogre for whom all the precious forms and beings are only the courses of a feast; but then, miraculously reborn, we are more than we were. (*Ibid.*, 162)

Prometheus' quest, like that of all heroes of myth, is, ultimately to find himself, that is, to recreate himself and the world:

His mother covers her eyes.
The mountain splits its sweetness.
The blue fig splits its magma.

Birth-hacked flesh-ripeness.
The cry bulging, a slow mire
Bubbles scalded.

The mountain utters
Blood and again blood.
Puddled, blotched newsprint.

Crocus evangels.
A mountain is flowering
A gleaming man.

Cloud-bird
Midwifes the upglare naphtha,
Opening the shell.

As Prometheus eases free
And sways to his stature
And balances, and treads

On the dusty peacock film where the world floats.
(*Prometheus on His Crag*, poem 21)

Prometheus' mother is the mountain, the whole earth, and the fruit of the earth. The earth itself, the chestnut, the fig, all are covered with a shell or skin within which is the magma (any crude mixture of mineral or organic matters in their pasty state; a stratum of fluid matter lying beneath the earth's crust). This 'slow mire' of unrealized life at the same time imprisons and cradles, entombs and enwombs that which is always waiting to be born. The crocus breaking through the lifeless winter earth is like a herald angel announcing the coming of the new man. For him what has to be broken through is the 'wordy earth' (poem 19), the hard shell of the ego and the whole pseudo-reality built up by a conspiracy of egos with their dependence on words to hold the world together, like a paste of blood-sodden newsprint. When the 'crucial knot' is unpicked the ego-shell splits open.

Prometheus sheds his human ballast. He is neither nailed to the world nor flying free of it. Prometheus gleams with newness, but the world itself is also renewed. Prometheus 'balances' the gift and the cost, humanity and godhead, heaven and earth:

> The universe flows through its full circuit, materialized spirit and spiritualized matter, undivided and reconciled to itself. (A. G. H. Smith, *Orghast at Persepolis*, 96)

The transfigured world is beautifully evoked in the last line with its delicate evanescence and weightless splendour. These last lines of his latest volume come clear of that sense of down-dragging, earth-bound mortality which the first lines of his first volume so powerfully conveyed:

I drown in the drumming ploughland, I drag up
Heel after heel from the swallowing of the earth's mouth.

The earth was then a dragon. Now it is resplendent as a peacock.[4]

Campbell describes the psychic journey of the mythological hero in terms extraordinarily appropriate to *Prometheus on His Crag:*

Fundamentally it is inward – into depths where obscure resistances are overcome, and long lost, forgotten powers are revivified, to be made available for the transfiguration of the world. This deed accomplished, life no longer suffers hopelessly under the terrible mutilations of ubiquitous disaster, battered by time, hideous throughout space; but with its horror visible still, its cries of anguish still tumultuous, it becomes penetrated by an all-suffusing, all-sustaining love, and a knowledge of its own unconquered power. Something of the light that blazes invisible within the abysses of its normally opaque materiality breaks forth, with an increasing uproar. The dreadful mutilations are then seen as shadows, only, of an immanent, imperishable eternity; time yields to glory; and the world sings with the prodigious, angelic, but perhaps finally monotonous, siren music of the spheres. (*The Hero With a Thousand Faces*, 29–30)

There is no sense, in *Prometheus on His Crag*, of any system being worked out. The poems are the stages of the psychic journey subjectively experienced, objectified as myth. The ending, however, is abrupt and elusive, since, up to that point, we have had no more than hints – butterfly, pearl, lizard, Helper – of the possibility of rebirth. For a more systematic, objective account of the process we must turn to *Orghast* itself, or rather, since *Orghast* is unpublished, to Hughes' own commentary on it in Smith's *Orghast at Persepolis*.

In the beginning was the Sun, Light, the creative fire (orghast itself), the Father, and Moa, incarnation, the womb of all things, the Mother. Their son in time is Krogon who is both Kronos and Zeus (the syllable Kr in Orghast means 'devour'). Krogon fractures the Divine Harmony of the universe, 'the bliss of making and unmaking', by trying to stop time, natural processes, replacement, in order to retain his own power for ever. He fears the energies of the universe, so he imprisons (represses) them. Krogon has thrown his shadow across the sun, so that his sickness is *within* all created beings. It is within Prometheus (here called Pramanath). But Prometheus has the vision to see beyond Krogon's world to the eternal harmonies:

Conscious in eternity, he has to live in time. And he cannot solve his dilemma.

He hangs between heaven and earth, almost torn apart, an open wound, immortal.

Something prevents him from solving his dilemma – Krogon. Krogon is in the soul of Pramanath like a demon, who regards his own arrangement as the only one truly suited to this impossible situation.

If Pramanath could abjure his mortal Moa nature, he would no longer be the victim of Krogon. But he remains loyal to his mortal human self. And if he foreswore his immortal nature, he would become one of Krogon's enslaved prisoners.

To solve this demon of disunity within himself, Pramanath descends into the warfare within himself, repeatedly. (94–5)

The vulture is the holy fire, the energies, but seen only through Krogon's sickness, seen as wholly destructive, dragonish, obscene, perhaps even become these things because denied. The only possible resolution of this conflict is to 'unriddle the Vulture', not as Oedipus had tried to unriddle the Sphinx, with an axe, nor as Crow had responded to the serpent (his mother), 'the sphinx of the final fact':

But Crow only peered.
                                        Then took a step or two forward,
Grabbed this creature by the slackskin nape,
Beat the hell out of it, and ate it
                                        ('A Horrible Religious Error')

nor as Hercules in the original myth simply shot the Vulture with a poisoned arrow. Hercules is a demented St George killing whatever he does not understand and does not like the look of. For every dragon he kills, many more appear. He ends in madness slaughtering his own wife and children whom he mistakes for monsters, as did St George in Crow's account of him.

And Agoluz (Hercules), the hero, will have to misunderstand and die in suffering as often as he is created... The cure, for Man, will be to understand this bird and come to some final reconciliation, not to heroify the sickness, as Agoluz does. (*Orghast at Persepolis*, 96–7)

Hughes sums up *Orghast* in these words:

Part I
is the story of the crime against material nature, the Creatress, source of life and light, by the Violater, the mental tyrant Holdfast, and her revenge. The first plan of her revenge is on the animal level, and it fails, because on the animal level the situation is unalterable, or rather inevitably reproduces itself; the second plan is on the truly human level, and it succeeds, transcending the conflict by creating a being which, like Prometheus (this is the story

of how he survives), includes the elemental opposites, and in whom the collision and pain become illumination, because it is the true account.

Part II

is the story of the tyrant Holdfast in the Underworld, the decomposition of the fallen ego among the voices of its crimes, oversights and victims. Hercules, his son, descends to raise him up, back into the world, but death gives instead the vulture (the mystery of Prometheus's physical/spiritual dilemma), transformed into a woman. (*Orghast at Peresepolis*, 132–3)

Thus Crow, the serpent, the dragon, the vulture, the fallen god, anathema, is restored as Anath, the supreme goddess who preceded Jehovah in Jerusalem, the goddess responsible for perpetuating the life of the gods and of the crops, for sacrifices and for the dew. The transformation is a direct result of the 'final reconciliation' of man and his suffering to which the 'negotiations with whatever happened to be out there', opened in *The Hawk in the Rain*, have brought Hughes.[5]

SEASON SONGS

As I have walk'd in Alabama my morning walk,
I have seen where the she-bird the mocking-bird sat on her nest
    in the briers hatching her brood.

I have seen the he-bird also,
I have paus'd to hear him near at hand inflating his throat and
    joyfully singing.

And while I paus'd it came to me that what he really sang for
    was not there only,
Nor for his mate nor himself only, nor all sent back by the echoes,
But subtle, clandestine, away beyond,
A charge transmitted and gift occult for those being born.
(Whitman, 'Starting from Paumanok')

After the limbo of *Prometheus on His Crag* Hughes needed to refresh himself at the source; after *Orghast* to rediscover the potency of the English language. In 1968 he had written the *Five Autumn Songs for Children's Voices*. Now, to cheer himself up, he turned aside from his confrontation with God to write some more nature poems for children, making these up into a set covering the four seasons. But they did not turn out to be quite that. Hughes discovered or rediscovered more than he had bargained for, amazed himself at the miracles which had been going on making and unmaking themselves on his farm, in his garden, under his bootsoles, while his eyes had been focused on the Needle of Elbruz or on the furthest stars. A little poem by a black schoolgirl I met in Texas has stayed with me:

I am as nature is,
Ugly when you see me ugly,
Beautiful when you see me beautiful.

Relaxing his will and opening his senses, Hughes found himself seeing many colours other than black, and many birds other than crows. If *Crow* had been his *Songs of Experience*, *Season Songs* was to be his *Songs of Innocence*:

In the little girl's angel gaze
Crow lost every feather
In the little boy's wondering eyes
Crow's bones splintered

In the little girl's passion
Crow's bowels fell in the dust
In the little boy's rosy cheeks
Crow became an unrecognizable rag

Crow got under the brambles, capitulated
To nothingness eyes closed
Let those infant feet pound through the Universe

The jacket of *Season Songs* tells us that it is 'intended primarily for young readers', but only the four poems carried over from *Autumn Songs* are strictly children's poems. The rest, though keeping 'within hearing of children', are really addressed to the child who is father of the man. That is, they are attempts to cut through the conditioned responses (or conditioned non-response) of adults to the natural world, to restore unfallen vision. Perhaps, in putting that note on the jacket, Hughes was simply being pessimistic about his chances.

No doubt the enthusiasm of the reviewers for *Season Songs* was partly a sign of their relief at finding themselves with so accessible and affirmative a book in their hands (a very beautiful book, too, in the American edition). But A. K. Weatherhead had exactly the right word – 'reifying', and thought them, as descriptions of nature, 'unapproached by any others in this century at least'; and Susan Fromberg Schaeffer went further:

> It is, so far, this century's necessary poultice, gigantic testimony to one undeformed will. At least for a while, it abundantly answers that numbing question: 'Why live?'

One would have thought there was little new to be said about the seasons. Hughes says little new, but it seems new because he has found words, images, rhythms, to make it new, and to embody autonomous reality, fullness of being, and wonder.[1] On every page there are precisely observed details:

Some buds have burst in tatters –
Like firework stubs
('Spring Nature Notes')

the more intangible differences of season, like the rays of strength emanating from a bare oak in April you did not feel in December; and the still larger spirit of a whole season:

Over the whole land
Spring thunders down in brilliant silence.
('Spring Nature Notes')

The poem 'April Birthday' is a prototype. April is everyone's birthday as the world (brought under your window for the occasion) staggers under nature's 'load of gift':

> And rabbits are bobbing everywhere, and a thrush
> Rings coolly in a far corner. A shiver of green
> Strokes the darkening slope as the land
> Begins her labour.

There is a great deal of wedding imagery, a strong sense of fruitful intercourse from which man is not excluded:

> Happy the grass
> To be wooed by the farmer, who wins her and brings her to church
> in her beauty,
> Bride of the Island.
> Luckless the long-drawn
> Aeons of Eden
> Before he came to mow.[2]
>
> ('Hay')

To balance such flights, there are poems like 'Apple Dumps' where the unearthly promise of blossom-time issues in pawky returns, like so many human marriages. But the failed attempts, the creatures and plants which don't make it, are just as much part of what Whitman called 'the procreant urge of the world', and seem, here, just as miraculous.

Man is not excluded unless he chooses to be. But not all the characters here are farmers, and some of the farmers are also huntsmen. Worse than the huntsmen are the disappointed car-loads who failed to be in at the kill. We see the same car-loads, another day, burning themselves on the beaches. But these are summer distinctions which winter obliterates:

> Your anklebone
> And your anklebone
> Lie big in the bed.
> ('Christmas Card')

Only one poem 'The Golden Boy', an astonishingly fresh and vivid reworking of the John Barleycorn story, makes full and overt use of myth. Part 3 of 'Autumn Nature Notes' tells of the quest of the chestnut to become another tree in the form of a fairytale:

> He rides to fight the North corner.
> He must win a sunbeam princess

From the cloud castle of the rains.
If he fails, evil faces,

Jaws without eyes, will tear him to pieces.
If he succeeds, and has the luck

To snatch his crown from the dragon
Which resembles a slug

He will reign over our garden
For two hundred years.

Other poems are variants of or imitation nursery rhymes, with the earthy candour of the best of those rhymes. In Hughes' version of 'Who Killed Cock Robin?' even Crow makes a fleeting appearance:

Who'll be their parson?
Me, says the Crow, for it is well-known
I study the bible right down to the bone.
I'll be their parson.

('Leaves')

Many of the poems are packed with imagery, much of it very lively and contemporary and colloquial, giving the poems an agility and lightness of touch, and establishing that Hughes is not concerned with some special Nature which only exists in poems or in the heads of Nature poets, but in the same world as tractors and traffic-jams and space-exploration. In 'Swifts' the mad rush of skidding metaphors projects the reader through giddy loops at breakneck speed.

A few poems, like 'Sheep', abjure even imagery, and just tell what happened like entries in a verse diary.

Whatever the method, the effect is the same. The poems are hierophanies, manifestations of the sacred. The book is a cornucopia of gifts. Each page opens a window onto a bright surging world, and the sun is

The golden and holy
Ground of the picture.

('The Seven Sorrows')

They are true gifts: we can take them outside and try them, like a new pair of eyes. The iron bar 'rusted sodden in the red soil' suddenly bears a leaf, and through the window of the salmon's egg we see an eager eye. Nature is non-stop. It won't wait to be interviewed. But if you missed that spring gift, here is a summer one, and you need only wait a year for another chance of the missed gift.

Death is ever-present in *Season Songs*. There are poems about the death of a lamb

> So he died, with the yellow birth-mucus
> Still in his cardigan.
>
> ('Sheep')

And of a fledgeling swift:

> The moustached goblin savage
>
> Nested in a scarf. The bright blank
> Blind, like an angel, to my meat-crumbs and flies.
> Then eyelids resting. Wasted clingers curled.
> The inevitable balsa death.
>
> Finally burial
>
> For the husk
> Of my little Apollo –
>
> The charred scream
> Folded in its huge power.
>
> ('Swifts')

Foxes and stags are hunted to death. A pheasant hangs from a hook with its head in a bag. A cranefly is going through with its slow death; the poet is a watching giant 'who knows she cannot be helped in any way'. But death does not cancel vitality, for all the deep compassion it evokes.

The first poem in *Season Songs*, 'A March Calf', is not about death, but includes it. The poem begins as though it is to be what we expect of an animal poem for children – visual, anthropomorphic, charming – the calf a 'little Fauntleroy – quiffed and glossy' in his natty Sunday suit. But that tone doesn't survive the first stanza. By the fifth he is

> Staring from every hair in all directions,
> Ready for the worst, shut up in his hopeful religion,
> A little syllogism
> With a wet blue-reddish muzzle, for God's thumb.

Since the worst comes so very often to calves, since his whole lineage is tied up in a system of butchers and markets, is that 'hopeful religion' merely pathetic?

> What did cattle ever find here
> To make this dear little fellow
> So eager to prepare himself?

The question is answered in the final stanza:

> Soon he'll plunge out, to scatter his seething joy,
> To be present at the grass,
> To be free on the surface of such a wideness,
> To find himself himself. To stand. To moo.

But is this bliss undercut by the calf's ignorance?

In his unpublished novel *Eleutheria* Beckett wrote:

> I am the cow, which, at the gates of the slaughterhouse, realises all the absurdity of pastures. A pity she didn't think of it sooner, back there in the long lush grass. Ah well. She still has the yard to cross. No one can take that away from her.

Hughes has devoted a great deal of his work to the crossing of that yard, being at the annihilating edge. Is it simply a matter, in *Season Songs*, of turning aside from his major preoccupations for a well-deserved repite? His original intention may have been no more than that, but I believe these poems have changed the direction of the mainstream of his work in a way which does not, perhaps, become evident until *Gaudete*.

Though the slaughter-house is present in 'A March Calf', it does not seem to me to imply 'the absurdity of pastures'. Beckett's image is, of course, only an image for all life, a variant of the more famous image in *Waiting for Godot*: 'They give birth astride of a grave'. The fact of death renders all life absurd. The mere demonstration that death is an essential part of the larger cyclic process would cut no ice with Beckett. In *Waiting for Godot* the bare tree suddenly has four or five leaves. If the inevitability of life simply guarantees the inevitability of suffering and death it is more of a curse than a blessing, and has no more significance than the song of the dog, which also perpetually renews itself and starts again. *Endgame* is Beckett's attempt to put a stop to all that. In Eliot, too, April is the cruellest month, and life is merely a circular dance around the bonfire:

> Keeping the rhythm in their dancing
> As in their living in the living seasons
> The time of milking and the time of harvest
> The time of the coupling of man and woman
> And that of beasts. Feet rising and falling.
> Eating and drinking. Dung and death.
> ('East Coker')

And the Leehallfae chapter of *A Voyage to Arcturus* is a savage parody, where these natural processes are speeded up to the point where life-cycles must be completed in minutes to make room for the teeming creation of new life.

The common assumption in Lindsay, Eliot and Beckett is that there is, or ought to be, such a thing as eternal life, which every human being has a right to. They assume that everything ephemeral or temporal is valueless. To be sacred is to be absolute, and nothing in time or space is absolute, so the world is crying out for redemption. The argument is theoretically strong, but whether it is *felt* to be true seems to be a matter of temperament, and of the individual's ability to recognize the sacred in unredeemed nature.

Of one of Beckett's heroes we are told:

> And if there were two things that Watt loathed, one was the earth and the other was the sky.

Most of us, I hope, are not as far gone as that. In the Lindsay chapter, what is obscene is not the processes but the speeding up of them. You can produce an equal obscenity by slowing them down, as in *Back to Methusalah*. The speed, relative to the creatures involved, is part of the rightness of the whole system. And Eliot gives us a strong sense of having, in youth, made the great refusal, and of everything afterwards being a sublimation of regret.

Against these we may set Whitman and Lawrence, who see no connection between time and value. There may even be a preference for the short-lived, which is frequently the more vivid and intense. Lawrence attempted to formulate this position in 'Reflections on the Death of a Porcupine', where his first 'law of life' is:

> Any living creature that attains to its own fullness of being, its own *living* self, becomes unique, a nonpareil. It has its place in the fourth dimension, the heaven of existence, and there it is perfect, it is beyond comparison.

By heaven or the fourth dimension he means 'not to be reckoned in terms of space and time'. This is completely different from Eliot's 'intersection of the timeless with time', which is really a ladder leading from time up into timelessness. Lawrence's heaven is a blossoming of timelessness, the absolute, within time, not going anywhere nor letting in anything from the outside, but sanctifying the world.

If the end product is sacred, then all the processes which go to make it and make way for it must also be sacred. In poem 6 of

'Song of Myself' Whitman makes this declaration of faith:

> The smallest sprout shows there is really no death,
> And if ever there was it led forward life, and does not wait
> at the end to arrest it,
> And ceased the moment life appeared.
>
> All goes onward and outward, nothing collapses,
> And to die is different from what any one supposed, and luckier.

Such a faith cannot be substantiated by abstract argument. But it can be substantiated by poems. It takes Whitman another forty-six poems to reach the end of 'Song of Myself' with that beautiful and moving finale:

> I bequeath myself to the dirt to grow from the grass I love,
> If you want me again look for me under your boot-soles.
>
> You will hardly know who I am or what I mean,
> But I shall be good health to you nevertheless,
> And filter and fibre your blood.
>
> Failing to fetch me at first keep encouraged,
> Missing me one place search another,
> I stop somewhere waiting for you.

What has passed in between is a world of witnessing. Hopkins wrote to Canon Dixon: 'The world is full of things and events, phenomena of all sorts that go without notice, go unwitnessed'. William Walsh comments:

> The witnessing by the mind, this investing a thing with an extra existence, is essentially a creative art. It saves part of the miraculous variety of the universe from waste. To know a thing – above all to know it through that finely developed sense of the particular which reveals unblurred a unique individuality – is a birth of new life, a release of possibility and an increment to being. (*The Use of Imagination*)

I don't understand how witnessing can be a matter of investing things with extra existence. The existence they already have is more than we can cope with.

Two more quotations from Hopkins:

> All things are charged with God, and if we know how to touch them give off sparks and take fire, yield drops and flow, ring and tell of him.

This Hughes would certainly endorse, but for the gender of that last pronoun – the transcendent God displacing the incarnate goddess. It is not, finally, the earth Hopkins is straining for union with; he values it as a springboard:

These things, these things were here, and but the beholder
Wanting, which two, when they once meet,
The heart rears wings bold and bolder,
And hurls for him, O half hurls earth for him, off under his feet.
('Hurrahing in Harvest')

What Hughes has strained so long for is balance on the earth, converting what had seemed mutually exclusive opposites into the poles of a single state, a single world of being:

When the Elm was full
When it heaved and all its tautnesses drummed
Like a full-sail ship

It was just how I felt.
Waist-deep, I ploughed through the lands,
I leaned at horizons, I bore down on strange harbours.

As the sea is the sail-ship's root
So the globe was mine.
When the swell lifted the crow from the Elm-top
Both Poles were my home, they rocked me and supplied me.

In summer it is relatively easy to feel at one with the earth, moving freely, yet rooted, balanced between wind and water, surging towards a rich future. It is perhaps too easy, in this buoyant mood, to feel oneself the measure of it all, riding time. Perhaps the truer epiphany comes from exposure, in the bareness and stillness of late autumn, to that sudden manifestation of something so other and so characteristically itself that one can no longer say:

It was just how I felt

and knows that the globe is its own:

But now the Elm is still
All its frame bare
Its leaves are a carpet for the cabbages

And it stands engulfed in the peculiar golden light
With which Eternity's flash
Photographed the sudden cock pheasant –

Engine whinneying, the fire-ball bird clatters up,
Shuddering full-throttle
Its three tongued tail-tip writhing

And the Elm stands astonished, wet with light,

And I stand, dazzled to my bones, blinded.
('Autumn Nature Notes')

He is stopped in his tracks, engulfed, by the revelation, yet his own poem is the photograph taken by that flash, his witnessing.

There is a similarity between this poem and Robert Graves' 'In Dedication', where the poet sails to distant regions in search of the goddess:

> Green sap of Spring in the young wood a-stir
> Will celebrate the Mountain Mother,
> And every song-bird shout awhile for her;
> But I am gifted, even in November
> Rawest of seasons, with so huge a sense
> Of her nakedly worn magnificence
> I forget cruelty and past betrayal,
> Careless of where the next bright bolt may fall.

One of the images Hughes used in that poem for his sense of atonement with the earth was:

> Waist-deep, I ploughed through the lands.

'Two Horses' expands that image into a whole long poem. It is a late addition to *Season Songs*, and rather different from anything else in it, gazing hypnotically at the plough-share and the haunches of the two great shire horses hauling it, simultaneously through the eyes of a ten-year-old boy and those of the poet thirty-five years on.

It is war-time, 1940, and the boy is helping on the land, supervised by an old ploughman. He imagines the piled earth-works as the castles and fortifications of his kingdom, a medieval kingdom always at war, where corn is wealth and power. His fantasy is more appropriate than he knows, as England digs for victory. And ploughing has not changed in all those centuries (it is to change the following year with the first tractor on that farm). The rhythm of the horses testifies to a rhythm of life other than that of wars, a continuity which must be maintained if man is to continue to live on the earth:

> Hauling earth's betrothal
> From an underworld, with crocus glints . . .
>
> Shaggy forest giants, gentle in harness
> Their roots tearing and snapping
> They were themselves the creaking boughs and the burden
> Of earth's fleshiest ripeness, her damson tightest
> Her sweetest
>
> Earth splayed her thighs, she lay back.

It is very like the opening of *The Rainbow*, in subject-matter, sexual imagery, repetitive rhythms:

> Their life and interrelations were such; feeling the pulse and body of the soil, that opened to their furrow for the grain, and became smooth and supple after their ploughing, and clung to their feet with a weight that pulled like desire.

And as the Brangwens there became mentally inert, saturated by sunshine during the day, hypnotized by the farming round, gazing into the fire all evening, so the boy here loses himself in a dream and drives his team into the thorns of the headland. The horses too had been in a deep sleep, which was also their worship, and had drawn the boy's consciousness into theirs:

> The last friendly angels
> Lifting their knees out of the earth, their clay-balled fetlocks
> Heads down praying
>
> And lifting me with them, into their furnace
>
> I walked in their flames.

The scene evokes Breughel's *Icarus*, where the ploughman seems not to notice the man falling from the sky. The boy does not notice

> The everlasting war behind the shoulder

which is the war of the gulls over the sheared worms, of the corn barons, of the bomber pilots. Against the heart-beat of the horses, 'the centuries are a stopped clock' ('The Ancient Heroes and the Bomber Pilot').

At the time of the Suez war and the Hungarian uprising Sylvia Plath wrote to her mother:

> The creative forces of nature are the only forces which give me any peace now, and we want to become part of them; no war, after these mad incidents, has any meaning for us. All I think of are the mothers . . .
>
> (*Letters Home*, 284)

The two horses have eyes 'like prehistoric mothers'. But they do not, to shield the child they have lifted into their bonfire, deny that 'the creative forces of nature' include death:

> Sudden yellow teeth of the nightmare and skull.

The poem ends with the horses

> Wading the earth's wealth
> In a steam of dung and sweat, to soft horse-talk
>
> Nodding and slow in their power, climbing the sky
>
> On the crumbling edge.

The lines magnificently balance strength and gentleness, life and death, wealth and dung, animal and human, earth and sky, time and permanence, with the suggestion, in those last words, that these 'last friendly angels' are on the point of passing into happy memory, along with another deeply satisfying ceremony.

Perhaps the phrase 'dung and sweat' is meant to echo Eliot's 'dung and death'. But the steam of dung and sweat is here 'the smoky foliage of their labour', the very flowering of their tree-strength.

These songs tell us, and what amazing news it is, what it is like to be alive in this world, with five senses and normal feelings. They embody, even more than Lawrence's own, the only kind of thought he approved of – 'a man in his wholeness wholly attending' ('Thought'). Hughes' earlier books record the struggle towards this wholeness. When it is achieved life's charge flows freely again and can be communicated to others through poems. The agony of Prometheus is behind the apparently spontaneous and joyful balance of these poems, and the humility of their thanksgiving:

> Thanking the Lord
> Thanking the Wheat
> Thanking the Bread
> For bringing them Life
> Today and Tomorrow
> Out of the dirt.
>
> ('The Golden Boy')

CAVE BIRDS

Beyond all anthropomorphic, atavistic, and symbolic meanings, one confesses to an infatuation with the formal allure of birds: the obsidian-like surface of the beaks, the crabbed fretwork of the legs and feet with their beaklike claws, the flutter of wings, feather, and down, and the bird's familial disorganization into a plethora of shapes and sizes, and in my favorites, their tessera-like, single-minded devotion to their ways of death. My pleasure has been to swell up owls, bloating them and fashioning them tun-like, surmounting their pneumatic bodies with small heads, with feet gross, monstrous, and with hooks beclawed; covering their breasts with a forest of bosses like a great Spanish door. My owls of night and ignorance, genitaled and sexless, hulking, brooding, wailing and screeching, distorted into my vision of aggressive predatory tyranny. (Leonard Baskin, *Sculpture, Drawings and Prints*)

In the spring of 1969 the great *Crow* project ground to a halt. Hughes thought he had exhausted Crow, could see no way forward for him. When he decided to publish some of the best of the poems already written, as *Crow*, he probably thought he was salvaging them from an abandoned project. But Crow refused to be killed off. He kept popping up. The full *Crow* is still not complete. Many scattered Crow poems are now published, but our main evidence for the direction it is to take is *Cave Birds*.

In 1974 Hughes saw a set of some twenty bird drawings by Leonard Baskin – marvellous vivid drawings of owls and eagles and many other birds, real and imaginary. They fired his imagination. Interpreting them in his own way, he wove a story round them, cast them as characters in a sort of static mystery play. At first there was simply a poem for each drawing – poems unusually studied and formal for Hughes. Then he felt the need to add a dozen more poems, outside the bird drama but parallel to it, giving the same story in direct and human terms, and in a free and simple style. Baskin then did eight more drawings to go with these.[1]

The protagonist is an innocent ('that is', says Hughes 'a guilty one'), an everyman. He has certain features in common with Socrates, whom Hughes holds responsible for the disastrous course of Western Civilization, the committer of the original sin:

> Socrates, in turning his back on poetic myths, was really turning his back on the Moon-goddess who inspired them and who demanded that man should pay woman spiritual and sexual homage: what is called Platonic love, the philosopher's escape from the power of the Goddess into intellectual homosexuality, was really Socratic love. . . . It was the male intellect trying to make itself spiritually self-sufficient. (Graves, *The White Goddess*, 11–12)

He is held responsible for dualism, rationalism, humanism; but since he is also an ordinary man trying to live in the modern world, he appears simply normal, no more guilty than any of us. In the bird drama the protagonist is, at this stage, a cockerel – a subtler version of what would have been called, in a mystery play, Pride of Life. All is apparently well with him: at least he thinks so. Suddenly, without warning, he suffers a psychic split; his consciousness is invaded by spectral birds who are representatives of an other-worldy court where he is to be tried for some nameless but apparently capital crime. The action passes to the underworld, where the protagonist is tried and condemned to death. Swallowed by a raven, he emerges as a crow, to a new adventure, new trials. He passes through various initiation ordeals, supervised by owls and eagles, culminating in a marriage (he is by now almost human) with an earthly woman (who is assumed to have been undergoing a parallel death), which is also his rebirth as a falcon.

In 'The Scream' we meet the protagonist. He is another egg-head who 'shuts out the world's knocking With a welcome' and 'resists receiving the flash Of the sun', his

> Braggart-browed complacency in most calm
> Collusion with his own
> Dewdrop frailty.
>
> ('Egg-head')

He treats life as a gift, drinks it 'like a newborn baby at the breast' and gives praise for it with the facility of any life-affirming romantic poet. (There are echoes of Hopkins, Lawrence, Dylan Thomas, Whitman and Yeats). He feels only the more 'brave and creaturely' the more he sees of the suffering of others. Suddenly, like Orpheus, he is struck dumb. He vomits his accumulated guilt

> Like an obsidian dagger, dry, jag-edged,
> A silent lump of volcanic glass.

This murderous savage weapon has been long forming within

him, with his own demon, his own innermost self, as its first victim.

It is this other self with whom he disputes in the second poem 'After the first fright':

> The disputation went beyond me too quickly.
> When I said: 'Civilization,'
> He began to chop off his fingers.
> When I said: 'Rule of Law and Protection of the Weak,'
> He hacked off his tongue.
> When I said: 'Sanity and again Sanity and above all Sanity,'
> He disembowelled himself.

This is Hughes' commentary:

> He is confronted in court with his victim. It is his own demon whom he now sees for the first time. The hero realizes he is out of his depth. He protests as an honourable platonist, thereby reenacting his crime in front of his judges. He still cannot understand his guilt. He cannot understand the sequence of cause and effect.

Nor, at this stage, can we. Those 'when's establish incontrovertibly that there is a cause and effect. It is not just that the platonic ideals are ineffectual against the horrors; they actually cause them. They assume that it is only necessary to shed enough light from the mind, and darkness will disappear.

Jung records a relevant dream:

> In a primeval forest. An elephant looms up threateningly. Then a large ape-man, bear, or cave-man threatens to attack the dreamer with a club. Suddenly the 'man with the pointed beard' appears and stares at the aggressor, so that he is spellbound. But the dreamer is terrified. The voice says, 'Everything must be ruled by the light'.

Jung interprets this as the intellect, cut off from the total psyche and become Mephistophelean, confronting the repressed and therefore threatening forces of the unconscious – Nietzsche's Dionysus:

> Dionysus is the abyss of impassioned dissolution, where all human distinctions are merged in the animal divinity of the primordial psyche – a blissful and terrible experience. Humanity, huddling behind the walls of its culture, believes it has escaped this experience, until it succeeds in letting loose another orgy of bloodshed. (*Psychology and Alchemy*, 86)

Hughes himself also refers to 'the agonies of an ancient Dionysus in a world of suddenly hardening sceptical intellect and morality'. (*A Choice of Shakespeare's Verse*, 188.) Hughes and Nietzsche are agreed that such 'wisdom' is a crime against nature. But they are also agreed that the criminal is 'honourable':

> One man is enthralled by the Socratic zest for knowledge and is persuaded that he can staunch the eternal wound of being with its help. . . . The kinds of illusion I have named answer only to noble natures, who resent the burden of existence more deeply than the rest and who therefore require special beguilements to make them forget this burden. What we call culture is entirely composed of such beguilements. (*The Birth of Tragedy*, 108–9)

The bird-court is not interested in honour, only in evidence and payment in kind.

The evidence is collected by the Interrogator, a vulturess, the first representative of the bird-court to make its appearance in the cycle. As in *Prometheus on his Crag*, the vulture is the representative of the sun. Whatever the sun exposes, the vulture watches for signs of life, which are also, automatically, the clues of guilt. She sees through the pitiful camouflage of flesh to the life not paid for. Under her interrogation the protagonist is as helpless as a skin-and-bone mule trying to hide in a desert but betrayed by the black shadow of its own inescapable physicality.

In 'She seemed so considerate' the protagonist recognizes at last that his world has died, and that he is somehow responsible. He humbly yields himself to the vulturess, who embraces him, saying:

> Look up at the sun. I am the one creature
> Who never harmed any living thing.

The saying is ambiguous. It could mean that he is already dead too; or that, by yielding to her he will find her to be his helper on the first stage of his journey towards birth.

The same line

> Who never harmed any living thing

had occurred in every draft of *Prometheus* 21 except the published text. It would, perhaps, have been out of place there since it operates in a different mode from the rest of that poem. There Hughes had sought to wring his resolution from the accumulated images in a concentrated complexity. There the ambiguity was on the surface in the straining diction, imagery, syntax and rhythm. It was the kind of poem which had to go through many drafts, like the refining of the alchemists. But some of the poems in *Cave Birds*, especially those outside the bird drama, achieve an apparently spontaneous and colloquial simplicity which is on the far side of such complexity, a pregnant and often shocking simplicity of which this line is a paradigm.

The defendant is brought face to face with his judge. This representative of natural law is a gross spider squatting obscenely at the centre of his cosmic web. He is

> The garbage-sack of everything that is not
> The Absolute

and therefore of everything that lives to disturb 'cosmic equipoise' and break 'the solar silence'. When he has removed the substance of 'those who have fouled His tarry and starry web' all that remains is 'the unalterable' – guilt and sentence.

In the last moments before sentence is passed, the defendant would like to say, to mitigate his offences, how 'imbecile innocent' he was, how he had empathized with all the world's suffering, even that of perfect strangers and animals, but his voice is supplanted by that of his victim, his shadow-self, who murmurs something very different – that he had turned his back on her coldly, that he had left her exposed to the cruel indifference of the earth, landslide and avalanche and flood:

> The whole earth
> Had turned in its bed
> To the wall.

Her sense of utter alienation is like that Catherine feels in *Wuthering Heights* when she imagines herself cut off from Heathcliff, the very ground of her being – 'the universe would turn to a mighty stranger: I should not seem a part of it'. It is interesting that Hughes should here project his hero's 'demon' as female, while Emily Brontë projects her heroine's as male; just as Jung would have us expect.

Killing one's own demon is only the start. The denial of the demon, which is a denial of nature and truth, sends destructive waves outwards in all directions. Hughes' introduction to the original version of 'The Plaintiff' ran:

> His crime implicates him in wider and wider responsibilities. His victim takes on a form which is progressively more multiple and serious, progressively more personal and inescapable.

Perhaps Hughes remembered from Nietzsche the image of Socratic man failing to 'staunch the eternal wound of being', for the protagonist here has nursed 'a bush of wounds'

And this festering, which your unconcern
Left to Mother Nature, is bulging

With a voice, with the unheard-of voice
That can no longer be stanched.

The poem went on, in that earlier version, to be too specific, mentioning Herod, Rome, autos-da-fe, death-camps, Stalin . . . But in the latest version it has gone cold in its formality.

The guilty one is sentenced to death, and his executioner is a Raven of Ravens. 'The Executioner' is a fine poem, its lapping rhythms inundating, saturating with darkness. We expect death to be expressed in negative terms, a draining, but here something already void is being filled up with something less barren than its life. There is no cruelty in this hemlock execution, rather a benediction. He is possessed by raven, swallowed by him. His cockerel body (including his 'hard brain – the sacred assassin') is rendered up for his atoms to be 'annealed of their blood-aberration'.

The next poem, one of the best, begins

First, the doubtful charts of skin
Came into my hands – I set out.

Swallowed by the raven, the hero is not dead, but embarked upon a new series of adventures. Possessed by raven, he is no longer a cockerel, but himself more like a crow. His journey is to the centre of himself, with no maps but the skin of his own hands. There are suggestions of Ulysses ('After the islands of women') who, like our hero, failed in all his relationships with women, and of whom Robert Graves wrote:

One, two, and many: flesh had made him blind,
  Flesh had one pleasure only in the act,
Flesh set one purpose only in the mind –
Triumphs of flesh and afterwards to find
  Still those same terrors wherewith flesh was racked.
('Ulysses')

What Cavafy tells Ulysses about the monsters is a clue to the reading of the whole of *Cave Birds*:

– you will not meet them
unless you carry them in your soul,
unless your soul raise them up before you.
('Ithaka')

But the stronger suggestion is of the questing grail knight at the Chapel Perilous, as in the final section of 'The Waste Land':

I came to loose bones
On a heathery moor, and a roofless church.

Wild horses, with blowing tails and manes,
Standing among graves.

And a leaning menhir, with my name on it,
And an epitaph, which read:
'Under this rock he found weapons.'

The only weapons he will need on his quest (unlike the heroes of 'Quest' and 'Gog' and 'Bones') are his own bones. The vision of his own grave is the first stage of his initiation, which Jessie L. Weston describes as the 'primary initiation, that into the sources of physical life', consisting of 'a contact with the horrors of physical death':

The actual initiation would probably consist in enlightenment into the meaning of Lance and Cup, in their sexual juxtaposition.

(*From Ritual to Romance*, 182–3)

The hero's rebirth, when it comes, is indeed to be a matter of discovering a right relation to woman, man and woman coming alive to each other again.

'The Knight' is the first poem in this sequence where it seems to me that the genius of Baskin has drawn out the genius of Hughes, has released it rather than restricted it. In Baskin's drawing the frail eyeless skeleton stands totally exposed to a wind which blows through it, flapping a few last ribbons of flesh. There is a tragic nobility in that high balanced skull.

This knight's conquest is over himself. He lowers his spoils, his engrossment, all his accumulated debts, onto 'the common wild stones of the earth' –

He has conquered in earth's name.
Committing these trophies

To the small madness of roots, to the mineral stasis
And to rain.

He is now the earth's champion, identifying his fibres with her roots, his bones with her stones, his blood with her rain. Her agents of decomposition help to dismantle him until 'nothing remains of the warrior but his weapons', the 'blades, shafts and unstrung bows' of his skeleton. The multicoloured flag of himself which the cockerel had flown, in self-assertiveness and self-sufficiency, is now in tatters:

He is himself his banner and its rags.

The verse moves in delicate small units:

> Here a bone, there a rag

reduced from elaboration to this simplicity.

Meanwhile, in the parallel real-world situation, the protagonist is no longer able to ignore the suffering of his victim, even when he does not witness it, but goes about his increasingly empty and disconnected daily routine. He is tempted to blame life itself, to identify it exclusively with suffering:

> And when I saw the emerald tufting the quince, in April
> And cried in dismay: 'Here it comes again!'
> The leather of my shoes
> Continued to gleam.

An earlier version of this poem had, instead of these last two lines:

> And thought about Hamlet
> Looking at Ophelia's corpse.

This suggests that Hughes may have been remembering a passage in *The Birth of Tragedy* where Nietzsche describes one aspect of the Dionysiac state:

> Everything that has been experienced by the individual is drowned. This chasm of oblivion separates the quotidian reality from the Dionysiac. But as soon as that quotidian reality enters consciousness once more it is viewed with loathing, and the consequence is an ascetic, abulic state of mind. In this sense Dionysiac man might be said to resemble Hamlet: both have looked deeply into the true nature of things, they have *understood* and are now loath to act. They realize that no action of theirs can work any change in the eternal condition of things . . . The truth once seen, man is aware everywhere of the ghastly absurdity of existence, comprehends the symbolism of Ophelia's fate: nausea invades him. (51–2)

'Something was happening' is an open, living poem where feeling flows freely, not diverted into complex canals as in too many of the bird poems. It ends with a startling image I cannot explain of the one person in the world who seems to be aware of him, who registers, who perhaps opens a path for him to a different and more hopeful dimension of existence:

> The earth, right to its far rims, ignored me
>
> Only the eagle-hunter
> Beating himself to keep warm
> And bowing towards his trap
> Started singing
>
> (Two, three, four thousand years off key.)

At this point the story, seduced no doubt by Baskin's drawings, seems to lose its way, dissipating the energy generated by the last three poems. There are hints of Hughes imitating himself and squeezing new images out of himself as an act of will. It is a relief to come to 'Only a little sleep' where, in the absence of a Baskin drawing at the time of composition, Hughes is able to be direct and warm again.

In 'A Loyal Mother' the eagle owl offers the hero an easy option, invites him under the comfort of her motherly feathers, each of which is a heaven and a lie. The original title of this poem was 'Father of Lying Constructions'. She offers a return to the womb, not for rebirth, but for cradling in endless bliss, the everlasting life promised by all the religions, without suffering or consciousness:

> This earth is heaven's sweetness.
>
> It is heaven's mother.
> The grave is her breast
> And her milk is endless life.
> You shall see
> How tenderly she has wiped her child's face clean
>
> Of the bitumen of blood and smoke of tears.

This balm of oblivion is attractive to our battered hero. It offers him Elysian Fields, the Isles of the Blest, a Lotus Land, Circe's Island where men are reduced to pigs simply by giving them permanent satisfaction of all their desires. In a wood he sees 'the festival of all the religions' in which all flora and fauna take part. All the birds are continuing for ever 'the performance of their feathers and eyes'; all the animals move

> In the glow of fur which is their absolution in sanctity.[2]

But that permanence of ecstasy, even if it were truly available to a human being, would be something less than human:

> And time was not present they never stopped
> Or left anything old or reached any new thing.

The only religion his deepest humanity sanctions for him is communion with a world in which gods are perpetually crucified and eaten and resurrected, and men move not in perpetual purified sanctity, but in the bitumen of blood and smoke of tears. There and only there is the ground of his striving, and, possibly, his atonement.

In 'A Riddle' the true mother offers to return him to that world:

I shall deliver you

My firstborn
Into a changed, unchangeable world
Of wind and of sun, of rock and water
To cry.

She is his daughter, bride and mother, and that is the riddle. At every stage of his life she has suffered for it; in his struggle she has taken the punishment. She is woman, the woman again of 'Crow's Undersong'. She is his victim, his rejected self, seen by him in his fear as a devouring eagle.

After three fine poems 'The Scapegoat Culprit' again gets in the way of what seems the natural development of the sequence towards the marriage poems. Hughes' own account of it goes:

His marriage, the opposite of a physical marriage, is celebrated by driving out of him a cockerel, as a scapegoat, a sacrifice to the eagles.

But there is no mention of marriage or the eagles in the poem, and it is difficult to see how, after all his scouring, there can be anything of the cockerel left in him to drive out. The poem has some striking lines, and considered simply as a fantasia on the splendid Baskin drawing, is impressive. But at this point in the larger scheme of *Cave Birds*, it cannot appear other than self-indulgent.

As the Loyal Mother was the false mother and false guide, the true mother is the Monkey-Eating Eagle and the true guide the Scarecrow Swift, who starts him on the last lap, the upward stage of his journey. 'The Guide' begins

When everything that can fall has fallen
Something rises.
And leaving here, and evading there
And that, and this, is my headway.

The true path is through the narrow interstices between all the 'lying constructions', landmarks, signposts, known reference points. I am reminded of Hughes' words in his *London Magazine* interview:

One had better have one's spirit invested in something that will not vanish. And this is a shifting of your foundation to completely new Holy Ground, a new divinity, one that won't be under the rubble when the churches collapse.

The loyal mother would have cuddled him warm in anaesthetic snow, but the true guide flies up with him into the wind, a red wind to empty him and a black wind to scour him. (These winds and their colours are found in Gnostic texts.)

> Then the non-wind, a least breath,
> Fills you from easy sources.

This is presumably the breath of life breathed into Adam's nostrils or into the dry bones in *Ezekiel.*

The hint of Eden is confirmed in the next poem, where the half-born hero finds a half-born earthly woman.

It seems that she has been passing through similar experiences in a parallel dimension, and now, almost human, they come together:

> And so when every part
> Like a bull pushing towards its cows, not to be stayed
> Like a calf seeking its mama
> Like a desert staggerer, among his hallucinations
> Seeking the hoof-churned hole
>
> Finally got what it needed, and grew still, and closed its eyes
>
> Then such greatness and truth descended
>
> As over a new grave, when the mourners have gone
> And the stars come out
> And the earth, bristling and raw, tiny and lost,
> Resumes its search
>
> Rushing through the vast astonishment.

This perfectly controlled and coherent flow of feeling, through one long sentence, is only possible because this poem is outside the bird-drama and not handcuffed to Baskin. Nor is the even finer poem 'Bride and Groom', a poem which will also appear in the complete *Crow* as the culmination of the process of repairing the damage of such poems as 'Lovesong', 'The Lovepet' and 'Actaeon':

> So, gasping with joy, with cries of wonderment
> Like two gods of mud
> Sprawling in the dirt, but with infinite care
>
> They bring each other to perfection.

Between the two marriage poems is 'Walking Bare', which is a sequel to 'The Guide'. Here the hero goes through the wind. He crosses a crystal desert. He is himself made of crystals. The 'blowtorch light' has reduced him to the 'gem' of himself:

> A bare certainty, without confection.

He is not, as I read it, 'immortal diamond', as Hopkins imagines himself after the resurrection. The 'gem' of himself is simply the irreducible core of selfhood, which, little though it is, is his true weight, and enough to balance him on the earth. It is not the same world which had died at the beginning of the cycle. That continues, but does not touch him:

> And the mountains of torment and mica
> Pass me by.
>
> Hurrying worlds of voices, on other errands,
> Traffic through me, ignore me.

He is himself the seed of a new world, the real world inside the husk flaking like mica, the dead skin of the old world. His gem is a speck of dust which the sun's breath will fan to a spark.

This mixing of metaphors is quite deliberate, and becomes more insistent in 'The Owl Flower', where the sun is simultaneously an owl and a flower (as it indeed appears to be in the Baskin drawing). The whirling corolla is now a maelstrom, and the speck of dust a mote in its eye, scalding in dews. The poem now takes up image after image from earlier in the sequence and reverses their charge. In the first poem the protagonist had claimed to ride the wheel of the galaxy. In the second his arrogance had collapsed to a 'stopping and starting Catherine wheel' in his belly. Now he is a mote at the core of a 'tightening whorl of plumes'. In 'The Plaintiff' the bird of light was his victim; his heart's winged flower:

> Her feathers are leaves, the leaves tongues,
> The mouths wounds, the tongues flames.

Now she is his mother. 'Wounds flush with sap'. The 'cauldron of tongues' is now the crucible in which the mummy grain cracks. (That image of the mummy grain is picked up from 'The Baptist' – 'a mummy bandaging . . . or a seed in its armour'.) She has come not to supplant him but to hatch him among her broody petals. The egg-stone bursts

> And a staggering thing
> Fired with rainbows, raw with cringeing heat,
>
> Blinks at the source.

The hero, as cockerel, as baboon, had

> Jumped at the sky-rump of a greasy rainbow.
> ('The Scapegoat Culprit')

Then his mudded body had been annealed, like an ore,

> To rainbowed clinker and a beatitude.
>
> ('Socrates' Cock')

Clinker is sterile, the mere dross of the alchemical process. Now, in 'The Owl Flower', rainbows are symbols of the charge of energy arcing between the creative source (the sun) and the new creation.

'The Owl Flower' is a packed, convoluted poem. For all the heat and movement of its content, and the crush of images, it seems to me never to get up off the page. It does not itself generate the charge or realize the miracle it purports to describe. Its obvious artificiality, its laborious craftsmanship, the absence of a speaking voice or any human orientation, casts doubt, retrospectively, on the authenticity of the whole bird-drama, (which seemed to have been moving towards a fusion of the human and bird protagonists), and leaves much weight for the final poem to carry.

'The Risen Falcon' is a more powerful poem, but essentially of the same kind as 'The Owl Flower'. The falcon is reborn from the sun, but breaks through the shell of earth 'weirdly as sunspots Emerge as earthquakes'. The imagery associates him with traditional theriomorphic images of resurrection – phoenix and snake; in him the long effort of the alchemists to transform dirt into God seems to have been accomplished. The image of the shell of earth, followed by earthquakes, a burning, and 'a leafless apocalypse' suggests that the falcon is somehow redeeming a ruined, devastated world. The risen falcon can apparently create a new Holy Ground. We are asked to believe that

> In the wind-fondled crucible of his splendour
> The dirt becomes God.

But the last lines suggest that this power is not yet accessible to man:

> But when will he land
> On a man's wrist.

This distinction seems to me to make nonsense of the whole conception, in which we have been encouraged to believe that the bird protagonist, whether as cockerel, crow or falcon, is a projection of human qualities and experiences, and, as the story progresses, becomes himself more human and more indistinguishable from the hero of the parallel human story, who has just achieved, in 'Bride and Groom', his godhead out of the mud. 'The

Risen Falcon' was in the first batch of poems to be written, all of which were bird-poems, and perhaps embodied a rather different ending then envisaged.

'The Risen Falcon' is not, in fact, the end. There is still the gnomic finale:

> At the end of the ritual
>   up comes a goblin.

Hughes had used exactly the same words in his *London Magazine* interview:

> We go on writing poems because one poem never gets the whole account right. There is always something missed. At the end of the ritual up comes a goblin. Anyway within a week the whole thing has changed, one needs a fresh bulletin. And works go dead, fishing has to be abandoned, the shoal has moved on. While we struggle with a fragmentary Orestes some complete Bacchae moves past too deep down to hear. We get news of it later . . . too late. In the end, one's poems are ragged dirty undated letters from remote battles and weddings and one thing and another.
>
> (15)

Some of the *Cave Birds* poems would have benefited from being a little more ragged, and with more of the directness and urgency of letters or bulletins. As it is the shape is lost under the baroque accretions.

Never before had Hughes worked so closely with Baskin or any artist. The two are obviously very close in spirit, and it is to be hoped that Hughes poems and Baskin drawings will continue to appear together. But their imaginations are not identical as my epigraph to this chapter amply demonstrates. As an artist Baskin is necessarily concerned with forms and surfaces and textures and the grotesque distortions to which they lend themselves. Hughes can do the verbal equivalent, and in some poems it is an appropriate thing for him to do, but it is not the way to the heart of his vision. That vision is revelatory not by distortion and construction but by far-seeing clarity and bare sensitivity, the qualities we find in most of the poems in *Cave Birds* which are outside the bird drama. Of the poems written to pre-existing Baskin drawings only two, 'The Knight' and 'The Loyal Mother' seem to me to approach the quality of the others.

The theme of psychic split, guilt, suffering, ego-death and rebirth, is so important and central for Hughes; and certain elements such as the use of marriage as a primary image of rebirth, are so new and crucial for his development, that, given the initial stimulus of the drawings, Hughes then needed all the freedom possible for his imagination to find its own framework without such exigencies as the need to write a poem to fit every Baskin drawing.

In attempting to organize the Baskin drawings into a bird-drama which would enable him to follow the stages in the destruction and renewal of an essentially human protagonist, Hughes was surely attempting the impossible – like going for a four-minute mile in a three-legged race. It is amazing that he came so near to bringing it off. He has given us a dozen fine poems, two or three great ones, some of which will, I hope, reappear in a less constraining context. For all its unevenness, *Cave Birds* constitutes a stage Hughes had to go through to find a way forward for Crow (towards his marriage in the Happy Land on the other side of the river), and to be able to write the Epilogue to *Gaudete*.

GAUDETE

No poet can hope to understand the nature of poetry unless he has had a vision of the Naked King crucified to the lopped oak, and watched the dancers, red-eyed from the acrid smoke of the sacrificial fires, stamping out the measure of the dance, their bodies bent uncouthly forward, with a monotonous chant of: 'Kill! kill! kill!' and 'Blood! blood! blood!'...

The poet is in love with the White Goddess, with Truth: his heart breaks with longing and love for her. She is the Flower-goddess Olwen or Blodeuwedd; but she is also Blodeuwedd the Owl, lamp-eyed, hooting dismally, with her foul nest in the hollow of a dead tree, or Circe the pitiless falcon, or Lamia with her flickering tongue, or the snarling-chopped Sow-goddess, or the mare-headed Rhiannon who feeds on raw flesh. *Odi atque amo*: 'to be in love with' is also to hate. Determined to escape from the dilemma, the Apollonian teaches himself to despise woman, and teaches woman to despise herself. (Graves, *The White Goddess*, p. 448)

In 1959 Hughes wrote his first play *The House of Taurus*. Sylvia Plath described it as 'a symbolic drama based on the Euripides play *The Bacchae*, only set in a modern industrial community under a paternalistic ruler' (*Letters Home*, 355). A few months later, after the play had been scrapped, she described it as 'only a rough, rather unpoetic draft, or redraft, of a theme from the *Bacchae* with an antiquated social message' (389). It is not surprising that he should have turned so soon to *The Bacchae*. Though Athens fell within a year of the death of Euripides, it was the prototype, in its glorification of the city, its humanism and rationalism, of all that followed in Western Civilization. Euripides, exiled (whether forcibly or voluntarily is not known) for the last two years of his life to remote, mountainous, semi-barbarous Macedonia, saw the dangers and issued his warning, incredibly early, but already too late. He saw that, in the words of E. R. Dodds:

To resist Dionysus is to repress the elemental in one's own nature; the punishment is the sudden complete collapse of the inward dykes when the elemental breaks through perforce and civilization vanishes. (273)

Euripides, at the beginning of this process, sought to avert it. Hughes, at the end, wonders what can be salvaged from the wreckage.

Dionysus was much more to the Greeks than the God of Wine. Some of his cult titles were: Power in the Tree, Blossom Bringer, Fruit Bringer, and Abundance of Life. In his edition of *The Bacchae* E. R. Dodds tells us:

> His domain is not only the liquid fire in the grape, but the sap thrusting in a young tree, the blood pounding in the veins of a young animal, all the mysterious and uncontrollable tides that ebb and flow in the life of nature.

When Dionysus entered Thebes, all the women of the city, young or old, came immediately under his spell, and flocked to the hills to join his rites. Every few years we seem to get, in England, a spate of similar, if small-scale, outbreaks. The newspapers make the most of them with their headlines about orgies, harems, covens, centring, very often, on a rogue vicar, who, when exposed, is hounded out. Something works beneath the surface of a typically genteel English village which erupts in this sensational way surprisingly frequently. In 1964 Hughes wrote a film scenario on such a theme, never used. From his attempt to understand the psychology of minister, women and husbands, he found himself with a potent myth on his hands, which he took up again in 1972 and developed in the form of a long narrative poem, an amazing and unique poem, which seems to me the most important poetic work in English in our time.

Gaudete is in three parts, a long central section, with relatively brief, but equally important, Prologue and Epilogue. The Argument runs:

> An Anglican clergyman is abducted by spirits into the other world. The spirits create a duplicate of him to take his place in this world, during his absence, and to carry on his work. [Prologue] This changeling interprets the role of minister in his own way. The narrative recounts the final day of events which lead to his cancellation by the powers of both worlds. [Main narrative] The original man reappears in this world, but changed. [Epilogue]

Because the interpretation of every part of *Gaudete* depends on one's sense of the shape and significance of the whole, and because that does not emerge at all clearly for several readings, I shall offer, before going on to the parts, a fuller Argument.

Lumb is abducted, apparently, in order to perform an act of healing in the other world, a situation common enough in Celtic folklore. It seems he is expected to heal the terribly scarred face of the goddess of that world, and to help her with a difficult birth. He is lashed to a lopped oak and flogged into unconsciousness.

Part of him, including his memory and sense of himself, passes into the oak, which becomes his double. When consciousness returns, it is to the changeling, who is subjected to a series of horrific initiatory rites before being released into this world to take up the life of Lumb as best he can. We see nothing more of the real Lumb until the Epilogue, except for a number of occasions when his consciousness leaks into that of his double, and one scene where, for a time, it completely supplants it. The changeling has been inadequately briefed both on how to be a human being, and on how to be a Christian minister. He misinterprets everything, woodenly, in accordance with his own essential nature as fertility spirit. He feels compelled to copulate as often as possible with as many women as possible. Soon he has all the women in the village in his harem. Those who need a religious sanction he tells that one of them is to be the mother of a god. Meetings of the Women's Institute become occasions for fertility rites. Suicidal and murderous passions are released, first in the women, then in their husbands. Two of the women kill themselves, one is murdered. The changeling is hunted down and shot and burned, together with the bodies of two of his brides, in a parody of a Beltane bonfire. His impact on the village has been an unmitigated disaster, both for himself and everyone else.

In the Epilogue the real Lumb returns to this world in the West of Ireland, transformed by his traumatic experiences in the other world. Though there is no full or continuous narrative of those experiences, we know something of them from the leakages into the main narrative – enough to know that he had been successful in his task and had been reborn. He appears to three little girls for whom he whistles an otter from the loch. He leaves with them a book of his poems, which they take to their priest. Their story causes the priest to have an experience of visionary splendour. He makes fair copies of the poems, forty-five short, beautiful, eerie lyrics, many of them prayers and hymns to an unnamed goddess.

The title *Gaudete* refers ironically to the Christmas hymn of that name from the *Piae Cantiones* of 1582, which begins:

> Gaudete, gaudete Christus est natus
> Ex Maria virginae, gaudete.
>
> Tempus ad est gratiae hoc quod optabamus,
> Carmina laetitiae devote redamus.

Deus homo factus est naturam erante,
Mundus renovatus est a Christo regnante.

Hughes' *Gaudete* celebrates a birth from the loins of a goddess who is far from virginal, a miracle which is not 'naturam erante' – in despite of nature – but is itself nature, as the goddess, if she must be given a name, is Nature.

It will be seen that the structure of the work is symmetrical – a crossover. Each Lumb is snatched against his will from his own world, thrust into a world he is not at all equipped to deal with, subjected to many horrors, and finally returned to his own world. But the differences are much more significant than the similarities, for one Lumb wreaks havoc and has to be 'cancelled'; the other performs his healing task, is reborn, and returns bringing inestimable gifts for mankind.

It will also be clear that the whole story is a psychological analogue, as all the many stories in myth and folklore of doubles, changelings, tanists, twins, weirds and shadows are. There is only one Lumb. He is undergoing a spiritual/psychological crisis. His way of life as a modern civilized Englishman, as a member of a tight little village community, as a minister in a puritanical religion (he was apparently practising voluntary celibacy), involves him in denying too much of himself, denying, as Euripides or Lawrence would have it, the god in himself. Seneca (anticipating Jung) wrote to Lucilius:

> A holy spirit indwells within us, one who works our good and bad deeds, and is our guardian. As we treat this spirit, so we are treated by it.

If you treat it badly enough, it becomes demonic and runs amok within the psyche, supplanting normal consciousness.

> And the vital twist, the mysterious chemical change that converts the resisting high-minded puritan to the being of murder and madness, is that occult crossover of Nature's maddened force – like a demon – into the brain that had rejected her. (*A Choice of Shakespeare's Verse*, 192)

Nature simply drives a wedge into an existing split, and produces two Lumbs who are imagined as acting independently of each other until the demon is exorcised and the psyche healed in the final atonement.

Hughes gives us more help than his brief Argument in how to read *Gaudete*. He gives us two epigraphs. The first is from Heraclitus:

If it were not Hades, the god of the dead and the underworld, for whom these obscene songs are sung and festivals are made, it would be a shocking thing, but Hades and Dionysos are one.

Discussing the place given in pagan religions, as opposed to Christianity, to intoxication and ecstasy, Jung comments:

Heraclitus doubtless saw what was at the back of it when he said, 'But Hades is that same Dionysus in whose honour they go mad and keep the feast of the wine-vat.' For this very reason orgies were granted religious license, so as to exorcise the danger that threatened from Hades. Our solution, however, has served to throw the gates of hell wide open. (*Psychology and Alchemy*, 136)

Heraclitus, incidentally, also provides Jung with his word for precisely the kind of crossover or psychic supplanting we have been discussing – enantiodromia – a 'conversion into its opposite'.

The other epigraph, from Wolfram von Eschenbach's *Parzival*, confirms that both Lumbs are one:

Contending here from loyalty of heart, one flesh, one blood, was doing itself much harm.

and also invites us to be open to further parallels between *Gaudete* and *Parzival*, where also the hero is drawn into a supernatural world where an act of healing is required of him for which he is ill-prepared, but eventually, after much suffering and bewilderment, accomplishes. I shall have more to say about *Parzival* and the grail/waste-land theme later.

Lumb's dislocation begins when, though he is the minister of a Southern country parish, he finds himself lost in a Northern industrial town whose streets are carpeted with corpses. This, I take it, is the waste land at its most blighted. His own people are in a wrong relationship with nature, but at least they cannot avoid it. Here natural life has withdrawn altogether, and the town is a mass grave.

The Prologue now becomes increasingly phantasmagoric as Hughes draws freely on what Jung calls 'the primordial images which have always been the basis of man's thinking – the whole treasure-house of mythological motifs'.

Lumb is conducted immediately to a woman 'tangled in the skins of wolves':

Lumb bends low
Over her face half-animal

And the half-closed animal eyes, clear-dark back to the first creature
And the animal mane
The animal cheekbone and jaw, in the fire's flicker
The animal tendon in the turned throat
The upper lip lifted, dark and clean as a dark flower.

He thinks she is dead, but when he lifts her eyelid 'the startling brilliant gaze knifes into him'. But she is grievously sick. He gathers that he has been brought to heal her:

He protests there is nothing he can do
For this beautiful woman who seems to be alive and dead.
He is not a doctor. He can only pray.

The woman is clearly 'the goddess of natural law and of love, who was the goddess of all sensation and organic life' (*A Choice of Shakespeare's Verse*, 187). She is Isis, mother of the gods, Graves' White Goddess. In psychological terms, she is Jung's Anima. For the present the nature of her sickness remains a mystery. When Parzival was first presented to the maimed Grail King Anfortas, he failed to cure him by responding to him inappropriately – according to the conventions of courtesy rather than spontaneously from his own full humanity. So here it is neither doctoring nor prayer which is required of Lumb. Parzival had only to ask what ailed Anfortas to heal him. He asked no questions; and Lumb asks none. The powers of that world must go a longer way about with him, and purge him of his own sickness first.

Lumb is forced to choose a tree. He chooses a young oak, which is felled and trimmed 'till the lopped trunk lies like a mutilated man, with two raised arms'. He thinks they are going to crucify him. They lash him to the tree and flog both the tree-bole and his own back, until he loses consciousness. The oak is associated with many vegetation gods, but specifically with Hercules. Graves reconstructs the death of Hercules thus:

At midsummer, at the end of a half-year reign, Hercules is made drunk with mead and led into the middle of a circle of twelve stones arranged around an oak, in front of which stands an altar-stone; the oak has been lopped until it is T-shaped. He is bound to it with willow thongs in the 'five-fold' bond which joins wrists, neck and ankles together, beaten by his comrades till he faints, then flayed, blinded, castrated, impaled with a mistletoe stake, and finally hacked into joints on the altar-stone. His blood is caught in a basin and used for sprinkling the whole tribe to make them vigorous and fruitful.

(*The White Goddess*, 125)

The joints are roasted and eaten and the remains burned. One of the names given to the ghost of Hercules after his midsummer sacrifice is Bran, the English Crow-god. His own original name, Heracles, means 'Glory of Hera'. Hera was the Queen of the Woods, the Life-Goddess, and also 'the Death-goddess who had charge of the souls of sacred kings and made oracular heroes of them'.

> He carries an oak-club, because the oak provides his beasts and his people with mast and because it attracts lightning more than any other tree. His symbols are the acorn; the rock-dove, which nests in oaks as well as in clefts of rock; the mistletoe; and the serpent. All these are sexual emblems. The dove was sacred to the Love-goddess of Greece and Syria; the serpent was the most ancient of phallic totem-beasts; the cupped acorn stood for the *glans penis* in both Greek and Latin; the mistletoe was an all-heal and its names *viscus* (Latin) and *ixias* (Greek) are connected with *vis* and *ischus* (strength) – probably because of the spermal viscosity of its berries, sperm being the vehicle of life. This Hercules is male leader of all orgiastic rites and has twelve archer companions, including his spear-armed twin, who is his tanist or deputy . . . His tanist, or other self, appearing in Greek legend as Poeas who lighted Hercules' pyre and inherited his arrows, succeeds him for the second half of the year; having acquired royal virtue by marriage with the queen, the representative of the White Goddess, and by eating some royal part of the dead man's body – heart, shoulder or thigh-flesh. He is in turn succeeded by the New Year Hercules, a reincarnation of the murdered man, who beheads him and, apparently, eats his head. This alternate eucharistic sacrifice made royalty continuous, each king being in turn the Sun-god beloved of the reigning Moon-goddess. (*The White Goddess*, 125–7)

Next comes the sacrifice of the colossal white bull; but when Lumb squeezes the pistol at the bull's head, the shot slams into his own brain. He is buried in the guts and drowned in the blood of many bulls. Though still, henceforth, called Lumb, this is, of course, the changeling, the oaken Lumb, undergoing his final initiation into the life of the body, his consecration to the task ahead, where he is to be the quasi-human embodiment of all the potency of the animal and vegetable worlds.

Bull sacrifice was an integral part (as well as human sacrifice) of the inauguration of the king in druidic rituals; and the name 'druid' means 'knowledge of the oak'. Mithras-worship was an oriental version of the Hercules cult, and it is with Mithras more than any other fertility god that bull-sacrifice is associated. In Mithraism the sacrifice of the Bull was the primal holy deed, for when the white bull died, and moved into the heavens as the moon, the world began. A bath in the blood of a dying bull was the standard rite for the washing away of sins and purification of the body. Mithraism (which was brought to England by the Romans) taught that the world was holy and celibacy a sin, men having a religious duty to work for the increase of the Good Creation. Taurabolism was common to the rites of Mithras, Cybele and Attis. Here is Frazer's description of the Attis rite:

> A bull, adorned with garlands of flowers, its forehead glittering with gold leaf, was then driven on to the grating and there stabbed to death with a consecrated spear. Its hot reeking blood poured in torrents through the apertures, and was received with devout eagerness by the worshipper on every part of his person and garments, till he emerged from the pit, drenched, dripping, and scarlet from head to foot, to receive the homage, nay the adoration, of his fellows as one who had been born again to eternal life and had washed away his sins in the blood of the bull. (*The Golden Bough*, 463)

The rites of Attis overlap those of Osiris, which in turn overlap those of Dionysus, who rode on a white bull, and in *The Bacchae* turns into one.

Though I have given some mythological background to the events and images of the Prologue, I don't want to suggest that it can only be understood with reference to such myths. Any such connections the reader can make are a bonus; the poetry would do its essential work in any case. The oak means to any Englishman masculine unbending strength, the vegetable world at its most thrusting and powerful. And the bull is the animal world at its most potent, full-blooded and dangerous. Hughes is not writing an allegory, where we should expect a precise connotation for every image and event. Symbols and myths work differently, sending out suggestions like ripples, touching chords often deep in the unconscious. And we need to share Lumb's own bewilderment and horror, his sense of something monstrous, nauseating, nightmarish, happening to him; yet we should feel that it is also mysteriously purposive, perhaps even sacred.

No-one can really invent new myths. It is a matter of selecting and recombining under high imaginative pressure from the mass of mythic material which most of us have forgotten, or relegated to ancient history or horror films at the conscious level, but which lies in suspended animation in the unconscious and invades our dreams. Myths which were ever true myths cannot die, since it is part of the definition of myth that it exists outside time, making intelligible the permanent realities. But they can become inoperative because we have died to them, after thousands of years of denial of the basic realities under the influence of all the isms which have conditioned our culture.

Hughes refuses to let all this, our inheritance of myth, gather dust on the shelves and become the domain of academics. He annihilates the safe distance of the material as we meet it in books on Celtic Mysteries or whatever. His rites take place in a slaughter-house, not a druidic circle. His fertility god is shortly to acquire a blue Austin van.

His myth in *Gaudete* has a quality common in all genuine myths: it can be interpreted equally well as applying to a supernatural cosmos of spirits and powers, to the natural world, or to the psychic world. It is at its richest if we can apprehend its relevance to all three at once; when it forces us to recognize the crassness of the distinction. And the power of Hughes' writing ensures that this is so. The reader is taken by the throat on the first page and held till the last, with the certainty that the most incredible events are indeed happening, because we see them and experience them.

Hughes has read very widely, and makes full use of his reading, but not, like Eliot in *The Waste Land*, in the form of quotation and allusion; everything has to be recycled through his imagination and experience, to emerge fused, charged, authenticated. Charged, that is, not with a few thousand volts of Hughes' patented 'verbal energy', as though that were something which could be switched on at will, but with the deepest contemporary human relevance and a deep compassion for all the suffering on earth. He knows that the myths hold all the keys to the psyche, and therefore to the sickness of the race.

In the main narrative the first character we meet is Major Hagen, and the first word, with a line to itself, is 'Binoculars'. Hagen, like so many of the men, is a voyeur. The world is looked at through lenses or glass – a window, a camera, the telescopic sights of a high-velocity rifle. He is a marksman

> Anaesthetised
> For ultimate cancellations

like the cancellation of the ring-dove, which he transforms into a feather mop, at the beginning, and his cancellation of Lumb at the end. He breeds bulls by artificial insemination. Other men in the village are also hunters and farmers. Nature is there to be used for human purposes, or misused.

Much is communicated by the style:

> The high-velocity rifles, in their glass-fronted cupboard,
> Creatures in hibernation, an appetite
> Not of this landscape.
> Coffee on the desk, untasted, now cold,
> Beside the tiger's skull – massive paperweight with a
> small man-made hole between the dragonish eye-sockets.

It is hardly poetry, rather fragmented prose, with all the links left out. It is a style which came into being, no doubt, as directions for the cameraman in the original film scenario. But it works here to create a sense of lifelessness, dissociation. Nothing is in a living relationship with anything else; and this is typical of the world our nature-spirit enters. It is a world of surfaces – veneers, wall-papers and skins; a world of 'polished modernity, the positioned furniture, in ultra colour, . . . like the demortalised organs of a body', of 'stuffed wild life', cactus windowsills, hall-chimes, souvenir ashtrays. It bears about the same relationship to nature, that is to say, to reality, as gravel to living rock. It cannot possibly accommodate Lumb, since it cannot accommodate even its domestic animals (a faithful retriever savages its master, who is savaging his wife; a cat becomes a demon and seduces its mistress), or real art (a Beethoven sonata havocks the house like a vandalising demon). It is a world wide open to the demonic because of the vacuum left by the absence of the sacred:

> In the old world God and divine power were invoked at any cost – life seemed worthless without them. In the present world we dare not invoke them – we wouldn't know how to use them or stop them destroying us. We have settled for the minimum practical energy and illumination – anything bigger introduces problems, the demons get hold of it.
>
> (*London Magazine*, January 1971, 10)

It is the waste land that modern literature has done so much to make us aware of, and so little (with the exception of Lawrence and the later Yeats) to cure. Here is Joseph Campbell's account:

> There has now spread throughout the Christian world a desolating sense not only of no divinity within, but also of no participation in divinity without: and that, in short, is the mythological base of the Waste Land of the modern soul, or, as it is being called these days, our 'alienation'. The sense of desolation is experienced on two levels: first the social, in a loss of identification

with any spiritually compelling, structuring group; and, beyond that, the metaphysical, in a loss of any sense either of identity or of relationship with a dimension of experience, being, and rapture any more awesome than that provided by an empirically classifiable conglomerate of self-enclosed, separate, mutually irritating organisms held together only by lust (crude or sublimated) and fear (of pain and death or of boredom).

(*Creative Mythology*, 394)

In *Gaudete* we feel that the underworld pushes up into this world with every grass-blade, explodes into it with every hatched egg, licks and flickers like green fire everywhere round the sterile houses. Every window is also

> . . . a door on to the furnace of the bright world
>
> The chill bustle
> Of the blossom-rocking afternoon
>
> The gusty lights of purplish silver, brightenings, sudden darkenings
> Teeming with wings and cries
> Under toppling heaven.
>
> (108)

To return to the first page of the main narrative (23), suddenly the camera pans away from Hagen to take in a whole world outside which dwarfs him, a rich, rolling, beautiful, infinite world:

> The parkland unrolls, lush with the full ripeness of the last week in May, under the wet midmorning light. The newly plumped grass shivers and flees. Giant wheels of light ride into the chestnuts, and the poplars lift and pour like the tails of horses. Distance blues beyond distance.

The usual prose/poetry distinction breaks down. Here the verse was prosaic, the prose is poetic, but rolls so much more spaciously and timelessly because unbroken into lines of verse. Hagen is as little 'of this landscape' as he was of India, when he shot tigers from his safe machan. The fullness of being of everything in the natural world continually invades the human world calling in question the reality of its inhabitants. Dunworth is almost extinguished by mere wafting scents:

> He leans at the door, emptied, merely his shape,
> Like a moth pinned to a board,
> While the nectars of the white lilac
> And the purple and dark magenta lilac
> Press through the rooms.
>
> (88)

Hughes seems able to draw on an inexhaustible fund of such images, with amazing freshness and fecundity, page after page, never the same. Cumulatively they give us an English Maytime, a whole flora and fauna, flowers and their scents, roistering young horses, trees rinsed with birdsong, shifting cloudscapes.

Against this, human life seems to be largely a series of devices to keep nature at bay. What undermines the safe cosiness from within is sex. The sense of desolation and sterility (none of the women have children) seems to be experienced much more strongly by women. Despite the recent improvements in their social position, Graves says that

> the White Goddess in her orgiastic character seems to have no chance of making a come-back, until women themselves grow weary of decadent patriarchalism, and turn Bassarids again. This is unlikely as yet, though the archives of morbid pathology are full of Bassarid case-histories. An English or American woman in a nervous breakdown of sexual origin will often instinctively reproduce in faithful and disgusting detail much of the ancient Dionysiac ritual. I have witnessed it myself in helpless terror.
>
> (*The White Goddess*, 458)

Lumb is able to exploit the explosive combination of sex and religion by promising the village women that one of them will become the mother of a god.

Into this world of sterile surfaces and brittle fragments, of cigarettes, cars, fashions, of Women's Institute meetings with cucumber sandwiches, of women owned by their husbands as domestic appurtenances, Hughes jams the elemental, the ithyphallic, in the form of his fertility god, his wood-demon, masquerading as Lumb. The girls and young women of the village are already walking incitements to devilry. The older women, with Lumb, are flung

> With more life than they can contain
> Like young dogs
> Unable to squirm free from their torturing infinite dogginess.
>
> (93)

Lumb impregnates the women with a reality too immense for their girdled bodies:

> She is gripped by the weird pathos of biochemistry, the hot silken frailties, the giant, gristled power, the archaic sea-fruit inside her, which her girdle bites into, which begins to make her suit too tight. She feels the finality of it all, and the nearness and greatness of death. Sea-burned, sandy cartilege, draughty stars, gull-cries from beyond the world's edge.
>
> (39)

Their ordinary world loses its reality:

She finds herself now in one room, now another, with a sensation of dropping through papery floors, falling from world to world.

(39)

The result is tragi-comic, as when Lumb and Mrs Garten, copulating on top of rickety rabbit-cages, overturn them and release two ferrets, 'creamy serpents', one of which, when recovered, is 'attached to a crying baby rabbit'. Janet Estridge, pregnant by Lumb, hangs herself, simultaneously releasing her father's imprisoned birds.

Life seems worthless without the energies Lumb releases; but, once released, those energies cannot be controlled, and destroy life. The women are in a trap. And so is Lumb. He cannot escape his own essential nature. All that underworld energy, that vegetable and animal procreative urge, channelled into a narrow man, can only express itself as frantic, priapic sexuality. His limited consciousness gropes to 'imagine simple freedom':

His possible freedoms, his other lives, hypothetical and foregone,
his lost freedoms.
As each person carries the whole world, like a halo,
Albeit a dim and mostly provisional world, but with a brightly
focused centre, under the sun,
Considering their millions
All mutually exclusive, all conjunct and co-extensive,
He sees in among them,
In among all the tiny millions of worlds of this world
Millions of yet other, alternative worlds, uninhabited,
unnoticed, still empty,
Each open at every point to every other and yet distinct,
Each waiting for him to escape into it, to explore it and possess it,
Each with a bed at the centre. A name. A pair of shoes. And a door.
And surrounded by still-empty, never-used limitless freedom.
He yields to his favourite meditation.
Forlorn, desperate meditation.

(50)

He is a creature of pure instinct, unadaptable, driven towards every unfertilized egg. But his survival instinct tells him that, in this human world, that act is increasingly desperate, like an oak which makes most mast when it fears death (as during severe drought). He feels his very blood is like the petrol in an engine out of control, accelerating towards danger. He feels he is being set up as a scapegoat. He is crucifying himself.

It is an extreme image of the biological duality of man, with his two brains, one clenched inside the other like a fist in a boxing-glove; 'the biological polarity of the life of the body and archaic nervous system and the life of the reflective cortex' (*A Choice of Shakespeare's Verse*, 199). Lawrence also expressed it as crucifixion:

It is the invariable crucifixion. The Cross, as we know, stands for the body, for the dark self which lives in the body. And on the Cross of this bodily self is crucified the self which I know I am, my so-called *real* self. The Cross, as an ancient symbol, has an inevitable phallic reference. But it is far deeper than sex. It is the self which darkly inhabits our blood and bone, and for which the ithyphallus is but a symbol. This self which lives darkly in my blood and bone is my *alter ego*, my other self, the homunculus, the second one of the Kabiri, the second of the Twins, the Gemini . . . And on this cross of division in the whole self is crucified the Christ. We are all crucified on it. (*Phoenix* 2, 619)

Perhaps the changeling thought he could best minister to the spiritual needs of his female parishioners by thus recharging their lives with power and animal joy. But far from healing or renewing, his activity only draws him into a fatal tangle of destructive passions. His own powers, compromised by the straitjacket of Lumb's human identity, cannot save him from becoming the plaything of jealous women and the victim of jealous men.

In a later meditation, the changeling sees in a Sheela-na-gig an image of the goddess he worships:

Lumb's eyes
Are locked
To an archaic stone carving, propped on his mantel, above the fire.

The simply hacked-out face of a woman
Gazes back at Lumb
Between her raised, wide-splayed, artless knees
With a stricken expression.
Her square-cut, primitive fingers, beneath her buttocks
Are pulling herself wide open –

An entrance, an exit.
An arched target centre.
A mystery offering
Into which Lumb is lowering his drowse.

(110)

It is the goddess at her most obscene:

The characteristic manifestation of the devouring-mother aspect of the goddess in Celtic symbolism – and analogous to the bloody Kali of the

> Hindus or the Coatlicue of the Aztecs – is graphically illustrated by the stone effigies known under the name of Sheela-na-gig, found in medieval churches and castles. The usual characteristics of Sheela-na-gig are 'an ugly, mask-like skull-face with huge scowling mouth, skeletal ribs, huge genitalia held apart with both hands, and bent legs', offering a fantasy of unlimited sexual licence but at the same time a comic reminder of our origins. (Sharkey, 8)

Lumb sees every woman as an incarnation of that goddess. Through that entrance he had hoped to draw up other spirits to transform the world. Failing that, it might be an exit, a way back to his own safe underworld. But too much is working against him. His promiscuous animality becomes merely degrading:

> When the physical presence of love has been degraded to lust, and forbidden lust has combined with every other forbidden thing to become a murderous devil, life itself has become a horror, the maiden has become a whore and a witch, and miraculous source of creation has become the empty hole through into Nothing. (*A Choice of Shakespeare's Verse*, 199)

He is obliged, for mere survival, to adopt a purely human, temporal strategy – to settle for a single woman, Felicity, and run away with her. In this he is perhaps falling back on a plan the original Lumb may have had before his split. Felicity may have been at the heart of that split. She is eighteen and 'the most exotic thing in the nursery':

> She is aware of it. She performs it a little, self-indulgently, with a flourish, as a leopard performs its frightening grace.
>
> Her overlong upsweeping nose, her flat calf's eye, her wide reckless mouth, were her father's real ugliness. For the time being they compound her enigmatic triangular beauty.
>
> Gypsy dark skin, intensifying into fierce wire hair. Lusty little moles on her upper lip, and on her cheek.
>
> (91)

This is Felicity's formal introduction to the story, but it comes after her first appearance.

The 'goat-eyed vicar' has been wounded in the head by Westlake's gun. He washes the wound at the river's edge in blazing sunshine. In the babel of waters

> He recognizes voices out of his past.
> Peremptory trivial phrases,
> Distinct and sudden, behind him and beside him.
> One voice is coming clearer, insistent.
> It calls his name repeatedly, searchingly.

It is his own voice.
As the other voices thicken over him
He manages, as from his deep listening, to answer: 'I'm here.'
(77)

We fade from the sparkling oily backwater of the river to an oil-still lake. It is evening with purple thunder-clouds gathering. He stands on an island fishing, while Felicity huddles in a boat nearby reading. But Lumb is interested only in his fish. This is surely a flashback to the old Lumb, resisting his feelings for Felicity, which rise nevertheless beneath the surface. It is the calm before the storm.

She watches his balancing form,
Black against the steely lake, under the electrical nearness of the mountains.
Lightning flutters, orange and purple, in the high silence
Over the peaks, behind the clouds,
And beneath the floor of the lake.

As the storm breaks, up from the lake comes the demon Lumb, who tries to drag Felicity into the lake with him. The two Lumbs fight over her in the violet glare:

And thunder trundles continually around the perimeter of the deeply padded heaven
And through the cellars of the lake
With splittings of giant trees and echoing of bronze flues and mazy corridors,
And repeated, closer bomb-bursts, which seem to shower hot fragments.

The antagonists 'lie face to face, gripping each other's hands'. It seems to be a prelude to the crossover which took place in the Prologue; but Lumb resisting, this time, to the point of tearing off the hand of his joyous, clowning double, who submerges howling. This is one flesh, one blood 'doing itself much harm', like Christian Parzival fighting his pagan brother before their reconciliation in love:

The life-desolating effects of this separation of the reigns of nature (the Earthly Paradise) and the spirit (the Castle of the Grail) in such a way that neither touches the other but destructively, remains to this day an essential psychological problem of the Christianized Western world.
(Campbell, *Creative Mythology* 393)

The tearing off of the hand has a hint of Beowulf's fight with Grendel.

This simplification has led, through dualistic theology, to the theory that death, evil, decay and destruction are erroneous concepts which God, the Good, the Right Hand, will one day disprove. Ascetic theologians try to paralyze or lop off the left hand in honour of the right; but poets are aware that each twin must conquer in turn, in an agelong and chivalrous war fought for the favours of the White Goddess. . . . The war between Good and Evil has been waged in so indecent and painful a way during the past two millennia because the theologians, not being poets, have forbidden the Goddess to umpire it, and made God impose on the Devil impossible terms of unconditional surrender. (*The White Goddess*, 446)

Gaudete is an invitation to the Goddess to resume that function.

Maud is one of the casualties of that indecent war, the maiden becomes old maid and murderous witch. Her true self, her capacity for joy in life (symbolized by her lost voice) is buried under a gravestone on which is engraved one lonely word 'Gaudete' – Rejoice! With boughs of apple-blossom, symbol of consummation, with which the White Goddess summoned Bran, she decorates her tomb, which is also the tomb of the goddess herself 'who seems to be alive and dead' and whose ghost walks the graveyard ahead of Maud. She tries to tear power from the heart of a white pigeon. She, not Felicity, must be Lumb's bride.

Mrs Davies, on the other hand, is a white witch, a troll woman, who has treated her demon kindly, as she treats her familiar, an adder which comes to her for milk and to which she sings. She is also expert at invoking power through drugs, as in the Dionysiac mushroom cults. Her mushroom sandwiches, her specially blended cigarettes, the din of archaic music, all conspire to release the women at the W.I. meeting from all their inhibitions and let the power flow. Lumb tries to channel it, as he has done before, into fertility rites, himself wearing the antlers and pelt of a stag.

We know, from Gallo-Roman carvings, of a horned god called Cernunnos, whose origins lie in the kind of deity whom anthropologists call the 'lord of the animals'. He was the god of the chase, and the quarry was in his power. He appears in British folklore as 'Herne the Hunter', and Shakespeare mentions his oak in Windsor Forest. The idea of a horned huntsman goes back to a very ancient level; cave paintings show a man in a wild animal's skin. The hunter identified with the stag in order to propitiate its ruling spirit. This is a very ancient mystery, although not a purely Celtic one: hunter and hunted are one.

Shape-shifting into our animal natures, whether as bull, stag, horse, boar, cat, bird or fish, is a common feature of Celtic tales. Such attempts at tapping latent powers and extending the range of consciousness through strictly observed rituals have long been recognized as the special gift of certain individuals. They enter a collective dream state where past and present, psychic and physical realities merge, to become the bridge between divine and animal aspects of man: these individuals, in all nomadic societies, are the shamans. (Sharkey, 12)

But Lumb is no shaman. He cannot hold the two worlds together. His plan to desert the women and elope with Felicity, known to Maud, deprives him of all authority. And Maud has another role in mind for Felicity, the sacrificial love-animal. Transformed by drugs Felicity feels 'the greatness and nobility of her role':

Somehow she has become a goddess.
She is now the sacred doll of a slow infinite solemnity.
She knows she is a constellation very far off and cold
Moving through this burrow of smoke and faces.
She moves robed invisibly with gorgeous richness.
She knows she is burning plasma and infinitely tiny,
That she and all these women are moving inside the body
of an incandescent creature of love,
That they are brightening, and that the crisis is close,
They are the cells in the glands of an inconceivably huge
and urgent love-animal
And some final crisis of earth's life is now to be enacted
Faithfully and selflessly by them all.

(142)

In the event, she is simply murdered by Maud, who miraculously recovers her voice only to denounce Lumb; he is going to run away with this girl

Like an ordinary man
With his ordinary wife.

The powers which have been released are insatiable. They will have no truck with order and ordinary. Maud has already made sure there will be no ordinary escape for Lumb, in his Bentley; she has thrown away the keys. He must go through with his destiny, first as hunted stag, then as burned vegetation god. But because he is hunted and burned not in a spirit of religious awe, but one of demented personal malignity and then getting rid of the evidence, nothing is achieved by his sacrifice.

The King of the Woods could reign for another year if he could outrun his pursuers. Lumb is confident of his powers:

He has plugged his energy appeal into the inexhaustible earth.
He imagines he is effortless Adam, before weariness entered,
leaping for God.
(163)

But the powers abandon him to the ordinariness he had compromised with, now that he no longer wants it:

He knows that the sky no longer ushers towards him
glowing hieroglyphs of endowment,
That he is now ordinary, and susceptible
To extinction,
That his precious and only body
Is nothing more than some radio-transmitter, a standard structure,
Tipped from an empty dinghy by a wave
In the middle of a sea grey and nameless.
(164)

A standard transmitter is of special value only according to what it transmits. When the powers with which he was invested in the Prologue are allowed to drain from him through the hole in his side, he loses his living relationship with the natural world. He loses his sense of the world as living, or at least as meaningful, and lapses into what Blake called 'Single vision and Newton's sleep' – a vision of the world mechanically fixed in its circular processes, and therefore absurd:

He sees the reeds sticking up out of the water
So conceitedly dull in their rootedness
Like books in a technical library.
He sees the lakewater
Simply waste liquid flowed in here, and collected by inertia,
From the gutters of space
Where it is worthless and accidental –
A spiritless by-product
Of the fact that things exist at all.
He knows now that this land
This embroidery of stems and machinery of cells
Is an ignorance, waiting in a darkness –
He knows at last why it has become so.
(165)

Fecundity, once his reason for living, he can no longer distinguish from waste. The passage gives us the essence of what is perhaps the dominant vision of twentieth-century literature, the vision which received its definitive expression in Sartre's *Nausea*:

All things . . . were abjectly admitting to one another the fact of their existence. . . . We were a heap of existents inconvenienced, embarrassed by ourselves, we hadn't the slightest reason for being there, any of us, each existent, embarrassed, vaguely ill at ease, felt superfluous in relation to the others. *Superfluous*: that was the only connection I could establish between those trees, those gates, those pebbles. (183–4)

This must have been the vision of the original Lumb after he lost his faith. Indeed the original Lumb seems to have been seeping back for some time, as the demon burns itself out. We see it in his willingness to give up his harem/coven and to settle for Felicity; and, more significantly, in the purely human compassion he shows when Felicity has been killed:

Lumb is kneeling.
He bows over her, close to her face,
His cheek almost touching her cheek
As he searches her face,
Hardly daring to breathe,
As if hardly daring to stir the air about her,
As if this were some horribly burned body
That has just dropped from a shocking height.
(148)

We are reminded of the other Lumb bending over the apparently dead goddess, and his implicit disclaiming of responsibility:

He is not a doctor. He can only pray.

This Lumb knows the depth of his responsibility; but we feel that, in any case, his compassion would be greater:

With all his gentleness
He pulls on the hilt of the dagger,
As if gentleness intense enough
Could force a miracle.
(148)

We can now return to a crucial passage (98ff) which gives us our most important glimpses into what has been happening, meanwhile, to the original Lumb, still stranded between two worlds. He imagines that a demon has taken the wheel of his car and caused a crash. He is thrown into the river. Bodies of water, river or lake, are always here the meeting point of the two worlds, leaking into each other, and mud is the primal substance out of which new life emerges. All the changeling's labours had brought no births. Of the two women who became pregnant to him one committed suicide and the other is contemplating it. In this passage are concentrated several births. The men in oilskins, cudgelling Lumb into the mud, are his midwives. The sodden paper they give him 'as if it were some explanation . . . disintegrates in his fingers, weak as a birth membrane'. Their malice drives him out of their world into the world of cattle and their slurry. The cattle 'churn in a vortex . . . bellowing outrage and fear'. They gore each other. It is like the churning of thwarted energies in madness; like the collapse of a civilization into anarchy, Lumb's dying to the old world and its false constructions; like a birth:

> It is like a dam bursting, masonry and water-mass mingled.
> (100)

In the stampede which follows the men are trampled to death, but Lumb, by running with the cattle, survives. He lets the rain clean his upturned face, lets it hurt his eyelids. His self-abandonment, though unconscious, is a positive act, the only way forward at that point, like the abandonment of Parzival who finds the Grail castle only by letting the reins lie loose on his horse's neck. The suffering the men have subjected him to releases his own compassion.

Afterwards he finds the crushed bodies of the men, then the heads of the women of his parish, all screaming, all buried to the neck in mud round the rim of a crater, from the bottom of which something is trying to squirm free. Lumb tries to rescue it. He draws it up, and it embraces him.

> The rain striking across the mud face washes it.
> It is a woman's face,
> A face as if sewn together from several faces.
> A baboon beauty face,
> A crudely stitched patchwork of faces,
> But the eyes slide,
> Alive and electrical, like liquid liquorice behind the stitched lids.
> (104)

It is the same woman he had failed to cure in the Prologue, now seen in her aspect of a composite of all the women in the world, and their disfigurement; a patchwork of all the living creatures mangled by men; the ravaged face of the earth itself. There are several shamanistic myths where the shaman is called upon to heal the goddess herself. In one the Lady of the Seals is infested about the head with parasites which represent all the aborted children and needlessly slaughtered animals on earth.

Lumb and the woman are clamped, knotted together. He cannot free himself.

> A swell of pain, building from his throat and piling downwards
> Lifts him suddenly out of himself.
> Somehow he has emerged and is standing over himself.
> He sees himself being delivered of the woman from the pit,
> The baboon woman,
> Flood-sudden, like the disembowelling of a cow
> She gushes from between his legs, a hot splendour
> In a glistening of oils,
> In a radiance like phosphorous he sees her crawl and tremble.
> (105)

But the calf-clamp is still on his twisted body:

> He feels bones give. He feels himself slide.
> He fights in hot liquid.
>
> . . .
>
> He crawls,
> He frees his hands and face of blood-clotted roping tissues.
> He sees light.
> He sees her face undeformed and perfect.
> (105–6)

We have followed through *Cave Birds* the process of ego-death, and of the mutual reconstitution of a man and woman:

> Like two gods of mud
> Sprawling in the dirt, but with infinite care
> They bring each other to perfection.

In several shamanistic myths, or Scots and Irish folktales, the task of the human being in the spirit world is to help with a difficult birth. Here the birth is doubly difficult. It is Lumb's own rebirth at which he must play the roles of mother and child. The woman, Nature, cannot give birth to him (rebirth is the only cure for his breakdown), until he has given birth to her, fertilized her, resacralized her, and thereby cured her deformity and sterility. As for Parzival, it is a simple matter of spontaneous human feeling, so long dammed up in Lumb, recognition, sympathy.

Lumb at this point is very like the ancient mariner, who had also failed in compassion towards Nature, been persecuted by his fellow-men and taken over by spirits, and who, after much suffering and madness, was released from his curse by a spontaneous act of recognition of the beauty and blessedness of the creatures of the great calm, which he had formerly seen only as slimy things crawling on a slimy sea. A spring of love gushed from his heart and he blessed them unaware. Then he fell into a deep healing sleep; when he awoke, it rained. We leave him moving about in the human world half-crazy, but able to open the hearts and eyes of others. The main narrative of *Gaudete* opened with the wanton shooting of a holy bird – a dove, sacred to the goddess. Though Lumb did not shoot it, he must, in the Epilogue, become that dove. By sharing its agony in the garden, he also shares its annunciation.

This passage ends with Lumb crawling out of the river

> Glossed as an exhausted otter, and trailing
> A mane of water.
>
> (106)

The otter, with its 'oil-of-water body, neither fish nor beast . . . of neither water nor land' ('An Otter'), is also a holy creature, denizen of both worlds; and, in spite of the hunt, a creature of joy.

Lumb's task may be simple, but it is far from easy, as we see in the tentative fearful steps he takes in the Epilogue, one back in recoil for every two forward, false starts, dead ends, panics and despairs. The object is to look Nature in the face, and love her, and be loved by her. The veils of falsification, sentimentality, anthropomorphism, conditioned responses, must be torn away; but not the veils which protect the Divine mysteries from profane eyes. Then there is the problem of seeing that face with joy when it is beautiful and with horror when it is ugly. The horror must not cancel the joy. It must deepen and complete it, as the joy of tragedy is ultimately so much more deep and complete than that of comedy. Under the veils there is yet the mask – the Venus mask of beauty or the Hecate mask of ugliness. Under the masks is the baboon beauty.

If the first requisite is compassion, the second is humility. And as the compassion is to be extended to all living things, so the humility is to be a humility of the race even more than of the individual. To look at life in an exclusively personal, ethical, social and historical context is always a falsification, since these contexts are invariably shaped and interpreted in exclusively human terms. Humanism is the racial equivalent of solipsism. It consigns the human race to a sterile, completely insulated capsule, as in Beckett's *The Lost Ones*. It crazily, hubristically, assumes, in the face of all the evidence, that the human race is self-sufficient, that such powers as there are outside the human world can be safely either exploited or ignored.

The moral of the main narrative of *Gaudete* is that modern, sophisticated secular society is not equipped to handle these forces, and if willy-nilly exposed to them, will respond with madness, murder, suicide, and a complete breakdown of humanistic civilized values. Yet cut off from them, it is sterile, and by denying them ensures that when they do erupt they will be the more debased, demonic and destructive. The rituals which formerly controlled them cannot now be reconstituted. They were grounded in a communal sense of the sacred which has completely gone.

The individual can always seek his own private salvation. But at a communal level, the only substitute we have for ritual is art. Matthew Arnold saw the poet replacing the priest, and the process has continued. In Shamanistic societies the two have always been one; and in our own Celtic past, as Graves has shown, the poets, often in opposition to the priests, held the ultimate secrets.

Speaking of shamanism, Hughes has said:

> The individual is summoned by certain dreams. The same dreams all over the world. A spirit summons him . . . usually an animal or a woman. . . . Once fully-fledged he can enter trance at will and go to the spirit world. . . . He goes to get something badly needed, a cure, an answer, some sort of divine intervention in the community's affairs. . . . Poets usually refuse the call. How are they to accept it? How can a poet become a medicine man and fly to the source and come back and heal or pronounce oracles? Everything among us is against it. (*London Magazine*, January 1971)

In *Gaudete* he has tried to circumvent this apparent impossibility by the strategy of making his protagonist, Lumb, begin as a failed priest and return as a 'half crazy' poet whose notebook contains forty-five of the finest poems Hughes has yet written.

Balancing, ultimately just outweighing, the disastrous eruption of the elemental into ordinary human society, is this other half of the crossover, the summoning of a single human being out of his world and into elemental nature. He is equally ill-prepared and ill-fitted for his task. His adventures are equally horrifying. He undergoes awful ego-deaths. But he survives. He even, almost inadvertently, carries out his healing task. He is reborn, and re-emerges in this world having recovered the buried capacity for joy, and a raw wisdom, and the capacity to perform small miracles.

The changeling was a log. He was blinkered and obsessed. He had no idea what was happening to him or why, but suffered mechanically as puppet and scapegoat, a transmitter of energies not his own. The real Lumb fights his battles in consciousness, and comes through, at the end, to a finely adjusted consciousness of nature and his place in it. His poems are the stages of his journey.

What Hughes is attempting, as a matter of life and death, is the recovery of the lost sense of the sacredness of Nature. Not, of course, the sentimental Nature of traditional English Nature poetry, but the savage, elemental, horrific (as well as incredibly lovely and tender and fresh) Nature all his work has gone to define. Sacredness, as Hughes understands it, has nothing to do with metaphysics. 'Sacred' means nothing more nor less than 'real'. To see something as real, in all its fullness of being, is to recognize it as a manifestation of the sacred, a hierophany.

No-one can, by taking thought, by reading a persuasive argument, by trying to live in accordance with the doctrines of a particular religion, begin to see things as sacred. Language is double-edged: by labelling or 'explaining' it can desacralize. 'What is that?' asks the wide-eyed child, and the mother replies 'Only an otter'. There is nothing extraordinary about it. It knows its place in the linguistic map of the world, where it is named and classified, and cannot, therefore, be either sacred or miraculous. Poetic naming, evocation, invocation, is just the opposite. The poet does not generate power, simply clears a channel for it. 'Through me the current and index', as Whitman said. And Whitman knew that the prototype miracle is the blade of grass:

> I believe a leaf of grass is no less than the journey-work of the stars,
> And the pismire is equally perfect, and a grain of sand, and the egg of the wren,
> And the tree-toad is a chef-d'oeuvre for the highest,
> And the running blackberry would adorn the parlors of heaven,

And the narowest hinge in my hand puts to scorn all machinery,
And the cow crunching with depress'd head surpasses any statue,
And a mouse is miracle enough to stagger sextillions of infidels.
('Song of Myself', 31)

Lumb's first 'miracle' is to draw an otter from the loch by whistling on the back of his hand. The three little girls for whom he performs it have not yet been brainwashed; they do not know what it is, and it is never named. But it is very real:

> It was like nothing the girls had ever seen, unless it was like a big weasel. It came up the gravelly beach below the rocks with that merry, hump-backed, snake-headed gallop of weasels. . . .
>
> Till at last the creature was sitting there in front of them, the size of a big cat, its dark fur all clawed with wet, craning towards the man, sniffing and shivering, so he could have reached out his hand and touched it, and the girls could smell the wild smell of the fish of the loch.
>
> (174)

The otter itself is a miracle. And the happy meeting of two worlds is a greater one, especially when we think of the earlier meeting with the joyous seal-like creature which came up out of a lake. Lumb performs effortlessly the miracle of summoning the sacred which the changeling Lumb had so laboriously failed to perform for his parishioners.

The girls run with their news and their notebook to their priest, who is 'gazing at an open page of St Ignatius'. At first he is inclined to pooh-pooh their 'miracle':

> 'If that is a miracle,' he said finally, 'To bring an otter up out of the loch, then what must that poor man think of the great world itself, this giant, shining beauty that God whistled up out of the waters of chaos?'
>
> And as he spoke the priest was suddenly carried away by his words. His thoughts flew up into a great fiery space, and who knows what spark had jumped on to him from the flushed faces of the three girls? He seemed to be flying into an endless, blazing sunrise, and he described the first coming of Creation, as it rose from the abyss, an infinite creature of miracles, made of miracles and teeming miracles. And he went on, describing this creature, giving it more and more dazzlingly-shining eyes, and more and more glorious limbs, and heaping it with greater and more extraordinary beauties, till his heart was pounding and he was pacing the room talking about God himself, and the tears pouring from his eyes fell shattering and glittering down the front of his cassock.
>
> (175)

This is a far cry from the *Spiritual Exercises* of St Ignatius: 'We must make ourselves indifferent to all created things.' Ignatius, recommending the chastizing of the flesh with hairshirts and iron chains, 'to overcome ourselves, so that sensuality will be obedient to reason and our lower inclinations be subject to higher ones', is the polar opposite of the changeling Lumb.

We are concerned very much with opposites here. The West Coast of Ireland is the opposite of Lumb's parish, relatively untouched by that kind of 'civilization', its Christianity, as Synge testified, all mixed up with paganism. The three girls are the opposite of the women of his parish, in their innocence, in the total absence of sexuality in his relationship with them, and in their relationship with their own priest, to whom they report what has happened like the three Maries reporting their morning miracle. The priest and Lumb are as opposite as priests can be (that is Lumb as he was when he was attempting to carry out his priestly duties). This priest, it seems, is more like a medieval anchorite, his faith grounded not in dogma and theology but in his personal sense of the sacred.

As Hopkins, to his horror, came close in spirit to Whitman, even in his commentary on the *Spiritual Exercises*, so perhaps this hermit priest is spiritually as close to Pantheism as Hopkins was. At least his religion is not so puritanical nor so far from pagan Nature-worship as Anglicanism. The Virgin Mary and the White Goddess are both personifications of the psychological/spiritual force Jung called the Anima. At least he is not so far removed in spirit from the reborn Lumb that a bridge cannot be built, a spark fly across, an imaginative fertilization take place. By bridging the chasm in his own psyche, Lumb has repaired the circuit which allows this charge to flow through him. When a shaman returns to the living, says Hughes,

> the results are some display of healing power, or a clairvoyant piece of information. The cathartic effect on the audience, and the refreshing of their religious feeling, must be profound. (*Listener*, 29 October 1964)

The priest, putting Ignatius aside, copies out Lumb's poems, which are 'hymns to a nameless female deity'.

As for Lumb himself, we assume his life henceforth will be to make his small contribution, here and there, to the great task of restoring to others a sense of the sacred, and a spiritual orientation towards life which makes it possible to experience nature as, in spite of everything, because of everything, healing, revivifying, and worthy of service.

When *Lumb's Remains* was given its first reading at the Ilkley

Festival in 1975, the poems (including several splendid ones not in *Gaudete*) were read in random order. Hughes must have had second thoughts about this, for the order of the poems in *Gaudete* does seem to me significant. They are progressive, not step by step, but with a wavelike surge and recoil, making almost imperceptible progress.

The first poem establishes the maturity and humility of Lumb. He has been dismantled, stripped to the bone, and knows his condition. He makes no protest. It is enough that he has survived. He is like the hero of *Cave Birds* in 'The Knight', the opposite of those knights, St Georges, who ride out blindly to strike at life with their little lances. He is more like a mature, humanized wodwo in his abandonment of identity, his vulnerability and exposure, his groping. This, not the riding forth in full armour, is the approach to life which requires real courage. The whole Epilogue reminds me very strongly of Lawrence's essay 'On Being a Man', where he defines man as a thought-adventurer:

> He dares take thought for what he has done and what has happened to him. And daring to take thought, he ventures on, and realizes at last.
>
> To be a man! To risk your body and your blood first, and then to risk your mind. All the time, to risk your known self, and become once more a self you could never have known or expected. . . .
>
> Today men don't risk their blood and bone. They go forth, panoplied in their own idea of themselves. Whatever they do, they perform it all in the full armour of their own idea of themselves. Their unknown bodily self is never for one moment unsheathed. All the time, the only protagonist is the known ego, the self-conscious ego. And the dark self in the mysterious labyrinth of the body is cased in a tight armour of cowardly repression. . . . And inside the armour he goes quite deranged. (*Phoenix* 2, 620–1)

The second poem begins:

> I hear your congregations at their rapture
>
> Cries from birds, long ago perfect
> And from the awkward gullets of beasts
> That will not chill into syntax.
>
> (176)

It seems that the higher we get up the evolutionary tree, the more difficult it is to join that congregation and share that rapture. Man's great evolutionary leap, language, should have freed him to express his rapture even more perfectly than the birds, but seems rather to have been 'sublimed' out of all contact with reality, usable now only as the small change of social intercourse.

The heat of naked feeling – pain, fear, joy, reverence – is an embarrassment we have developed language to cool and clothe:

> Words buckle the voice in tighter, closer
> Under the midriff
> Till the cry rots, and speech
>
> Is a fistula

Part of the fascination of Shakespeare's language, for Hughes, is that this had not yet happened:

> It was even worse bad luck for Shakespeare's language that the crippled court-artifice of Restoration speech should have been passed on to the military garrison of the Empire, where the desirable ideal of speech for all Englishmen became the shrunken, atrophied, suppressive-of-everything-under, bluffing, debonair, frivolous system of vocal team-calls which we inherit as Queen's English. (*A Choice of Shakespeare's Verse*, 198)

Some of the Turtons and Burtons of E. M. Forster's British Raj retired to Lumb's parish. The image of a 'stupid or crafty doctor' reminds us of Dr Westlake's inadequacy:

> And the finality of that dead girl lies at the centre of the day
> Like an incomprehensible, frightful dream.
> And her live sister is worse – all that loose, hot, tumbled softness,
> Like freshly killed game, with the dew still on it,
> Its eyes seeming alive, still strange with wild dawn,
> Helpless underbody still hot.
>
> (72)

The turbulence of her body destroys his detachment, her voice scorches him, and the insanity in her eyes

> Her irises clear and nimble-delicate as a baboon's
>
> (57)

makes 'something in his marrow' shrivel with fear. It was, of course, the goddess herself he was exposed to. And Lumb had been almost as inadequate in the same situation:

> He is not a doctor. He can only pray.

Prayer was, in a sense, what was needed, but not the sort he had in mind – the professional formulas of his church. He is now occupied in learning how to pray, so that he can join her congregation.

The third poem introduces a theme which is to recur, that of the willing death:

> The spider clamps the bluefly – whose death panic
> Becomes sudden soulful absorption.

A stoat throbs at the nape of the lumped rabbit
Who watches the skylines fixedly.

(177)

Many of the cries which make up the rapture of nature's congregation are death-cries.[1] The first image, where only insects are involved, can be easily accepted; the second with difficulty. But the third is another matter:

Photographs of people – open-mouthed
In the gust of being shot and falling.

These are people, unwilling victims of members of their own species who are not killing them for food. Nature herself revolts against it:

And you grab me
So the blood jumps into my teeth

And 'Quick!' you whisper, 'O quick!'
And 'Now! Now! Now!'

Now what?

That I hear the age of the earth?

That I feel
My mother lift me up from between her legs?

This is indeed the magnitude of what is required of him. That he re-establish his life in the most basic realities of his nature and the world's. No tinkering, no 'sanguinary nostrums' will cure that sickness.

The fourth poem is another version of the meeting with the ailing goddess. He faces the world with a fragmented soul – superficial, dehumanized relationships, absurd, clownish gods, instincts and repressions fighting among themselves, yet feels himself able to 'use' the world, like a 'thrilling weapon', or to walk happily through it, though his steps have no aim. But he cannot go on much longer ignoring the goddess deep in the cave behind him, his own capacity for wholeness, which he has turned his back on.

The whole earth is 'groaning in labour'; the lark's song labouring at the sun; everything labouring to bring itself into fullness of being:

A prickling fever
A flush of the swelling earth –

(178)

Touching the mere grains of earth, he cannot withstand the prophesy that he is to be atoned with it.

There are two ways of seeking atonement with the whole world. One is to try to contain it, to extend one's consciousness until one becomes, like Whitman in 'Song of Myself', a cosmos. In the sixth poem Lumb develops this kind of awareness, but it is mere romantic afflatus which exalts the self and excludes the goddess. He cannot come to wholeness simply by inflating his soul and violently taking possession of nature like a forced bride:

> I neglected to come to degree of nature
> In the patience of things.
>
> I forestalled God –
>
> I assailed his daughter.
>
> Now I lie at the road's edge.
> People come and go.
>
> Dogs watch me.
>
> (179)

Such pride, selfyeast of spirit, must be humbled in the dirt. Now he must sue like a beggar at her gate. Nature's smile is not, as Hopkins put it, to be wrung. Or, in Kafka's terms, there is no road from man to God, only from God to man. One can only wait for grace in humility, that is, emptied to receive it should it come, a willing prisoner. A poem in *Lumb's Remains*, unfortunately dropped from *Gaudete*, expresses the possibility that such service, if not perfect freedom, can be thriving and fecundity, even if the goddess never comes; growing and fruiting, life issuing out of mud and rubble, the fecund ditch, being her permanent benediction:

> If searching can't find you
>
> Show me that corner
> Where I can sit, your prisoner,
> Till you come.
>
> As my blood, waiting for food – its god,
> Is a prisoner in my darkness,
> And cannot thrive anywhere else.
>
> As a fig-tree burdened with figs,
> In its trench of rubble
> Is a prisoner.

The eighth poem gives us another image for the same condition of self-abandonment and disorientation:

> A kelp, adrift
> In my feeding substance.
>
> (180)

The kelp, a large seaweed, drifts in water which contains what it feeds on, but drifts also in its own substance which, burned, is a rich fertilizer.

In the next poem Lumb reduces his effort from trying to be the world to trying to be a leaf. For a moment he succeeds:

> And your fulness comes
>
> And I reel back
> Into my face and hands
>
> Like the electrocuted man
> Banged from his burst straps.
>
> (180)

If we compare this little poem with the description at the beginning of 'Egg-Head' of the effect of letting in on one's sense 'a leaf's otherness' we can see how far Hughes has come from the insistent rhetoric, confident in its own impressiveness, of *The Hawk in the Rain.*

'This is the maneater's skull' (183) takes another look at the tiger's skull Major Hagen used as a paperweight. The maneater is on the goddess's leash, is the goddess in one of her aspects. Not until he has been devoured, emptied and abandoned, can she rescue him, fulfilling his vision of

> An unearthly woman wading shorewards
> With me in your arms
>
> The grey in my hair.
>
> (183)

That vision is sustained by the relationship he perceives between the oak and the earth, its bride, which is simultaneously a crucifixion and a love-act. The oak sheds twigs as tokens of its pain and bliss, brown leaves as tokens of its death, and acorns as tokens of its rebirth. Lumb lies beneath it in 'perilously frail safety', as his twin had tried to make an ash-tree his prayer. There is no safety for him either,

> For nothing can be sole or whole
> That has not been rent.
>
> (Yeats, 'Crazy Jane and the Bishop')

And the soul must be wholly lost before it can regain the world.

'Waving goodbye' (185) is a splendid example of Hughes' ability to ground his larger themes, which could so easily become abstract, cold or contrived, in very moving common experience in the contemporary world. The protagonist's helplessness is like that of one visiting in hospital someone desperately ill, in whom one's whole world is invested – a world which can be lost as easily as knocking off a flower-vase while waving goodbye. The world which was a hospital is now a morgue, soon a cemetery. In the unreal world where people still live as though life were something other than a grievous funeral, he feels like a lonely survivor from a forgotten past, exposed, deprived of function, a curio:

> Like a pillar over Athens
>
> Defunct
>
> In the glaring metropolis of cameras.
>
> (186)

Under the pressure of pain and loss and alienation, there comes a strong temptation to see the world itself as lost, and well lost, and to seek to live like a disembodied spirit. It is the temptation voiced by the soul in Yeats' 'Dialogue of Self and Soul':

> Think of ancestral night that can,
> If but imagination scorn the earth
> . . .
> Deliver from the crime of death and birth.

We have seen Hughes wrestling with himself on this ground in the 'coming clear' poems, and doing himself much harm, for the part of himself (everything which is not spirit) which rolls away towards non-being on the rejected earth, stands out there

> His howling transfigured double ('Song of Woe')

like the wailing mutilated demon floundering in the lake.

In 'I said goodbye to earth', the speaker again steps off into non-being. But the image of crucifixion

> I saw the snowflake crucified
> Upon the nails of nothing

generates the image of holy communion

> I heard the atoms praying
> To enter his kingdom
> To be broken like bread
> On a dark sill, and to bleed

which also suggests to me the homely image of feeding birds at an open window. The atoms and snowflakes seem to be striving in the opposite direction to the man, towards being, incarnation, at any cost. They pray to enter the kingdom of death and birth, and God would rather be a man on a cross than not be a man at all.

Hughes has described the disciplines of the Sufis as

a highly refined course of moral self-development, annihilating themselves without heaven or hell or religious paraphernalia of any kind, and without leaving life in the world, into the living substance of Allah, the power of Creation. (*Listener*, 29 October 1964)

This describes quite closely what he is attempting himself in the Epilogue of *Gaudete*.

As the self in the Yeats dialogue is content to pitch

Into the frog-spawn of a blind man's ditch

so Lumb swings back from outer space to the example of the swallow, which, rebuilding –

Collects the lot
From the sow's wallow.
(187)

But Lumb feels he has completely dispersed himself, is nothing but his own obituary, his own absence. His prayer is that the goddess gather the scattered particles of dust and rebuild him. He sees her now as his keeper 'sitting in the sun'. We are reminded of the penultimate poem in *Prometheus on his Crag* where Prometheus first recognizes the vulture as his 'helper', and midwife to his rebirth. If she is a falcon, must she devour him before he can be reborn?

In 'The night wind' he is very much back in the world, a world suggesting a return to Neanderthal beginnings, or at least to the condition of Mad Tom in the storm:

A night
To scamper naked
To the dry den
Where one who would have devoured me is driven off
By a wolf.
(187)

That devouring is only deferred until 'I skin the skin' (196), with the reconstitution in the following poem.

In 'The viper fell from the sun' Lumb is bombarded with miracles and teeming miracles.

I stirred, like a discarded foetus,
Already grey-haired,
In a blowing of bright particles.

The particles are his own dust, his own atoms, in the process of being reassembled. The discarded foetus is adopted by heaven, which enters, for the first time, into a maternal relationship with him:

A hand out of a hot cloud
Held me its thumb to suck.

Lifted me to the dug that grew
Out of the brow of a lioness.
(188)

The next poem is about the opposite process, the false cure which consists of extracting from him everything that connects him with nature – tusk, mountain-root, seven-seas' spring, clouds and stars, and then dedicating the remainder to a crazed matricidal God.

The Fifth Proposition of Marinetti's Futurist Manifesto was to 'hymn the man at the steering wheel whose ideal axis passes through the centre of the earth'. Hughes' vision is at the opposite pole from this of man riding the earth like a car and steering it in his chosen direction, imposing his will on it. In 'The coffin, spurred by its screws' man cannot even screw down a coffin lid without sending it off in some wrong direction; and the earth isn't going anywhere.

As for me
All I have

For an axle

Is your needle
Through my brains.
(189)

The image is excruciatingly painful; but it is better than no axle at all, a needle of many Norths. The needle is his orientation and his commitment, like the loyalty of the grass-blade, and the precariously balanced banner of the blackbird,

Gold on black, terror and exultation.

When he sees the greater agony and deeper commitment of the badger

Biting spade-steel, teeth and jaw-strake shattered

the end of his alienation is in sight; he knows where he belongs:

Me too,
Let me be one of your warriors.

Let your home
Be my home. Your people
My people.
(190)

Lumb will invest his faith in something which, because it is not an erection cannot collapse. But even nature is not infallible, shrinking back under the inquisitory eyes and fingers of men, under the bulldozers, and obliged to withdraw so much of her beauty. She remains, in spite of her 'veils of wrinkle and shawls of ache', the only saviour.

Lumb's achievement is to be to let into the world again, as if for the first time, 'the untouched joy'. Joy is not the same as pleasure, which is what Mrs Davies was able to make life yield without too much difficulty. It did not help her at the crisis. It involves not caring too much. Everything true and strong has to be paid for; and what buys joy is pain. As the drunkard's song is paid for by the treading of the grapes, so his soul must be trampled by the earth into full realization of its horror, or his joy will be worthless. It is as though (193) he had placed his soul under the eyelid of the goddess, which is also the 'chiselled threshold' between the worlds, the granite bedrock of everything. The lid sinks and grinds his soul's kernel 'till blood welled', but that blood, anointing her, revives her, and is perhaps the only balm.

Suffering is the universal bond and truth, and therefore itself a form of atonement. 'Faces lift out of the earth' returns to the unanswered questions of 'Who are you?'. The faces lifting out of the earth are not specified – animal or human, new-born or dying – but their cries are like the half-cry

> Of a near-fatally wounded person
> Not yet fallen, but already unconscious

like the people – open-mouthed

> In the gust of being shot and falling

in the earlier poem. What good would it do to 'hear the age of the earth'? Now he hears it:

> From age to age
> Nothing bequeathed
> But a gagged yell
>
> A clutchful of sod
>
> And libraries
> Of convalescence.
>
> (195)

That yell is all the cries ever uttered in extremity and ignorance, but also in affirmation:

And these are the ones
Who are trying to tell
Your name.

It is not an effort history can help with. It has to be undertaken anew by every generation and every individual. The 'gagged yell', like the skylark's song, may be an attempt to cry either 'Joy' or 'Help'. The 'clutchful of sod' may be a clawing of the earth in a spasm of pain, or what has in fact been grasped of the goddess – 'eating the medical earth' as Hughes put it in 'Littleblood'. The accumulated knowledge of the race records neither the name of the goddess nor the experience of her, only the aftermath, the slow recovery, the replacement of the layers of insulation.

Orphanhood is used in several of these poems as an image of the state of separation from the mother, the goddess, nowhere more powerfully than in 'Calves harshly parted from their mamas':

After some days, a stupor sadness
Collects them again in their field.
They will never stray any more.
From now on they only want each other.
(197)

This is the stupor in which most of us live, so conditioned to loss that it is almost forgotten. The tiger cannot experience such loss. Still, he is 'like left luggage', confident of being shortly reclaimed. Moving, he is equally safe:

Heaven and hell have both adopted him.

He centres both worlds; he is Hughes' image for the Marriage of Heaven and Hell. His hide is his banner, like the blackbird's

Gold on black, terror and exultation

reconciling apparent opposites, like the magpie's plumage in *Parzival*:

Blame and praise alike are inevitable for the man whose courage is undaunted, mixed of white and black as it must be, like a magpie's plumage. Such a one may nevertheless know blessedness, though both colours have a part in him: that of Heaven, that of Hell.

Tigers featured prominently in the visions of subjects injected with harmaline in Santiago, though there are, of course, no tigers in the New World. Claudio Naranjo sums up his analysis of these visions in highly relevant terms:

The complex of images discussed first as portraying the polarity of being and becoming, freedom and necessity, spirit and matter, only set up the stage for the human drama. This involves the battle of opposites and eventually their reconciliation or fusion, after giving way to death and destruction, be this by fire, tigers, drowning, or devouring snakes. The beauty of fluid fire, the graceful tiger, or the subtle and wise reptile, these seem most expressive for the synthetic experience of accepting life as a whole, or, better, accepting existence as a whole, life and death included; evil included too, though from a given spiritual perspective it is not experienced as evil any more. (Harner, 190)

Hughes' most vivid expression of this is in 'Crow's Table Talk':

> The tiger
> Kills like the fall of a cliff, one-sinewed with the earth,
> Himalayas under eyelid, Ganges under fur –
> Does not kill.
>
> Does not kill. The tiger blesses with a fang.
> The tiger does not kill but opens a path
> Neither of life nor of death:
> The tiger within the tiger:
> The tiger of the earth.
>
> O tiger!
> O brother of the viper! O beast in blossom!

The tiger, in a sense, is the goddess.

'A Bang – A Burning – ' (197) expresses Lumb's first full empathy with another creature. The crack of a rifle (Hagen's, presumably) jolts his consciousness into that of the shot dove, or the dove's, through its cries, bleeds into his. He becomes a rainbow-breasted dove in its agony. He is becoming one flesh with nature.

The image of the dead man with which the next poem opens reminds us of all those Baskin images of dead men. Hughes wrote, of one of these:

> 'The Hanged Man' is not dead: it is the Angel, shattered by death, dispersed to the Universe, re-assembled by joy.

The bullet of death and the kiss of joy are both the touch of the Angel, here the goddess, otherwise buried 'a hundred faces behind the human face'. Without that touch we stay dead, yield up our humanity to the dead world of 'inescapable facts'. With it we are received into the dance, the 'suffering vitality of nature'. The question and answer of Hughes' essay on Baskin apply equally to himself:

> How deep is agony and how deep is joy and what can survive the answer. The thing that survives guides the blade that cuts these images from the mass of the world's ashes.

I come to the end of my comments on these poems with a strong sense of more than usual inadequacy, of having talked round them without really coming to grips, of having given the impression that they are tendentious, when perhaps their greatest strength is that they are not in the least. They are deeply personal and felt and immediate, but at the same time objective – their authenticity guaranteed by the complete lack of self-consciousness or artifice or straining for merely verbal effects and impact: so much so that they make even the Prometheus poems seem contrived. They are poems not to be explicated but to be possessed by. The distinction between thought and feeling breaks down utterly here. They are intense feelings at that point where they articulate themselves as images. They are whistled up from the depths, and affect us often as Lumb's whistle affected the girls, like a fine bloody thread being pulled through our hearts.

In the main narrative fullness of being seemed all around, dwarfing the human action, but no-one taking much notice of it. Here we have a bleak psychic landscape of error, absence and negation, with Lumb 'trying to split a glimpse through his black blindness', to throw images like ropes across the abyss between being and non-being. The images oscillate between the personal and the cosmic, and the reader strains to connect them. But though the poems often start with what look like startling but disconnected images, by the end they have been shaped by the controlling religious feeling into a unity which makes it appropriate to think of them as hymns.

Thus each poem is enacting what the whole epilogue, indeed the whole of *Gaudete*, is reaching for – atonement. The basic image of the whole work has been that of the split, the split psyche, the split between man and woman, man and nature, the profane and the sacred. This split is the wound to be healed. What is sought is an adjustment in consciousness and feeling which will enable us to recognize these 'opposites' as polar rather than dual, that is parts or phases of a single whole, connected to each other ('one flesh, one blood'), dependent on each other, complementing each other. Dualism inevitably leads to the setting up of one 'opposite' against the other, and the attempt to destroy the indestructible 'opposite', which is racial suicide.

In *Cave Birds* that adjustment was called marriage. Here it is called love. It is far removed from the lust of the changeling who funnelled his whole consciousness into the black hole of the Sheela-na-gig. Lumb has been violently cured of that:

> Something grips by the nape
> And bangs the brow, as against a wall
> Against the untouchable veils
> Of the hole which is bottomless
> Till blood drips from the mouth.
> (185)

It is equally far removed from the arid spirituality of St Ignatius. But it spiritualizes the physical by taking the affective drives and diffusing them through the whole of nature, and simultaneously grounds spirit in nature, finding all it needs of holiness there.

In so far as *Gaudete* can be said to have any progenitor in modern English literature, it is *The Waste Land*. Most of the great books and poems since then have been variations on its themes, new testimonies to the same social, cultural, psychological and spiritual conditions. Many writers have simply paraded their symptoms in the hope that they would turn out to be, as Eliot's were, or Kafka's, symptomatic of a whole culture. Some have offered a more conscious diagnosis. The few who have offered cures have been, in their very different ways, inadequate, doomed. There is a sense in which the great writers of this century have tended to cancel each other out. The orthodox religious/mystical answers won't stand up. In *The Four Quartets* they are vacuous, the product of desperation and repudiation. Imagine a critique of it by Lawrence. The life-affirming answers have been too naive, taken too much for granted. Imagine a review of *Lady Chatterley's Lover* by Beckett. The nihilists and absurdists have allowed themselves the irresponsible luxury of despair. Imagine a review of *Waiting for Godot* by Brecht. The Marxists and meliorists have been so busy pulling up one bucket they have not noticed the other going down, nor the dead body in the well. Imagine a review of Brecht by Ionesco.[2]

Hughes is searching for a position which cannot be outflanked, which maintains human dignity and purpose without falsifying the facts, which recovers the sane and the sacred without evasion, abstraction or doctrine. In *Gaudete* he has come close to achieving that.

NOTES

THE HAWK IN THE RAIN

1. It is a language which matches T. E. Hulme's definition of the language of poetry:

> 'It is a compromise for a language of intuition which would hand over sensations bodily. It always endeavours to arrest you, and to make you continuously see a physical thing, to prevent you gliding through an abstract process.'

But language can be vital and arresting without being in any literal sense concrete, visual or sensual. There are many sources of poetic energy capable of energizing abstractions and ideas. We can follow the dynamics of 'The Hawk in the Rain' in its verbs. What nature does is expressed in a succession (like hammer-blows) of violent monosyllabic verbs. The weather 'drowns' the man, 'drums' the sodden land under his feet, 'bangs' and 'kills' the hedges (his bearings and moorings), 'thumbs' his eyes, 'throws' his breath, 'tackles' his heart, 'hacks' his head. Meanwhile the earth also takes part in the 'drowning' and 'drumming', 'swallows' him (or tries to), 'clutches' his feet, 'grabs' and 'dazes' him. He suffers the effects of twelve violent verbs, six from above, six from below, in so far as, in all that turmoil, they can be separated. By disguising some of the verbs as participles and gerunds (including two in the first two lines), Hughes avoids expending the energies they generate. The one-way process does not exhaust itself, but is a dogged habit of nature. Meanwhile the man himself has few verbs, and they are passive or reflexive:

> and I,
> Boodily grabbed dazed last-moment-counting
> Morsel in the earth's mouth, strain . . .

The strain is already there in the waiting for the verb, and by the time we reach it, it is doomed. The hawk's verbs perfectly balance active with passive. It effortlessly, masterfully, straddles the line and stanza endings:

> but the hawk
> Effortlessly at heights hangs his still eye.
>
> . . . the master
> Fulcrum of violence where the hawk hangs still.

2. In May 1957 Hughes had published in *Granta* a splendid short story called 'O'Kelly's Angel'. O'Kelly captures an Angel and puts it on show on Salisbury Plain. Inevitably, a Protestant mob marches from the north to liberate the Angel, and the Catholics mass to take it to Rome. O'Kelly finds there is more money in instant religion and founds the O'Kellians who soon

number ten million fanatics. The army is powerless to prevent the ensuing massacre.

Meanwhile the Angel hangs in its cage:

> 'a flung tense uprighteness, as though it were holding itself by pure intensity in the very tiptop of heaven. Its great eyes stared fixedly beyond the world . . . Its huge unfocussed eyes stared into nothing.'

The Angel shows no awareness of the battle raging around it. In a desperate effort to remove the cause of the chaos the army shells the stadium. The third shell hits the cage, killing O'Kelly and bringing sudden peace to the plain.

> 'From the little grisly pyre the Angel was rising. Its head flung back, as ever, its wings were folded motionless, and its great eyes gazed out beyond the battlefield, beyond the world, beyond the end of the end.'

A ring of angels descends to meet it.

> 'Then, as slowly, all the Angels rose together.
>
> All those thousands of bloody eyes stared up.
>
> The Angels rose.
>
> Smaller and smaller grew the bright ring. At last it was only a star. For five long minutes it was a star.
>
> Then the star went out.
>
> Life came back to the Plain terribly. The wounded and the dead lay like the furrows of ploughland. The living stood and looked at their hands, and their arms bloody to the armpits. Then they looked out across the reeking stilled plain. Then they looked at the twisted remains of the cage, and the whitening ashes of O'Kelly's pulpit. Then they looked at the blue zenith of heaven, which was darker now, and where the ordinary stars were beginning.
>
> Then, finally, they looked at each other.'

The Hawk has much in common with this Angel.

3. It is not just 'civilization'. It is what Don Juan calls the 'tonal' – 'everything we know and do as men':

> 'As long as his *tonal* is unchallenged and his eyes are tuned only for the *tonal*'s world, the warrior is on the safe side of the fence. He's on familiar ground and knows all the rules. But when his *tonal* shrinks, he is on the windy side, and that opening must be shut tight immediately, or he would be swept away. And this is not just a way of talking. Beyond the gate of the *tonal*'s eyes the wind rages. I mean a real wind. No metaphor. A wind that can blow one's life away. In fact, that is the wind that blows all living things on this earth.' (Castaneda, *Tales of Power*, 176)

4. Emily Brontë described Heathcliff's eyes as 'the clouded windows of hell'. The house described in 'Wind' is at Heptonstall, not far from the Brontë moors. In *Wuthering Heights* the window does come in. Its breaking is associated with violent emotions, bloodshed, violation and the supernatural. What has there been shut out is not only the stormy elements, but a child from her rightful physical and spiritual home and her inheritance. You cannot shut out death and danger without also shutting out life and love. Yet the body cannot bear total exposure. Heathcliff and Cathy reject book, thought, and (in the sense that they never recognize each other as *separate* people) each other. They dare to be struck dead and are struck dead, finding, in death, that heaven which is forbidden to the living.

5. Between *The Hawk in the Rain* and *Lupercal* there slipped through a magnificent prophetic poem 'Quest', published in an obscure periodical in February 1958 and never reprinted. It is quite unlike anything else of the period in its visionary intensity.

> I know clearly, as at a shout, when the time
> Comes I am to ride out into the darkened air
> Down the deserted streets. Eyes, terrified and hidden,
> Are a weight of watching on me that I must ignore
> And a charge in the air, tingling and crackling bluely
> From the points and edges of my weapons, and in my hair.
> I shall never see the monster that I go to kill.
>
> And how it is ever to be killed, or where it is,
> No one knows, though men have ridden a thousand times
> Against it as I now with my terror standing in my hair,
> Hardly daring risk into my lungs this air the same
> As carried the fire-belch and boistering of the thing's breath
> Whose mere eye unlidded anywhere were a flame
> To stir the marrow deep under most ignorant sleep.
>
> I ride, with staring senses, but in
> Complete blackness, knowing none of these faithful five
> Clear to its coming till out of the blind-spot
> Of the fitful sixth – crash on me the bellowing heaving
> Tangle of a dragon all heads all jaws all fangs,
> And though my weapons were lightning I am no longer alive.
> My victory to raise this monster's shadow from my people
>
> Shall be its trumpeting and clangorous flight
> Over the moon's face to its white-hot icy crevasse
> With fragments of my body dangling from its hundred mouths.

'Quest' may well have grown out of 'Bayonet Charge'. There too the man responds to some incomprehensible but inescapable cosmic imperative:

> In what cold clockwork of the stars and the nations
> Was he the hand pointing that second?

He runs, apparently alone (at least in his own consciousness) towards an enemy he cannot see, nor, with his single bayonet, hope to kill. His terror is like a charge of electricity in 'that blue crackling air'. The relationship with 'Bayonet Charge' might suggest an interpretation of 'Quest' as a war poem. A volunteer soldier goes to raise the shadow of war from his people. Thousands will die and their deaths will buy a brief period of peace. Then thousands more must march to feed the insatiable monster.

Such an interpretation is, by itself, much too small for the poem, though the poem certainly includes it. Too much would be left unaccounted for, or explicable only as exaggeration or posturing – an explanation which the sweep, power and coherence of the poem rules out. 'Quest' is terrifying in the hero's quiet acceptance of the inevitable horror. And the terror is not in the description of the dragon, of which there is only a line, but in that complete blackness in which it must be faced, with all five senses straining but sealed, relying on the unreliable sixth sense to give a moment's warning which would, in any case, be quite useless against such an antagonist, with any weapons. This is some metaphysical horror.

'Quest' could also be an image of the necessary self-surrender of the artist. The artist is a hero who seeks to open negotiations with whatever happens to be out there, who dares to be struck dead, exposing himself to 'manslaughtering shocks', and, far from peeping through his fingers, or watching it on television, rides into the blackness 'with staring senses'. His people on whose behalf he goes would rather he stayed at home with a nice cigarette and a nice view of the park and wrote poems about waiting for the bus. We have become expert at living (or partly living) as though there were no dragon.

But the hero of 'Quest' is obviously not going to negotiate. Nor is he going naked. He is going as fully armed as he can, in darkness possibly because he dare not open his helmet. He is going theoretically to kill, actually to be killed. To what end?

There are several sequels to 'Quest' notably 'Gog', 'A Horrible Religious Error', 'Crow's Account of St George' and 'Bones'.

6. 'It is a return to an alliterative poetry that, pounding, brutal and earthbound, challenges the Latinate politeness of artificial society with ruthless energy and cunning, and so drags the Latinate words into its unruly, self-ruling world that even *they* come to sound northern and Germanic. The pummelling trochees and lead-weighted, bludgeoning spondees have a mesmeric effect, beating and rooting out of us those once apparently safe underlying rhythms of rhetorical and philosophical discourse, mental scene-painting and nostalgic or evocative reflection, with which the iambic pentameter is so closely associated. Quite literally, by asserting the naked, deeper rhythms of our Germanic (and also onomatapoeic) heritage, Ted Hughes is taking the English language back to its roots. Yet such a bold counter-revolution necessarily involves, for Hughes at least, a ferocious reaction against nine hundred years of Christianity, humanism and rationalism, a reaction that, because it must be ferocious, acts as if the trunk, branches and leaves of nine hundred years of humane and literary culture had borne little but rotten fruit.' ('"Natural" Rhythms and Poetic Metre', an unpublished essay by A. S. Crehan)

Most readers were able to accept the rhythms of *The Hawk in the Rain* on the grounds that they mimed the violent content of the poems, but as, in later books, Hughes used the old rhythms for wider and wider purposes, they began to sense that more than their ear was under assault, and to stiffen their resistance. Even *Crow* got past many reviewers because they were able to consign it to the appropriate pigeon-hole of nihilism or black comedy. *Gaudete*, finally, left them no way of avoiding a confrontation, and they responded with a chorus of mindless abuse – a poor advertisement for the humane, rational culture they purported to be defending.

WODWO

1. Several of Hughes' works, especially those for children, are remakings of that 'suspect' legend of St George and the Dragon.

The Iron Man, for example, offers an alternative to ruthless cruelty. A terrible space-dragon lands on the earth. Mankind tries to destroy it:

> 'They want to bring the whole world back to the status quo of no space monsters, no intrusion from the unknown. They want the whole world to be settled back to its worldly affairs and to be able to ignore the terrible energies of space.' ('Myth and Education', 65)

In a traditional story, the Iron Man, St George, would kill the dragon. In a more realistic story he would be killed by it. Neither story does anything to resolve the problem, to cure the sickness. The St George story simply advocates 'the complete suppression of the terror':

> 'In other words it is the symbolic story of Christianity, it's the key to the neurotic-making dynamics of Christianity. Christianity in suppressing the devil, in fact suppresses imagination and suppresses vital natural life. (*Ibid*, 66)

The little boy and the Iron Man make friends with the dragon. They 'Invite space to take part in the life of the world'. His story, Hughes claims, connects you 'with the deepest and most alien seeming powers in your own mind, which are the correspondents of the outermost demon powers of space'.

If Hughes regards the fable of St George as 'suspect', he wholeheartedly approves of Beauty and the Beast. In his own version of this story, the Beast is again a bear. Floreat, the rich man's daughter, is sick in her mind. She dreams she is visited at night by a horrible beast. But when her father and the doctor hide in her bedroom they too see it. They shoot and wound it. It escapes, leaving its blood on mirror and powder-compact. To entertain Floreat they hire a bearkeeper with his dancing bear. (It is the same bear the brother killed 'with claws like garden-forks'.) The bear is bandaged, but dances. Floreat dances with the bear. When her father goes for his camera the bear picks up Floreat and runs off with her. It keeps her in its cave and seems gentle. She comes to love the bear and is happy, cured. But the father comes and shoots the bear again. When he goes into the cave to finish him off, he finds a young man:

I am the bear. I am the monster in the night.
Give your belief time. For fifteen years
I have been a bear in the sight of men and women.
And at all other times, a flying dragon.
I would have been a bear and a flying dragon
To the end of my days
If Floreat had never said she loved me.
Those were the words I needed to break the spell.

Of course the words 'befriend' and 'love' are appropriate only within a fantasy, a children's tale. You cannot really befriend or love an angel or a dragon. The dragon, however, is not an actual space being, but the shape given within the psyche to powers which are terrifying and felt to be hostile. Some of them really are hostile, possibly even evil, in which case it is perhaps even more important to recognize them in their true nature. To abolish Satan puts him 'beyond control – gives him complete freedom. As if we should deny an enemy, rather than pin him down in everlasting negotiations' (*Ibid.*, 69).

2. The source is, in fact, *The Golden Bough* (p. 869) where Frazer writes of the brotherhood of the Green Wolf:

> 'Thus it has been shown that the leading incidents of the Balder myth have their counterparts in those fire-festivals of our European peasantry which undoubtedly date from a time long prior to the introduction of Christianity. The pretence of throwing the victim chosen by lot into the Beltane fire, and the similar treatment of the man, the future Green Wolf, at the midsummer bonfire in Normandy, may naturally be interpreted as traces of an older custom of actually burning human beings on these occasions; and the green dress of the Green Wolf, coupled with the leafy envelope of the young fellow who trod out the midsummer fire at Moosheim, seems to hint that the persons who perished at these festivals did so in the character of tree-spirits or deities of vegetation. From all this we may reasonably infer that in the Balder myth on the one hand, and the fire-festivals and custom of gathering mistletoe on the other hand, we have, as it were, the two broken and dissevered halves of an original whole. In other words, we may assume with some degree of probability that the myth of Balder's death was not merely a myth, that is, a description of physical phenomena in imagery borrowed from human life, but that it was the same time the story which people told to explain why they annually burned a human representative of the god and cut the mistletoe with solemn ceremony. If I am right, the story of Balder's tragic end formed, so to say, the text of the sacred drama which was acted year by year as a magical rite to cause the sun to shine, trees to grow, crops to thrive, and to guard man and beast from the baleful arts of fairies and trolls, of witches and warlocks. The tale belonged, in short, to that class of nature myths which are meant to be supplemented by ritual; here, as so often, myth stood to magic in the relation of theory to practice.'

3. Lawrence tried to restore the older pagan meanings of the dragon symbolism in Revelation:

> 'The dragon and serpent symbol goes so deep in every human consciousness, that a rustle in the grass can startle the toughest "modern" to depths he has no control over . . .
>
> From earliest times, man has been aware of a "power" or potency within him – and also outside him – which he has no ultimate control over. It is a fluid, rippling potency which can lie quite dormant, sleeping, and yet be ready to leap out unexpectedly...
>
> It is swift and surprising as a serpent, and overmastering as a dragon. It leaps up from somewhere inside him, and has the better of him...
>
> A hero was a hero, in the great past, when he had conquered the hostile dragon, when he had the power of the dragon *with him* in his limbs and breast...
>
> The usual vision of the dragon is, however, not personal but cosmic. It is in the vast cosmos of the stars that the dragon writhes and lashes. We see him in his maleficent aspect, red. But don't let us forget that when he stirs green and flashing on a pure dark night of stars it is he who makes the wonder of the night, it is the full rich coiling of his folds which makes the heavens sumptuously serene, as he glides around and guards the immunity, the precious strength of the planets, and gives lustre and new strength to the fixed stars, and still more serene beauty to the moon. His coils within the sun make the sun glad, till the sun dances in radiance. For in his good aspect, the dragon is the great vivifier, the great enhancer of the whole universe.' (*Apocalypse*, ch. XVI)

4. Hughes read *The Rainbow* when he was about eighteen. He read it in a tent in a field which held horses. During the night a heavy rainstorm came on, and the horses spent the whole night charging from one corner of the field to the other around his tent. But there were several other sources for 'The Rain Horse' including a recurrent dream when he was a boy.

5. 'A man has a persistent fear-dream about horses. He suddenly finds himself among great, physical horses, which may suddenly go wild. Their great bodies surge madly round him, they rear above him, threatening to destroy him. At any minute he may be trampled down...

Examining the emotional reference we find that the feeling is sensual, there is a great impression of the powerful, almost beautiful physical bodies of the horses, the nearness, the rounded haunches, the rearing. Is the dynamic passion in a horse the danger-passion? It is a great sensual reaction at the sacral ganglion, a reaction of intense, sensual, dominant volition. The horse which rears and kicks and neighs madly acts from the intensely powerful sacral ganglion. But this intense activity from the sacral ganglion is male: the sacral ganglion is at its highest intensity in the male. So that the horse-dream refers to some arrest in the deepest sensual activity of the male. The horse is presented as an object of terror, which means that to the man's automatic dream-soul, which loves automatism, the great sensual male activity is the greatest menace. The automatic pseudo-soul, which has got the sensual nature repressed, would like to keep it repressed. Whereas the greatest desire of the living spontaneous soul is that this very male sensual nature, represented as a menace, shall be actually accomplished in life. The spontaneous self is secretly yearning for the liberation and fulfilment of the deepest and most powerful sensual nature.' (D. H. Lawrence, *Fantasia of the Unconscious*, 167–8)

6. Hughes wrote 'The Suitor' on the day after the birth of his son Nicholas. When he read it to Sylvia she said 'That is your best story. But the girl is me, and the flute player is death.'

7. 'The Wound' is what Hughes managed to retain and put into shape of a dream. The dream was of a film, complete, very long, with many episodes. Along with the action, in which he was Ripley, he dreamed a very full written text which was both dramatic and descriptive at the same time, by John Arden. (He had just read *Sergeant Musgrave's Dance*.) He woke up feeling very disappointed that Arden had written something Hughes felt to be absolutely his own. Then he realized that it was his own. He drifted back to sleep and dreamed the whole thing again, in exact detail, perfectly repeated. He woke up and wrote down all he could remember. It faded rapidly, but he managed to get the main thread and most of the episodes. At the time Hughes was working on the Bardo Thodol and that too was in the dream. His first interpretation was that this was his parallel Gothic–Celtic version. When he came later to write up 'The Wound' for radio he changed a great deal and lost much of the original dream which was too cinematic to convert.

8. Of his male tortoise Lawrence wrote:

> Poor little earthy house-inhabiting Osiris,
> The mysterious bull tore him at adolescence into pieces,
> And he must struggle after reconstruction, ignominiously.

The cross on which the tortoise is broken is sexuality. The bull is Dionysus, the torn adolescent Pentheus, or his cousin Actaeon, or Adonis.

9. One of Lawrences's finest poems 'Tortoise Shout' comes very close here. The cry of the tortoise *in extremis* is also interpreted as 'incomprehensively both ways':

> A scream,
> A yell,
> A shout,
> A paean,
> A death-agony,
> A birth-cry,
> A submission

All tiny, tiny, far away, reptile under the first dawn.
War-cry, triumph, acute-delight, death-scream reptilian,
Why was the veil torn?
The silken shriek of the soul's torn membrane?
The male soul's membrane
Torn with a shriek half music, half horror.

Lawrence goes on to list cries, including 'the nightingale's piercing cries and gurgles' which have startled the depths of his soul. They are the cries of both joy and pain. What they have in common is that they are torn from us

Torn, to become whole again, after long seeking for what is lost,
The same cry from the tortoise as from Christ, the Osiris-cry of
    abandonment,
That which is whole, torn asunder,
That which is in part, finding its whole again through the universe.

The secret Lawrence learns from the tortoise is that giving up the ghost is also receiving the ghost. The spear through the side of the tortoise is sexuality, the command to 'seek his consummation beyond himself'. Lawrence, like Hughes, sees sexuality as a tragic condition. But the last words of self-abandonment 'Consummatum Est' mean not only 'it is finished' but also 'it is accomplished', and Yeats knew that Hamlet and Lear, even in the moment when heaven blazed into their heads, were gay.

10. In Yeats' play *The Death of Cuchulain*, Cuchulain is butchered by a blind old man for twelve pennies and says bitterly: 'Twelve pennies! What better reason for killing a man?' Yeats gives him these last words:

There floats out there
The shape that I shall take when I am dead,
My soul's first shape, a soft feathery shape,
And is not that a strange shape for the soul
Of a great fighting-man?
I say it is about to sing.

In 'Cuchulain Comforted' Yeats follows him beyond the grave where he sews his shroud and joins a chorus of birds who are all the ghosts of 'convicted cowards'.

11. Nietzsche knew the type:

'Today I saw a sublime man, a solemn man, a penitent of the spirit:
oh, how my soul laughed at his ugliness!
Hung with ugly truths, the booty of his hunt, and rich in torn clothes;
many thorns, too, hung on him – but I saw no rose.
There is still contempt in his eye, and disgust lurks around his mouth.
He rests now, to be sure, but he has never yet lain down in the sunlight.
His countenance is still dark; his hand's shadow plays upon it.
The sense of his eyes, too, is overshadowed.
To be sure, I love in him the neck of the ox: but now I want to see the
eye of the angel, too.' (*Thus Spake Zarathustra*, 139–40)

12 Einstein believed that the miracle of the universe was its comprehensibility. Nietzsche knew this type too:

> 'You first want to *make* all being conceivable. . . . It must bend and accommodate itself to you! Thus will your will have it. It must become smooth and subject to the mind as the mind's mirror and reflection.' (*Thus Spake Zarathustra*, 136)

CROW

1. His efforts to understand the world in which he finds himself bring him into contact with the products of human culture, with religion and literature and science, all of which seem to him to have got it all wrong, according to what he has seen of the world, so he rearranges the traditional elements in a way which seems to him more in accordance with the facts, in 'Apple Tragedy' and 'Song for a Phallus', for example. Also he tries his hand at original composition with notes for some little plays, always with the same two characters.

He becomes curious about his own nature and purpose, and wonders who could have created him. He finds himself embarked on a quest for this creator. His adventures bring him into contact with various women and female monsters. Because they are ugly, often horrific, he fights them, or evades them, or in some way mismanages the situation, not realizing that each time he is meeting his own mother, his intended bride. He comes to a river. Beside it sits a gigantic horrible female, an ogress, who will not let him cross unless he carries her on his back. As they cross, she gets heavier and heavier, driving Crow into the river-bed until the water is up to his mouth. Then she asks him a question to which he must sing the right answer, quickly. The questions recapitulate the various mistaken encounters he has had with her in the past; that is, they are all, in some sense, questions about love. He knows little about it, and desperately tries the principle of permutation, singing every answer he can think of until one satisfies her, and her weight decreases again. This happens seven times before they reach the other side. 'Lovesong' is one of Crow's answers to the question: 'Who paid most, him or her?'. 'The Lovepet' is an answer to the question: 'Was it an animal? Was it a bird? Was it an insect? Was it a fish?'. The right answer to the question: 'Who gives most, him or her?' is the lovely poem 'Bride and groom lie hidden for three days', also in *Cave Birds*.

2. The publication, in *Crow*, of a mere selection of poems from the early part of this story, without the story, allowed several hostile critics to approach the work as though Crow were merely a mouthpiece for Hughes. Sometimes Hughes admires Crow, sometimes is horrified by him, sometimes both at once. Often we can have no idea where he stands, since he withdraws from the poems. Crow is a technique for total objectivity, like the hypothetical Martian observing this world and its denizens without preconceptions or habituation. Crow's attitudes are frequently mistaken, confused, or wildly contradictory. It is ridiculous to say, as David Holbrook does, that 'Lovesong' gives us Hughes' own fixed attitude to sexual love.

3. The copy of *Newsweek* in which *Crow* was reviewed carried on the front cover a photograph of Lieutenant Calley and the bodies of a few of his victims. Inside, a Gallup poll showed that 50% of those questioned thought that such incidents were common. 79% disapproved of the verdict, 20% because they thought that what happened at My Lai was not a crime.

4. The poem which balances 'A Horrible Religious Error' is 'A Lucky Folly'. Here Crow quite inadvertently, out of sheer desperation and cowardice, does the right thing. Suddenly he finds himself cast as unwilling St George when he stumbles upon a screaming maiden about to be devoured by a dragon:

> The dragon surrounded him like a seaquake
> And the maiden cried lamentably.
> Crow cut holes in his nose. He fingers this flute,
> Dancing, with an occasional kick at his drum.
>
> The dragon was dumbfounded – he was manic
> For music. He began to grin.
> He too began to dance. And in horror and awe
> The maiden danced with him, incredulous.
> 'O do not stop,' she whispered, 'O do not stop.'
> So the three danced – and Crow dared not stop –
>
> To the creaking beak pipe and the kicked drum.
>
> But, at last, Crow's puff ran out and he stopped.
> The maiden paled.
> But the dragon wept. The dragon licked Crow's foot
> He slobbered Crow's fingers –
> 'More, more' he cried, and 'Be my god.'

5. The tablet of which this is a fragment is probably the Smaragdine or Emerald Tablet on which were engraved the thirteen precepts of Hermes Trismegistus. These precepts formed the basis of both Alchemy and Gnosticism. Any reader well grounded in Alchemy, Gnosticism and Manichaeism (as I am not) will find many new insights and connections in *Crow*.

6. J. M. Newton adduces two highly relevant passages from Alan Watts:

> 'Every individual is an expression of the whole realm of nature, a unique action of the total universe. This fact is rarely, if ever, experienced by most individuals. Even those who know it to be true in theory do not sense or feel it, but continue to be aware of themselves as isolated "egos" inside bags of skin.
>
> The first result of this illusion is that our attitude to the world outside us is largely hostile. We are forever "conquering" nature, space, mountains, deserts, bacteria, and insects instead of learning to co-operate with them in a harmonious order. In America the great symbols of this conquest are the bulldozer and the rocket...' (*The Book: On the Taboo Against Knowing Who you Are*)

'Obviously, I exist only in relation to everything else, but I did not come into that relation from somewhere outside – in such a way that "everything else" would be foreign to or other than myself. I did not alight in this universe like a bird arriving upon a branch from some alien limbo. I grew upon that branch like a leaf. For I am something which everything is doing: I am the whole process waving a flag named me, and calling out "Yoo-hoo!" ' (*Beyond Theology*)

7. One underlying meaning is suggested by Jung:

'*Perfection* is a masculine desideratum, while woman inclines by nature to *completeness*. If a woman strives for perfection she forgets the complementary role of completeness, which, though imperfect by itself, forms the necessary counterpart to perfection. For just as completeness is always imperfect, so perfection is always incomplete, and therefore represents a final state which is hopelessly sterile.' (*Answer to Job*)

In the Kundalini yoga system there are six bodily centres corresponding to six psychological states, and the object of the system is to activate these centres one by one, by awakening the sleeping power called Kundalini, the serpent. This serpent is 'the feminine, form-building, life-giving and -supporting force by which the universe and all its beings are rendered animate' (Campbell, *Myths to Live By*, 108). The first centre is torpid and of the earth. The second, situated in the genitals, is sexuality

(She has come amorous it is all she has come for).

Its name, Svadhishthana, means 'her favourite resort', and its element is water

(She comes as far as water no further).

The first two centres are not specifically human, as distinct from animal, and if further centres are not activated, there is no power (3) or enlightenment (4), no coming clear of this world and exposure to 'the terrifying, devastating aspects of the cosmic powers in their ego-shattering roles' (5), no perception of them in 'their bliss-bestowing, fear-dispelling, wondrous, peaceful, and heroic forms' (6), and no ultimate reconciliation (7). (Campbell, *op. cit.*, 114)

8. Several of these are what Hughes calls Bedtime Stories. He planned a separate book of these before *Crow*, which was to have included 'Song of Woe', 'Existential Song' and 'Crow's Elephant Totem Song', as well as, from *Crow*, 'Lovesong', 'Criminal Ballad' and 'Crow's Account of the Battle', and from *Crow Wakes*, 'Anecdote' (but not, strangely, the poem in *Crow* actually called 'Bedtime Story'). Some later poems also probably come into this category, including 'Crow's Song About England' and, possibly, 'Crow's Song About God'. It was in 'Earth-Moon' that Hughes had first hit upon the form, and he developed it to great effect.

Those bedtime stories which do not actually begin 'Once upon a time', or 'There was a person', could easily do so. They have a wide-eyed childlike simplicity, eschewing all 'effects', just recording the elementary facts. This matter-of-fact unadorned style generates a remarkable tension between the linguistic innocence and the horrific content of the stories. They have the inevitability, incontrovertability, of fairy stories, ballads and myths. Some of them are the great myths retold, but so stripped-down they are hardly recognizable. The dispassionate, understated narrative seduces the reader to give his total attention and credence. It is only a fairy-tale, about the once-upon-a-time world which is not our world. It is too late to draw back when the realization comes that it is very much our world.

9. There are several poems in *Crow* in which laughter, or a grin, or a smile, seems to have a life of its own. A grin is, of course, the permanent expression of a skull, and takes over the living face at moments other than those of amusement, the face of a woman in labour or a man in a crashing car, a murderer's face or 'the face in the electric chair' ('A Grin'). Such grins are not laughter. But even laughter is perhaps, as Shaw puts it, 'the natural recognition of destruction, confusion, and ruin'. And Beckett defines the 'mirthless laugh' (the 'risus purus', 'the laugh laughing at the laugh') as the laugh at that which is unhappy.

'The Smile' has a different dimension. Like the grin it ranges the earth

Looking for its occasion.

And its occasion is also death. But to die grinning is surely different from to die smiling. At one extreme there is the sordid, vulgar, derisive rictus of Crystalman in David Lindsay's *Voyage to Arcturus*, signifying that there is nothing beyond physical death, and that physical death is obscene. At the other extreme is the expression on the face of the dying Lear, whose heart, like Gloucester's, bursts 'smilingly', signifying a momentary vision of eternity. If Hughes' Grin is nearer the former, his Smile is nearer the latter:

And the crowd, shoving to get a glimpse of a man's soul
Stripped to its last shame,
Met this smile
That rose through his torn roots
Touching his lips, altering his eyes
And for a moment
Mending everything

Before it swept out and away across the earth.

If creation fails every time in its attempt to adjust man to the universe, at least it ultimately mends everything by returning him to the kind darkness of nothingness.

PROMETHEUS ON HIS CRAG

1. As part of their research into the Manichean themes of the myths and of Calderon's *La Vida Es Sueno*, Peter Brook's company studied a book by

Victor Serge called *Men in Prison*. In prison Serge had gradually learned to separate his inner world, which nothing could touch, from the outer world in which he was helpless: 'My lucidity, my freedom are irrevocably mine... Among those who succeed in resisting madness, their intense inner life brings them to a higher conception of life, to a deeper consciousness of the *self*, its values, its strength. At certain moments you feel astonishingly *free*.' Hughes never read the book.

2. My quotations from *Prometheus on His Crag* differ in three places from the Rainbow Press text. These are Hughes' revisions. Poem 5 should read ' – the woman again' not ' – that woman'. Poem 20 should end as quoted on p. 154, and poem 21 is now as quoted on p. 156.

3. In *Orghast* the vulture reaches into the womb saying:

> come from darkness
> come through nothingness
> come into peace
>
> I am the god from beyond division
>
> ...
>
> it is your fate
> your fear your truth is your terror
> this is your nothingness
> come into light
> and be devoured by truth
> give yourself to god
> surrender to me your god of truth
> of light your god of light your light
> come and lose your darkness

Hughes found that the Prometheus myth fused with, almost subsumed, Crow, St George, Beauty and the Beast, The New World. It also comes close to the Manichean vision of one of the neglected masterpieces of this century, David Lindsay's *A Voyage to Arcturus* (1920). There the protagonist, an Everyman figure called Maskull, goes to the planet Tormance in the system of Arcturus in search of the source of Muspel, a pure white radiance which is God. As he crosses the continents of Tormance he meets with life in an amazing variety of forms. He meets with beauty and love and kindness in purer forms than they are ever known on earth, but he has to learn to reject them all, since they are all deceiving manifestations of Crystalman, whose obscene rictus disfigures even the most beautiful face at the moment of death. (The grin has a similarly independent existence in several Hughes poems.) The Crystalman principle is precisely the attachment to self and to the created world, whose varied colours and forms have been produced by Crystalman (also called Shaping) casting his shadow across the face of Muspel so that the white radiance is split and stained as by a prism, broken down into colours, shapes, phenomena, the whole material universe. Maskull is accompanied on his quest by Krag, who is pain, and who puts him through many ordeals.

Lindsay himself had seen the relevance of the Prometheus myth. Panawe, the first man Maskull meets on Tormance, identifies him with Prometheus. At the half-way stage of his journey Dreamsinter says to him: 'You came to steal Muspel-fire, to give a deeper life to men.' And Maskull's last vision before he dies and is reborn as Nightspore is so close to the image of Prometheus on his Crag as to suggest that Krag's name derives from it:

> 'He floated towards an immense perpendicular cliff of black rock, without top or bottom. Half-way up it Krag, suspended in mid-air, was dealing blows at a blood-red spot with a huge hammer. The rhythmical, clanging sounds were hideous . . .
>
> 'What are you doing, Krag?' he asked. Krag suspended his work and turned round.
>
> 'Beating on your heart, Maskull,' was his grinning response.' (239)

Krag's other name, Surtur, suggests both vulture and wounds. Surtur, in Teutonic myth was a fire-giant. Krag's name on earth is Pain. Maskull had thought Krag (the midwife at the birth of Nightspore) to be his enemy and persecutor until the eleventh hour.

He comes ultimately to realize that it is only with Krag's aid, only through the most complete renunciation and self-exposure to redemptive pain that Muspel can be reached.

4. Joseph Campbell, speaking of regression and rebirth experienced in a therapeutic session using L.S.D., uses similar images, including the peacock:

> '. . .a regression to this level may be carried to culmination in an utterly terrifying crisis of actual ego-death, complete annihilation on all levels, followed by a grandiose, expansive sense of release, rebirth, and redemption, with enormous feelings and experiences of decompression, expansion of space, and blinding, radiant light: visions of heavenly blue and gold, columned gigantic halls with crystal chandeliers, peacock-feather fantasies, rainbow spectrums, and the like. The subjects, feeling cleansed and purged, are moved now by an overwhelming love for all mankind, a new appreciation of the arts and of natural beauties, great zest for life, and a forgiving, wonderfully reconciled and expansive sense of God in his heaven and all right with the world.' (*Myths to Live By*, 262)

Laing, in recording a very similar experience, found the image of a Bird of Paradise:

> 'Garden. Cat at bird. Shoo off nasty cat, and catch bird. How elusive she is, and I am turning into a cat myself. Stop. Cat is a cat is a bird is a non-bird of ineffably frail space suddenly spreading in parabolic grace of authority. How foolish to worry, to try to save her, or grasp her. Perhaps the cat was trying to save her. Let be. Cat and bird. Begriff. The truth I am trying to grasp is the grasp that is trying to grasp it.

I have seen the Bird of Paradise, she has spread herself before me, and I shall never be the same again.

There is nothing to be afraid of. Nothing.

Exactly.

The Life I am trying to grasp is the me that is trying to grasp it.'

(*The Bird of Paradise*, 156)

5. The only respite ever granted Prometheus was when the vulture stopped, like the rest of creation, to listen to the strains of Orpheus as he charmed Pluto in the Underworld. If we feel that the reconciliation, the ultimate harmony desiderated in *Orghast* is merely theoretical, and that evoked in *Prometheus* 21 a declaration of faith and hope rather than fully substantiated experience, perhaps 'Orpheus', certainly the most beautiful expression of this mystery, is also the most accessible. We can understand and imaginatively share the experience of Orpheus at every stage. The myth, especially in the fresh and moving way Hughes handles it, relates much more easily than the lofty Prometheus myth to common human experience and to familiar tragic art. This treatment, simplified for children, is of course very different from the treatment Hughes would have given the same material had he been writing for adults.

Orpheus plays music so magic that it makes not only the animals but even the trees and stones dance. The secret of his music is happiness, and the secret of his happiness is his wife Eurydice. But a voice (a bird? a spider? a serpent?) keeps coming to Orpheus telling him that every song must be paid for. Orpheus believes that the world is a gift and plays on. Suddenly his hand goes numb and a terrible cry announces that his wife has been bitten by a snake and is dead. Orpheus mourns for a month in silence, then decides to go down to the underworld to find Eurydice. Using his guitar like the drum of a shaman (Orpheus was the first shaman) he beats a path through space:

It carries him
Through the storm of cries,
The last cries of all who have died on earth,
The jealous, screaming laments
Of all who have died on earth and cannot come back.

He lays his road of sound across the heavens.
His guitar carries him.
Into the storm of blood,
The electrical storm of all the blood of all who have died on earth.
He is whirled into the summit of the storm.
Lightnings strike through him, he falls –

He falls into the mouth of the earth.
He falls through the throat of the earth, he recovers.
He rides his serpent of sound through the belly of the earth.
He drives his spear of sound through the bowels of the earth.
Mountains under the earth fall on him, he dodges.
He flies through walls of burning rock and ashes.

His guitar carries him.
He hurtles towards the centremost atom of the earth.
He aims his beam of sound at the last atom.

He smashes through the wall of the last atom.
He falls
He falls
At the feet of Pluto, King of the kingdom of the dead.

Beside Pluto sits Persephone, her face, made of white ivory, 'the pointed, eyeless face of a maggot'. Persephone is also Hecate, the snake goddess, or Agriope ('savage face'), the underground form of Demeter or Aphrodite or Semele. Orpheus was a priest of Dionysus and repeats the journey to the underworld made by Dionysus himself to recover from Persephone his mother Semele. Eurydice is a name for the underground form of the triple goddess, therefore she *is* Persephone, and Orpheus' task is to transform Persephone who has never spoken in the underworld, whose face, a flower on earth, Pluto has never seen open. Orpheus plays, a new solemn music, and gradually her face, 'the white beak of the first sprout of a flower', begins to open. Orpheus offers Pluto a wife for a wife. Pluto can give him only the soul of Eurydice. She returns to earth with him and once again he plays for her, but not as he once played. His new music is tragic art, the opposite of that art which exists only to deceive grief. It creates a context within which experiences otherwise intolerable can be confronted and accommodated. It enables humanity to be reconciled to its losses in the knowledge that they are the price of its joys, of living itself. The roots of life and beauty and joy are in death and corruption and horror (the underworld). It is the music of nature itself:

The trees did not dance. But the trees listened.
The music was not the music of dancing
But of growing and withering,
Of the root in the earth and the leaf in the light,
The music of birth and of death.
And the stones did not dance. But the stones listened.
The music was not the music of happiness
But of everlasting, and the wearing away of the hills,
The music of the stillness of stones,
Of stones under frost, and stones under rain, and stones in the sun,
The music of the seabed drinking at the stones of the hills.
The music of the floating weight of the earth.
And the bears in their forest holes
Heard the music of bears in their forest holes,
The music of bones in the starlight,
The music of many a valley trodden by bears,
The music of bears listening on the earth for bears.
And the deer on the high hills heard the crying of the wolves,
And the salmon in the deep pools heard the whisper of the snows,
And the traveller on the road
Heard the music of love coming and love going

And love lost forever,
The music of birth and of death.
The music of the earth, swaddled in heaven,
 kissed by its cloud and watched by its ray.
And the ears that heard it were also of leaf and of stone.
The faces that listened were flesh of cliff and of river.
The hands that played it were fingers of snakes and a tangle of flowers.

SEASON SONGS

1. Hughes has described the poems as 'verses of simple observation', and observation is certainly the central discipline – observation grounded in knowledge, familiarity, inwardness. In 1956 Sylvia Plath wrote of Hughes:

> 'I am constantly amazed at his vast fund of knowledge and understanding: not facts or quotes of second-hand knowledge, but in organic, digested comprehension which enriches his every word.' (*Letters Home*, 251)

That knowledge has grown and understanding deepened immensely since then, especially where nature is concerned. The poems are intensely visual, but not at all photographic or aesthetic; the visual images are simply clues about what is going on underneath the surface.

2. Introducing this poem on radio Hughes commented:

> 'Growing grass and making hay of it and bringing the loads in across a land crawling with slow loads is one of the deepest ceremonial satisfactions in farming, and every farmer feels it, no matter how mechanized or exhausted he might be.'

CAVE BIRDS

1. The exact sequence of events was as follows. Leonard Baskin showed Hughes a set of nine drawings. Hughes, not suspecting that there were to be more, made a complete cycle of poems to go with them. These drawings (and poems) were:

A Hercules-in-the-Underworld Bird ('The Summoner')
A Desert Bittern ('The Advocate')
A Titled Vulturess ('The Interrogator')
An Oven-Ready Pirhana Bird ('The Judge')
A Hermaphroditic Ephesian Owl ('The Plaintiff')
A Raven of Ravens ('The Executioner')
A Tumbled Socratic Cock ('The Accused'; now 'Socrates' Cock')
A Ghostly Falcon ('The Risen'; now 'The Risen Falcon')
Goblin ('Finale')

At this point Baskin became enthusiastic and produced another ten birds. These are the ten which appear in the Scolar Press edition. To accommodate them Hughes had to invent a whole series of further stages between execution and resurrection.

A Death-Stone Crow of Carrion ('The Knight')
A Double Osprey ('The Gatekeeper')
A Flayed Crow ('A Flayed Crow in the Hall of Judgement')
A Maze Pelican ('The Baptist')
A Sunrise of Owl ('A Loyal Mother')
A Monkey-Eating Eagle ('Incomparable Marriage'; now 'A Riddle')
A Stud Cockerel Hunted into a Desert ('The Culprit')
A Scarecrow Swift ('The Guide')
A Crow of Prisms ('Walking Bare')
An Owl Flower ('The Good Angel'; now 'The Owl Flower')

For relief and contrast Hughes then added several poems not intended to go with any drawings, most of them, in fact, quite outside the bird-drama:

'I was just walking along' (now 'The Scream')
'After the first fright'
'She seemed so considerate'
'Your mother's bones wanted to speak'
'In these fading moments'
'First, the doubtful charts of skin'
'Something was happening'
'Only a little sleep'
'As I came, I saw a wood'
'After there was nothing there was a woman'
'His legs ran about'
'Bride and groom'

These are the 31 poems which were read at the Ilkley Festival in 1975, with the 19 Baskin drawings projected. Subsequently Baskin did eight more drawings to go with eight of the new poems. Four of the poems read at Ilkley have now been dropped: 'The Summoner', 'The Advocate', 'Your mother's bones' and 'After there was nothing'. Others have been radically revised.

2. This is strongly reminiscent of a fine poem by James Dickey called 'The Heaven of Animals', which ends:

They stalk more silently,
And crouch on the limbs of trees,
And their descent
Upon the bright backs of their prey

May take years
In a sovereign floating of joy.
And those that are hunted
Know this as their life,
Their reward: to walk

Under such trees in full knowledge
Of what is in glory above them,
And to feel no fear,
But acceptance, compliance.
Fulfilling themselves without pain

At the cycle's centre,
They tremble, they walk
Under the tree,
They fall, they are torn,
They rise, they walk again.

GAUDETE

1. The idea of the willing victim is not simply a rationalization; it can be observed in the field. Several lions come upon an old buffalo in the middle of a pool. They will not go out of their depth, so the buffalo could outwait them. Or it could fight for its life. It does neither. It walks slowly towards them, and slowly bows its head, exposing its spinal cord to the lioness already on its back.

2. The scope of this study allows me to throw out here only a few hints and gestures towards the possible lines of a comparative study of Hughes and his great predecessors and contemporaries. To develop and substantiate them would be material for another book, and this I have begun to write. It will be called *Worshippers of Nature*.

BIBLIOGRAPHY

A. WORKS BY TED HUGHES

(Publication London unless otherwise stated)

The Hawk in the Rain, Faber and Faber, 13 September 1957. First American edition, Harper, 18 September 1957. First paperback edition, Faber and Faber, 1968.

REVIEWS: *Birmingham Post*, 26 Nov. 1957 (Sir Ifor Evans); *Books and Bookmen*, Nov. 1957 (J. C. Hall); *Church Times*, 28 Mar. 1958; *The Daily Telegraph*, 4 Oct. 1957 (Kenneth Young); *Delta*, Spring 1958 (W. I. Carr); *Encounter*, Nov. 1957 (Graham Hough); *English*, Spring 1958 (Howard Sergeant); *Gemini* 3, 1957 (Roger Hubank); *Halifax Courier*, 6 Dec. 1957; *Irish Times*, 14 Sept. 1957 (Austin Clarke); *Isis*, 23 Oct. 1957 (Judith Spink); *Library Journal*, 1 Dec. 1957; *Listen*, Spring 1958 (Alan Brownjohn); *The Listener*, 23 Jan. 1958; *London Magazine*, Jan. 1958 (Roy Fuller); *Manchester Guardian*, 4 Oct. 1957 (Robin Skelton); *New Statesman*, 28 Sept. 1957 (Edwin Muir); *New York Times*, 6 Oct. 1957 (W. S. Merwin); *The Observer*, 6 Oct. 1957 (A. Alvarez); *Oxford Magazine*, 22 May 1958 (G. J. Warnock); *Oxford Times*, 20 Sept. 1957 (E.E.); *Poetry*, June 1958 (Galway Kinnell); *Saturday Review*, 9 Nov. 1957 (Philip Booth); *Spectator*, 11 Oct. 1957 (Robert Conquest); *The Sunday Times*, 3 Nov. 1957 (John Press); *Time and Tide*, 19 Oct. 1957 (John Heath-Stubbs); *The Times*, 23 Jan. 1958; *Times Literary Supplement*, 18 Oct. 1957; *Voices* 165, Jan.–Apr. 1958; *Yorkshire Post*, 30 Apr. 1959 (Leonard Clark).

Pike. A broadside poem, woodcut illustration by Robert Birmelin; Gehenna Press, Northampton, Mass., 1959. Limited edition, 150.

Lupercal, Faber and Faber, 18 March 1960. First American edition, Harper, 3 August 1960. First paperback edition, Faber and Faber, 1970.

REVIEWS: *Atlantic*, Nov. 1961 (Peter Davison); *Audience*, Summer 1960; *Christian Science Monitor*, 25 Aug. 1960 (John Holmes); *Critical Quarterly*, Summer 1960 (Alun Jones); *The Daily Telegraph*, 14 Apr. 1960 (Kenneth Young); *Delta*, Winter 1961 (J. M. Newton); *English*, Autumn 1960 (Ralph Lawrence); *Essence*, Winter 1960; *Granta*, 30 Apr. 1960; *Guardian*, 18 Mar. 1960 (Robin Skelton); *Halifax Courier*, 8 Mar. 1960; *Harper's*, Sept. 1960 (Stanley Kunitz); *Hudson Review*, Winter 1960 (John Thompson); *Irish Times*, 9 Apr. 1960 (Austin Clarke); *Isis*, 11 May 1960 (Greysteil Ruthven); *Library Journal*, Aug. 1960 (B. A. Robie); *Listener*, 28 July 1960 (Graham Hough); *New Statesman*, 9 Apr. 1960 (Donald Hall); *New York Herald Tribune*, 22 Jan. 1961 (Paul Engel); *New York Times*, 14 Aug. 1960 (Philip Booth); *The Observer*, 27 Mar. 1960 (A. Alvarez); *Oxford Times*, 15 Apr. 1960 (E.E.); *Partisan Review*, Jan./Feb. 1961 (Kenneth Koch); *Poetry*, Jan. 1961 (Thom Gunn); *Poetry Dial*, Winter 1961; *Poetry Review*, July 1960 (Robert

Armstrong); *Prairie Schooner*, Fall 1962; *Sewanee Review*, Spring 1962 (E. Lucas Myers); *Spectator*, 22 Apr. 1960 (Norman MacCaig); *Sunday Times*, 3 Apr. 1960 (John Press); *Time and Tide*, 14 May 1960; *The Times*, 25 Aug. 1960; *The Times Literary Supplement*, 15 Apr. 1960; *Tomorrow*, 4, 1960 (Clive Jordan); *Virginia Quarterly*, Winter 1961; *Voices 174*, Jan.–Apr. 1961; *Yorkshire Post*, 24 Mar. 1960 (Leonard Clark).

Meet My Folks! Illustrated by George Adamson; Faber and Faber, 7 April 1961. First American edition, illustrated by Mila Lazarevitch, Bobbs-Merrill, 1973. This edition omits 'My Grandpa' and 'Grandma' and adds four new poems 'My Uncle Mick', 'My Aunt Flo', 'My Granny' and 'My Own True Family'. First paperback edition, Puffin Books, 1977. This edition omits 'My Aunt Flo' and adds two new poems, 'My Fairy Godmother' and 'My Other Granny'; there are also four new drawings by George Adamson.

REVIEWS: *Christian Science Monitor*, 7 Nov. 1973; *Kirkus*, 1 Aug. 1973; *Library Journal*, 15 Sept. 1973; *Saturday Review*, 4 Dec. 1973; *The Tablet*, Oct. 1961 (Terence M. Cluderay); *Times Literary Supplement*, 19 May 1961.

Selected Poems, Thom Gunn and Ted Hughes; Faber and Faber, 1962.

How the Whale Became, with drawings by George Adamson: Faber and Faber, 8 November 1963. First American edition, with drawings by Rick Schreiter, Atheneum, 1964. First paperback edition, illustrated by George Adamson, Penguin, 1971.

REVIEWS: *Birmingham Post*, 26 Nov. 1963; *Book Week*, 22 Nov. 1964 (M. S. Libby); *Guardian*, 6 Dec. 1963 (Robert Nye); *Horn Book*, Oct. 1964 (E.L.H.); *Irish Times*, 7 Dec. 1963; *Library Journal*, 15 October 1964 (W. M. Crossley); *Listener*, 21 Nov. 1963 (Elizabeth Brewer); *New Statesman*, 8 Nov. 1963 (Christopher Ricks); *New York Review of Books*, 3 Dec. 1964 (J. A. Smith); *New York Times Book Review*, 8 Nov. 1964 (Gloria Vanderbilt); *School Librarian*, March 1964 (Laurence Adkins); *The Sunday Telegraph*, 24 Nov. 1963; *The Sunday Times*, 24 Nov. 1963 (Oscar Turnhill).

The Earth-Owl and Other Moon People, with drawings by R. A. Brandt; Faber and Faber, 22 November 1963. All these poems are also in *Moon-Whales*.

REVIEWS: *Agenda*, Dec.–Jan. 1963–4 (Anita Auden); *Birmingham Post*, 26 Nov. 1963 (Pauline Smith); *English*, Summer 1964 (Howard Sergeant); *Guardian*, 22 Nov. 1963 (Richard Keel); *Hudson Review*, Autumn 1964 (Ian Hamilton); *Irish Times*, 4 April 1964 (Michael Longley); *New Statesman*, 6 Dec. 1963 (Christopher Ricks); *Observer*, 22 Dec. 1963 (A. Alvarez); *Outposts*, Spring 1964 (Philip Hobsbaum); *Review*, Jan. 1964 (P. Marsh); *Scotsman*, 4 Jan. 1964 (Martin Seymour-Smith); *Spectator*, 27 March 1964 (Elizabeth Jennings); *Teacher*, 24 Jan. 1964 (Ray Sparkes); *The Times*, 5 Dec. 1963; *Times Literary Supplement*, 27 Feb. 1964; *Tribune*, 7 Feb. 1964 (Jeremy Robson); *Western Daily Press*, 18 Nov. 1963 (Keith Turner).

Nessie the Mannerless Monster, with pictures by Gerald Rose; Faber and Faber, 24 April 1964. First American edition illustrated by Jan Pyk. Bobbs-Merrill, 1974 (as *Nessie the Monster*).

REVIEWS: *Coventry Evening Telegraph*, 30 Apr. 1964 (Susan Hill); *Guardian*, 10 July 1964 (Robert Nye); *The Listener*, 28 May 1964 (Anthony Thwaite); *New Statesman*, 15 May 1964 (Mary Scrutton); *The Sunday Telegraph*, 29 November 1964 (Ian Serraillier); *Teacher*, July 1964; *Times Literary Supplement*, 9 July 1964.

The Burning of the Brothel, Turret Books, October 1966. Limited edition, 300 (75 signed).

Recklings, Turret Books, 1966. Limited edition, 150, signed.

Scapegoats and Rabies, Poet and Printer, March 1967. Limited edition, 400.

REVIEWS: *New Statesman*, 16 June 1967 (Julian Symons); *Spectator*, 28 July 1967 (C. B. Cox.)

Wodwo, Faber and Faber, 18 May 1967. 'Logos' and 'Gog' II and III not in the American edition. First American edition, Harper, 22 Nov. 1967; contains two poems 'Root, Stem, Leaf' and 'Scapegoats and Rabies' not in the English edition. First paperback edition, Faber and Faber, 1971.

REVIEWS: *Birmingham Post*, 17 June 1967 (Barbara Lloyd-Evans); *Books and Bookmen*, Nov. 1967 (Michael Baldwin); *Book World*, 24 Dec. 1967 (Chad Walsh); *Cambridge Evening News*, 8 July 1967; *Cambridge Quarterly*, Autumn 1967 (J. M. Newton); *Carleton Miscellany*, Summer 1968 (D. Galler); *Church Times*, 15 Sept. 1967 (Norman Nicholson); *Delta 42*, Feb. 1968 (Sydney Bolt); *English*, Spring 1968 (Howard Sergeant); *English Studies*, June 1968 (M. Thorpe); *Far Point*, Fall 1968 (John Ferns); *Glasgow Herald*, 17 June 1967 (Charles Senior); *Guardian*, 19 May 1967 (Donald Davie); *Hudson Review*, Spring 1968 (A. Hecht); *Irish Times*, 20 May 1967 (Eavan Boland); *Kentish Gazette*, 18 July 1967 (R.A.F.); *Kenyon Review* 30, 1968 (Robin Skelton); *Library Journal*, 1 Nov. 1967 (Jerome Cushman); *The Listener*, 6 July 1967 (Graham Martin); *New Statesman*, 16 June 1967 (Julian Symons); *New Yorker*, 30 March 1968 (Louise Bogan); *New York Review of Books*, 1 Aug. 1968 (John Thompson); *Northwest Review*, Summer 1968 (R. Mariels); *The Observer*, 21 May 1967 (A. Alvarez); *Poetry*, September 1968 (H. Carruth); *Poetry Review*, Autumn 1967 (L. Clark); *Punch*, 5 July 1967 (John Press); *Scotsman*, 24 June 1967 (Martin Seymour-Smith); *Sheffield Star*, 1 July 1967 (Byron Rogers); *Spectator*, 28 July 1967 (C. B. Cox); *The Sunday Times*, 28 May 1967 (Jeremy Rundale); *The Tablet*, 8 July 1967 (John Juniper); *The Times*, 13 July 1967 (Derwent May); *Times Literary Supplement*, 6 July 1967; *Tribune*, 30 June 1967 (Jeremy Robson); *Virginia Quarterly*, Summer 1968 (S. F. Morse); *Yorkshire Post*, 6 July 1967 (Leonard Clark).

Animal Poems, Richard Gilbertson, Bow, Crediton, Devon, 1967. Limited edition, 100, signed.

Poetry in the Making. An Anthology of Poems and Programmes from 'Listening and Writing', Faber and Faber, 6 December 1967. First American edition as *Poetry Is*, Doubleday, 1970; lacks 'Writing a Novel' and 'Words and Experience'. First paperback edition, Faber and Faber, 1969
REVIEWS: *English Journal*, March 1971; *Horn Book*, Feb. 1971; *Kentish Gazette*, 23 Jan. 1970 (C.R.E.P.); *Library Journal*, 15 Dec. 1970 (M. A. Dorsey); *New Statesman*, 9 Feb. 1968 (Julian Symons); *New Yorker*, 5 Dec. 1970; *New York Book Review*, 8 Nov. 1970 (Thomas Lask); *Saturday Review*, 14 Nov. 1970 (Zena Sutherland); *Times Literary Supplement*, 14 March 1968; *Tribune*, 12 Sept. 1969 (Robert Nye).

Gravestones. A series of 6 poster poems designed by Gavin Robbins. 'Bowled Over', 'Fern', 'Still Life', 'Theology' and 'Thistles' from *Wodwo*; 'As Woman's Weeping' from *Recklings*. Each printed from silk screen in black and red or green. Exeter College of Art, 1967. Limited Edition 40, signed.

Poems: Ted Hughes, Linocuts: Gavin Robbins. The same poems and designs as *Gravestones*. Bartholomew Books, Exeter College of Art, 1968. Limited edition 300, signed.

The Iron Man, with drawings by George Adamson, Faber and Faber, 26 Feb. 1968. First American edition, as *The Iron Giant* with drawings by Robert Nadler, Harper, 23 Oct. 1968. First paperback edition, Faber and Faber, 1971. Adaptation for children learning to read, with illustrations by Colin Smithson, Penguin 1973.
REVIEWS: *Books and Bookmen*, Dec. 1971; *Book World*, 23 Feb. 1969; *Guardian*, 29 March 1968 (J.R.T.); *Horn Book*, Dec. 1968 (V.H.); *Library Journal*, 15 Dec. 1968 (Elva Harmon); *Listener*, 16 May 1968 (Naomi Lewis); *New York Times Book Review*, 3 Nov. 1968 (Robert Nye); *Spectator*, 14 June 1968 (Colin MacInnes); *The Tablet*, 27 April 1968 (Janet Bruce); *Teacher*, 13 Sept. 1968 (Margery Fisher); *Teachers' World*, 19 April 1968; *The Times*, 13 April 1968 (Robert Nye); *Times Educational Supplement*, 8 March 1968; *Times Literary Supplement*, 14 March 1968.

Five Autumn Songs for Children's Voices, Richard Gilbertson, Bow, Crediton, Devon, December 1968. Limited edition, 500 (188 signed).

The Demon of Adachigahara. Music by Gordon Crosse, words by Ted Hughes; Oxford University Press, 1969. First performed 27 March 1968.

I Said Goodbye to Earth. A poster poem designed by Gavin Robbins; 1969. Limited edition, 75, signed. Exeter College of Art.

Seneca's 'Oedipus' adapted by Ted Hughes; Faber and Faber, 8 December 1969. First American edition, illustrated by Reginald Pollack, Doubleday 1972.
REVIEWS: *Listener*, 1 Jan. 1970 (Christopher Ricks); *The Observer*, 25 Jan. 1970; *Spectator*, 21 March 1970 (Martin Seymour-Smith).

The Martyrdom of Bishop Farrar, Richard Gilbertson, Bow, Crediton, Devon, 4 March 1970. Limited edition, 100, signed.

The Coming of the Kings and other plays, Faber and Faber, 1 September 1970. First American edition (as *The Tiger's Bones*) illustrated by Alan E. Cober, Viking, 1974. Also contains 'Orpheus'. All these plays are available in acting editions from the Dramatic Publishing Co., Chicago.

REVIEWS: *Horn Book*, April 1974; *Library Journal*, 15 March 1974; *The Observer*, 27 Sept. 1970; *Spectator*, 5 Dec. 1970; *Teachers' World*, 19 Feb. 1971 (Sidney Robbins); *Times Literary Supplement*, 30 Oct. 1970; *Use of English*, Spring 1971 (David A. Male).

Crow, Faber and Faber, 12 October 1970. First American edition, Harper, 3 March 1971; contains 7 poems not in the first English edition: 'Crow Hears Fate Knock on the Door', 'Crow's Fall', 'The Contender', 'Crow Tries the Media', 'Crow's Elephant Totem Song', 'Crow Paints Himself into a Chinese Mural' and 'The Lovepet'. Second English edition, Faber, 1972; contains all the poems in the American edition with the exception of 'The Lovepet' and with the addition of 'Crowcolour'. Limited edition, with drawings by Leonard Baskin, Faber, December 1973, 400, signed; contains three further poems: 'Crow Rambles', 'Crow's Courtship' and 'Crow's Song about Prospero and Sycorax'.

REVIEWS: *Agenda*, Spring–Summer 1971 (Peter Dale); *Ambit 46*, 1971 (Martin Bax); *Birmingham Post*, 17 Oct. 1970 (Barbara Lloyd-Evans); *Book World*, 2 Jan. 1972; *Books and Bookmen*, Dec. 1970 (Derek Stanford); *Cambridge Quarterly*, Autumn 1971 (J. M. Newton); *Christian Science Monitor*, 29 April 1971 (Victor Howes); *Church Times*, 27 Nov. 1970 (Norman Nicholson); *Commonweal*, 17 Sept. 1971 (B. Wallenstein); *Contemporary Literature*, Winter 1973 (Marjorie G. Perloff); *Critical Quarterly*, Spring 1971 (David Lodge); *Delta*, Spring 1972 (N. Roberts); *Encounter*, March 1971 (Douglas Dunn); *English*, Spring 1971 (Howard Sergeant); *Erasmus Review* 1, 1971 (Lee J. Richmond); *Guardian*, 15 Oct. 1970 (Peter Porter); *Hudson Review*, Summer 1971 (H. Carruth); *Human World*, Nov. 1972 (I. Robinson and D. Sims); *Irish Times*, 31 Oct. 1970 (Eavan Boland); *Library Journal*, July 1971 (Sanford Dorbin); *The Listener*, 29 Oct. 1970 (Derwent May); *London Magazine*, Jan 1971 (Tony Harrison); *Malahat Review*, April 1971 (R.S.); *Mediterranean Review*, Fall 1971 (Dabney Stuart); *Nation*, 16 March 1974; *National Observer*, 31 May 1971; *New Statesman*, 16 Oct. 1970 (Alan Brownjohn); *Newsweek*, April 1971 (J. Kroll) *New York Review of Books*, 22 July 1971 (Stephen Spender); *New York Times Book Review*, 18 April 1971 (Daniel Hoffman); *The Observer*, 11 Oct. 1970 (A. Alvarez); *Partisan Review*, Winter 1971/2 (G. S. Fraser); *Platform*, Summer 1971 (Luke Spencer); *Poetry*, Feb. 1972 (C. Kizer); *Prairie Schooner*, Fall 1972 (Mordecai Marcus); *The Review*, Dec. 1970 (John Fuller); *Saturday Review*, 2 Oct. 1971 (J. Kessler); *Scotsman*, 31 Oct. 1970 (Martin Seymour-Smith); *Shenandoah*, Winter 1972 (Peter Cooley); *Southern Arts*, Jan. 1971 (John Fairfax); *Southern Review*, Spring 1975 (Steve Utz); *Spectator*, 6 March 1971 (Christopher Hudson); *Stand*, Vol. 12, No. 2, 1971 (Anne Cluysenaar); *The*

Sunday Telegraph, 11 Oct. 1970 (Brian Cox); *The Sunday Times*, 25 Oct. 1970 (Lyman Andrews); *Sydney Morning Herald*, 5 June 1971 (Philip Roberts); *The Tablet*, 21 Nov. 1970 (Damian Grant); *Time*, 5 April 1971 (Christopher Porterfield); *The Times*, 17 Dec. 1970 (Richard Holmes); *Times Literary Supplement*, 8 Jan. 1971 (Ian Hamilton); *Tribune*, 11 Dec. 1970 (Jeremy Robson); *Use of English*, Vol. 22, No. 3, 1971 (Sandy Cunningham).

A Few Crows, illustrated by Reiner Burger: Rougemont Press, Exeter, Oct. 1970. Limited edition, 75, signed.

Four Crow Poems ('Crow and the Birds', 'King of Carrion', 'That Moment', 'Crow's Last Stand'). Silkscreen prints by R. J. Lloyd, 1970. Limited edition, 20.

A Crow Hymn, Sceptre Press, Frensham, Surrey, 1970. Limited edition, 100 (26 signed).

Fighting for Jersualem. Graphics by Ron Brown. Mid-NAG Poetry Poster, No. 7, 1970.

Shakespeare's Poem, Lexham Press, March 1971. Limited edition, 150 (75 signed).

Crow Wakes, Poet and Printer, April 1971. Limited edition, 200.

Poems – Ruth Fainlight, Ted Hughes, Alan Sillitoe, Rainbow Press, May 1971. Limited edition, 300, signed.

Eat Crow, Rainbow Press, 1971. Limited edition, 150, signed.

Autumn Song, poster poem by Nina Carroll, Kettering, 1971.

Selected Poems 1957–1967, Faber 1972 (paperback only). First American edition with drawings by Leonard Baskin, Harper, 1973.
REVIEWS: *America*, 16 March 1974 (Thomas Kinsella); *Baltimore Evening Sun*, 13 March 1974 (Jane Conly); *Buffalo News*, 2 March 1974 (Jeff Simon); *Dublin Magazine*, Winter/Spring 1973 (R. Weber); *Hartford Courant*, 3 March 1974 (Paul H. Stacey); *International Herald Tribune*, 20 Feb. 1974 (Marjorie Perloff); *Kirkus*, 1 Nov. 1973; *New Republic*, 16 Feb. 1974; *New York Review of Books*, 7 March 1974 (Karl Miller); *New York Times Book Review*, 13 Jan. 1974 (Calvin Bedient); *St. Louis Globe-Democrat*, 30 March 1974 (Brian Taylor); *Saturday Review World*, 20 Nov. 1973; *Southern Humanities Review*, 1974, pp. 551–2 (John M. Ditsky); *Virginia Quarterly*, Spring 1974.

Sunday (*Wodwo*), first separate publication, illustrated by Graham Humphreys, Leopards, Cambridge University Press, 1972.

In the Little Girl's Angel Gaze. A broadsheet designed by Ralph Steadman, Steam Press 1972. Limited edition, 50, signed.

Prometheus on His Crag. Rainbow Press, November 1973. Limited edition, 160, signed.

The Story of Vasco, Libretto by Ted Hughes from the play by Shehadé, Oxford University Press, March 1974. The opera by Gordon Crosse first produced by Sadler's Wells at the London Coliseum, 13 March 1974.

Spring, Summer, Autumn, Winter, Rainbow Press, September 1974. Limited edition, 140, signed.

The Interrogator (*Cave Birds*), with facsimile of early draft, and drawing by Leonard Baskin. Scolar Press, May 1975. Limited edition 250.

Cave Birds. Ten poems with facsimilies of early drafts, and ten drawings by Leonard Baskin. Scolar Press, 1975. Limited edition 100, signed by poet and artist.

Season Songs, illustrated by Leonard Baskin, Viking Press, Oct. 1975. Contains all the poems in *Spring*, *Summer*, *Autumn*, *Winter*, except 'Hunting the Summer', with the addition of 'Swifts', 'Hay', 'Sheep', 'Autumn Nature Notes' and 'December River'. First English edition Faber and Faber, May 1976, which omits 'The Defenders' and adds 'March Morning Unlike Others', 'Icecrust and Snowflake', 'Apple Dumps', 'A Cranefly in September', and 'Two Horses'.

REVIEWS: *Art Teacher*, Spring 1976; *Booklist*, 15 Dec. 1975 (B. Hearn); *Cambridge Quarterly*, Vol. 7 No. 1 (John Newton); *Chicago Tribune*, 26 Oct. 1975 (Susan Fromberg Schaeffer); *Choice*, Feb. 1976; *Daily Mail*, 20 May 1976; *Encounter*, Nov. 1976 (Douglas Dunn); *English*, Autumn 1976 (John Stokes); *Guardian*, 20 May 1976 (Martin Dodsworth); *Horn Book*, April 1976 (P.H.); *Kirkus*, 15 Oct. 1975; *The Listener*, 20 May 1976 (Ronald Blythe); *New Times*, 28 Nov. 1975 (Geoffrey Wolff); *New York Times Book Review*, 21 Dec. 1975 (Thomas Lask); *Northwest Review*, Vol. 15 No. 3 (A. K. Weatherhead); *Observer*, 4 July 1976 (Peter Porter); *Poetry Nation*, 1, 1976 (David Day); *School Library Journal*, Dec. 1975 (Merrie Lou Cohen); *Scotsman*, 29 May 1976 (George Mackay Brown); *Spectator*, 17 July 1976 (Nick Totton); *Times Educational Supplement*, 25 June 1976 (Peter Fanning); *Times Literary Supplement*, 16 July 1976 (Edwin Morgan); *Tribune*, 6 Feb. 1976 (Martin Booth).

Earth-Moon, illustrated by the author, Rainbow Press 1976. Limited edition 226, signed. All these poems are also in *Moon-Whales*.

Eclipse, Sceptre Press 1976. Limited edition 250, 50 signed.

Moon-Whales, illustrated by Leonard Baskin, Viking Press, Oct. 1976. Contains all the poems in *The Earth-Owl* and *Earth-Moon*.

REVIEWS: *Bulletin of the Centre for Children's Books*, May 1977; *Choice*, June 1977; *Delap's F. & S.F. Review*, April 1977 (Mary S. Weinkauf); *Horn*

Book, April 1977; *Hudson Review*, Summer 1977 (David Bromwich); *Kirkus*, 15 Oct. 1976; *New York Times Book Review*, 9 Jan. 1977 (William Stafford); *School Library Journal*, Dec. 1976; *Washington Post Book World*, 7 Nov. 1976 (Joseph McLellan).

Gaudete, Faber and Faber, 18 May 1977. First American edition Harper and Row, Dec. 1977, containing a longer Argument.

REVIEWS: *Agenda*, vol. 15, nos. 2–3, 1977 (Peter Dale); *Ambit* 71, 1977 (Edwin Brock); *British Book News*, Aug. 1977 (Shirley Toulson); *Cambridge Quarterly*, vol. 7, no. 4, 1977 (J. M. Newton); *Chicago Tribune Book World*, 12 Feb. 1978 (Susan Fromberg Schaeffer); *Church Times*, 1 July 1977 (Norman Nicholson); *Critical Quarterly*, Summer 1977 (C. B. Cox); *The Daily Telegraph*, 26 May 1977 (Elizabeth Jennings); *Delta* 57, 1977 (Neil Roberts); *English*, Autumn 1977 (W. W. Robson); *The Financial Times*, 7 July 1977 (Anthony Curtis); *Guardian*, 19 May 1977 (Martin Dodsworth); *The Listener*, 2 June 1977 (John Bayley); *London Magazine*, Nov. 1977 (Craig Raine); *New Statesman*, 27 May 1977 (Peter Conrad); *New York Times Book Review*, 25 Dec. 1977 (Robert Pinsky); *Observer*, 22 May 1977 (Philip Toynbee); *St. Louis Globe*, 31 Dec. 1977 (Brian Taylor); *Spectator*, 11 June 1977 (Peter Ackroyd); *Spectrum* 2, Huddersfield New College, 1977 (Mark Hinchliffe); *Stand*, vol. 19, no. 2, 1978 (Terry Eagleton); *The Sunday Times*, 29 May 1977 (Julian Symons); *Thames Poetry*, Nov. 1977 (A. A. Cleary); *The Times*, 7 July 1977 (Robert Nye); *Times Educational Supplement*, 10 June 1977 (Herman Peschmann); *Times Literary Supplement*, 1 July 1977 (Oliver Lyne); *Tribune*, 3 June 1977 (Martin Booth).

Chiasmadon, with etching by Claire Van Vliet, Charles Seluzicki, June 1977. Limited edition, 185 copies, 120 for sale, signed.

Sunstruck, Sceptre Press, August 1977. Limited edition, 300 copies, 100 signed.

Moon-Bells, Chatto and Windus, 2 Feb. 1978.

REVIEWS: *Guardian*, 30 March 1978 (Martin Dodsworth); *Times Literary Supplement*, 7 April 1978 (John Mole).

Orts, Rainbow Press, Spring 1978. Limited edition, 200 copies, signed.

Moortown Elegies, Rainbow Press, Summer 1978. Limited edition. 150 copies, signed.

Cave Birds, Faber and Faber, 16 Oct. 1978. With drawings by Leonard Baskin.

Calder Valley Poems, Rainbow Press, late 1978. Limited edition.

B. HUGHES IN TRANSLATION

Ted Hughes: Der Eisenmann, Julius Steeger 1969. *The Iron Man* is also published in Japanese (1971).

Ted Hughes, Gedanken-Fuchs Gedichte, ed. Faas, Literarisches Colloquium, Berlin, 1971.

Ted Hughes, Antologia Poetica, ed. Pardo, Plaza and Janes, S.A., 1971.

Ted Hughes, Wiersze Wybrane, Wydawnictwo Literackie Krakow, 1972.

Ted Hughes, Pensiero-Volpe e Altre Poesie, ed. Pennati, Arnoldo Mondadori, 1973. All but two of the *Crow* poems in this selection are also in *Almanacco Dello Specchio* 2, 1973.

Ted Hughes: Kråka, ed. Lundkvist, Tuppen På Berget 1975.

Ted Hughes: Krage, ed. Thorborg, Husets Forlag 1977. Contains only about half the poems.

C. WORKS EDITED BY TED HUGHES

(Publication London unless otherwise stated.)

New Poems, Hutchinson, 1962. Edited Ted Hughes, Patricia Beer and Vernon Scannell.
REVIEWS: *Times Literary Supplement*, 23 Nov. 1962.

Five American Poets, Faber and Faber, 1963. Edited by Thom Gunn and Ted Hughes; contains foreword by the editors.
REVIEWS: *Encounter*, Jan. 1964 (John Hollander); *Critical Quarterly*, Autumn 1963 (John Stallworthy); *Times Literary Supplement*, 1 Nov. 1963.

Selected Poems, Keith Douglas, Faber and Faber, 1964. Contains introduction and biographical note by Ted Hughes. First American edition, Chilmark Press, 1964.
REVIEWS: *English*, Summer 1964 (Howard Sergeant); *Saturday Review*, 2 Jan. 1965 (Chad Walsh); *Spectator*, 27 March 1964 (Elizabeth Jennings); *Stand*, Vol. 6 no. 4 (Geoffrey Hill); *Times Literary Supplement*, 19 March 1964.

Modern Poetry in Translation, 1–10, 1966–71. Co-edited by Ted Hughes.

A Choice of Emily Dickinson's Verse, Faber and Faber, 1968. Selected with an introduction by Ted Hughes.
REVIEWS: *The Listener*, 1 Aug 1968 (Margaret Drabble); *New Statesman*, 16 Aug. 1968 (Elizabeth Jennings); *Times Literary Supplement*, 25 July 1968.

Crossing the Water, Sylvia Plath, Faber and Faber, 1971. Contains note by Ted Hughes.

A Choice of Shakespeare's Verse, Faber and Faber, 1971. Selected with an introduction by Ted Hughes. First American edition as *With Fairest Flowers While Summer Lasts*, Doubleday, 1971.

REVIEWS: *Books and Bookmen*, April 1972 (Marie Peel); *Guardian*, 25 Nov. 1971 (Martin Dodsworth); *Irish Times*, 20 Nov. 1971 (Elgy Gillespie); *The Sunday Times*, 16 Jan. 1972 (Christopher Ricks), and Ted Hughes replied to this review the following Sunday.

Johnny Panic and the Bible of Dreams, Sylvia Plath. Faber and Faber, 1977. Introduction by Ted Hughes.

D. CONTRIBUTIONS BY TED HUGHES TO BOOKS AND PERIODICALS

I. UNCOLLECTED POEMS

(i.e. Poems not included in any of the publications listed in A.)

'Wild West': *Don and Dearne*, Mexborough Secondary School, 1946; *Scotsman*, 14 Sept. 1968; *Young Winter's Tales*, Macmillan, 1970.

'The Little Boys and the Seasons': *Granta*, 8 June 1954; *Accent*, Spring 1957; *Poetry from Cambridge 1952–4*, ed. Karl Miller, Fantasy Press, 1955.

'The Court Tumbler and Satirist': *Poetry from Cambridge 1952–4*.

'The Woman With Such High Heels She Looked Dangerous': *Delta 5*, Spring 1955.

'Scene Without an Act': *Granta*, 12 May 1956.

'The Drowned Woman': *Poetry* LXXXIX, 5, Feb, 1957.

'Letter': *New Statesman*, 28 Sept. 1957.

'Quest': *The Grapevine*, University of Durham Institute of Education, Feb. 1958.

'Constancy': *London Magazine*, Aug. 1958.

'Shells': *New Yorker*, 1 Aug. 1959; *London Magazine*, March 1961.

'Gulls Aloft': *Christian Science Monitor*, 15 Dec. 1959.

'Snails': *Christian Science Monitor*, 15 Dec. 1959.

'Fable': *Times Literary Supplement*, 9 Sept. 1960; *Mademoiselle*, March 1961.

'Lines to a Newborn Baby': *Texas Quarterly*, 3, 4, Winter 1960.

'To F.R. at Six Months': *Western Daily Press*, 22 Feb. 1961 (as 'For Frieda in her First Months'); *Sewanee Review*, LXXI, i, January 1963.

'Dully Gumption's College Courses': 'Semantics'; 'Political Science'; 'Theology' (*Wodwo; Selected Poems*); 'Humanities' (*Recklings*); *London Magazine*, March 1961.

'My Uncle's Wound': broadcast 26 July 1961; *Poetry at the Mermaid*, Poetry Book Society, 1961.

'The Road to Easington': broadcast 24 July 1962; *English Poetry Now*, *Critical Quarterly Supplement* 3, 1962; *New Lines 2*, ed. Robert Conquest, Macmillan 1963.

'Sunday Evening': *Atlantic Monthly*, May 1963.

'Era of Giant Lizards': *Poetry*, Vol. CIII, 3, Dec. 1963.

'On Westminster Bridge': *Poetry*, Vol. CIII, 3, Dec. 1963.

'After Lorca': *Poetry*, Vol. CIII, 3, Dec. 1963; *New Poetry 1964*, *Critical Quarterly Supplement*, 1964.
'Poem to Robert Graves Perhaps': *Poetry*, Vol. CIII, 3, Dec. 1963.
'Small Hours': *Poetry*, Vol. CIII, 3, Dec. 1963.
'Bad News Good!': *Agenda*, Dec./Jan. 1963/4.
'Dice': *Critical Quarterly*, Vol. 6, No. 2, Summer 1964.
'O White Elite Lotus': *Critical Quarterly*, Vol. 6, No. 4, Winter 1964.
'The Brother's Dream': broadcast 22 Nov. 1965; *Poetry 1900–1965*, ed. MacBeth, Longman with Faber and Faber, 1967.
'Carol': *Sunday Times Weekly Review*, 19 Dec. 1965.
'Gibraltar': *New Statesman*, 8 April 1966.
'Folk-Lore': *Critical Quarterly*, Vol. 8, i, Spring 1966.
'Warm Moors': *Critical Quarterly*, Vol. 8, i, Spring 1966.
'Birdsong': *London Magazine*, Sept. 1966.
'The Last Migration': *The Animal Anthology*, ed. Diana Spearman, 1966.
'To W. H. Auden': *The Sunday Times*, 19 Feb. 1967.
'Three Legends' (the first of these is the first of the 'Two Legends' in *Crow*): *Journal of Creative Behaviour*, 1, 3, July 1967.
'TV On': *Listener*, 28 Sept. 1967.
'A Motorbike': *The Listener*, 30 Nov. 1967.
'Dog Days on the Black Sea': *Critical Quarterly*, Vol. 10, Nos. 1, 2, 1968; *Word in the Desert*, Oxford, 1968.
'?': *Critical Quarterly*, Vol. 10, Nos. 1, 2, 1968; *Word in the Desert*, 1968.
'Crowquill': *Poetry Gala*, 1968.
'The New World' (Three Choirs Festival Programme, 1972) 1 'It is Not Long You'll be Straddling the Rocket'; 2 'When the Star was on Her Face'; 3 'A Star Stands on Her Forehead'; 4 'I said Goodbye to Earth' (Poster Poem, Gavin Robbins, 75 numbered and signed, 1969); 5 'The Street was Empty and Stone'; 6 'Where Did We Go?' These poems were set by Gordon Crosse in 1969.
'Ballad on Bauble-Head': *New American Review* 8, Jan. 1970.
'Song of Woe': *Critical Quarterly*, Vol. 12, no. 2, Summer 1970.
'Though the pubs are shut': *A Folio of British Poetry*, ed. Lucie Smith, Unicorn Press, 22 May 1970.
'Fighting for Jerusalem': *Mid-NAG* Poetry Poster No. 7; *Times Literary Supplement*, 9 Oct. 1970.
'A Lucky Folly': *Workshop* 10, 1970; *Say It Aloud*, Hutchinson 1972.
'Existential Song': *London Magazine*, July/August 1970; *Corgi Modern Poets in Focus 1*, 1971; *New Poems 1971–2*, Hutchinson, 1972.
'The Space Egg was Sailing': *New Poems 1970–1*, Hutchinson, 1971.
'An Alchemy': *Poems for Shakespeare 2*, ed. Graham Fawcett, The Globe Playhouse Trust Publications, 1973.
'Welcombe': *Bananas* 1, Jan.–Feb. 1975.
'Exits': *Bananas* 1, Jan.–Feb. 1975.
'Festival of Poets': *Bananas* 1, Jan.–Feb. 1975.
'Beware of the Stars': *New Departures*. 7/8, 10/11, 1975.
'The Lamentable History of the Human Calf' (from *Difficulties of a Bridegroom*): *New Departures*, 7/8, 10/11, 1975.

'X': *Poetry Supplement*, Poetry Book Society 1975.
'The Virgin Knight': *New Statesman*, 19 March 1976: *Words*, Broadsheet 25, 1976.
'Light', 'Air', 'Skin': *Granta*, April 1976.
'Actaeon': *Atlantic*, Sept. 1976.
'Postcard from Torquay': *New Statesman*, 29 Oct. 1976.
'The Womb': *New Statesman*, 26 Nov. 1976.
'The fallen oak': *Boston University Journal*, XXIV, 3, 1976.
'And the falcon came', 'The Wild Duck', 'The Unknown Wren', 'And the owl floats', 'And the Phoenix has come' (all *Adam and the Sacred Nine*): *New Poetry*, Arts Council, 1976.
'A God': *New Poems* 1976–7, Hutchinson, 1977.
'Eye went out to hunt you': *Aquarius* 9, 1977.
'Nefertiti': *Times Literary Supplement*, 24 June 1977; *New Poems 1977–8*, Hutchinson, 1977.
'Who lives in my skin with me?' (*Caprichos*); *Mars* 1, 1977.
'I walk' (*Caprichos*): *Mars* 1, 1977.
'If you doubt this face' (*Caprichos*): *Mars* 1, 1977.
'Dead, she became space-earth' (*Caprichos*): *Boston Univ. Journal*, XXV, 2, 1977.
'After the grim diagnosis', *Poetry Supplement*, Poetry Book Society 1977.
'Old age gets up', *Poetry Supplement*, Poetry Book Society 1977.
'Unknown Warrior': *New Poems 1977–8*, Hutchinson, 1977.

2. TRANSLATIONS

Poems by Janos Pilinszky, *Modern Poetry in Translation* 7, June 1970.
Selected Poems of Yehuda Amichai, Penguin, 1971.
'Under the Winter Sky' by Janos Pilinszky, Mencard 2nd series 9, Menard Press 1975.
Selected Poems by Janos Pilinszky, translated by Ted Hughes and Janos Csokits, Carcanet, Sept. 1976. Introduction by Ted Hughes.
REVIEWS: *Agenda* 14,3, 1976 (Michael Hamburger); *Guardian*, 28 Oct. 1976 (Martin Dodsworth); *Observer*, 12 Dec. 1976 (Peter Porter); *PN Review* 3, Spring 1977 (Clive Wilmer); *Times Literary Supplement*, 21 Jan. 1977 (Henry Gifford).
'The Portuguese Synagogue in Amsterdam', 'A Dog After Love', 'Like the Inner Wall of a House' and 'A Song About Rest' by Yehuda Amichai, *Times Literary Supplement*, 29 Oct. 1976.
Amen by Yehuda Amichai, Harper 1977. Introduction by Ted Hughes.
REVIEWS: *Hudson Review*, Winter 1977–8 (Vernon Young); *New York Times Book Review*, 3 July 1977 (M. L. Rosenthal).

3. STORIES

'Bartholomew Pygge Esq.': *Granta*, 4 May 1957.
'O'Kelly's Angel': *Granta*, 18 May 1957.

'The Rain Horse' (*Wodwo*)*: Harper's*, Jan. 1960; *London Magazine*, Feb. 1960; *Introduction*, Faber, 1960; broadcast, 29 Aug. 1960; *Listening and Writing*, Autumn 1961.

'Snow' (*Wodwo*)*: Introduction*, Faber, 1960; *Harper's Bazaar*, Oct. 1961; broadcast 8 Jan. 1963.

'Sunday' (*Wodwo*): *Introduction*, Faber, 1960.

'The Caning': *Texas Quarterly* III, 4, Winter 1960.

'The Harvesting' (*Wodwo*): broadcast 17 Dec. 1960; *London Magazine*, April 1961.

'Miss Mambrett and the Wet Cellar': *Texas Quarterly*, IV, 3, Autumn 1961.

'The Suitor' (*Wodwo*): *Encounter*, May 1964.

4. DRAMA
(including unpublished plays)

'The House of Aries': broadcast 16 Nov. 1960; *Audience* 8, 2, Spring 1961; *Two Cities*, Summer 1961 (3 excerpts); *Texas Quarterly*, Autumn 1961 (2 excerpts).

'The Calm': produced in Boston, 1961.

'A Houseful of Women': broadcast 1961.

'The Wound' (*Wodwo*), broadcast 1 Feb. 1962. First stage production at the Young Vic, 17 July 1972.

REVIEWS: *The Daily Telegraph*, 18 July 1972 (Keith Nurse); *The Financial Times*, 18 July 1972 (B. A. Young); *Guardian*, 18 July 1972 (Michael Billington); *Stage and Television Today*, 20 July 1972 (D.F.B.); *The Times*, 18 July 1972 (Charles Lewson).

'Difficulties of a Bridegroom': broadcast 21 Jan. 1963.

'Epithalamium': performed at the Royal Court Theatre, London, 18 July 1963.

'Dogs': broadcast 12 Feb. 1964.

'Eat Crow' (1971): written 1964; part published in *Encounter*, July 1965.

'The House of Donkeys': first broadcast 30 Sept. 1965; *Living Language*, Autumn 1970 (first half only).

'The Tiger's Bones' (*The Coming of the Kings*): first broadcast in two parts, 26 Nov. and 3 Dec. 1965; *Listening and Writing*, Autumn 1965.

'Beauty and the Beast' (*The Coming of the Kings*): first broadcast, 2 Dec. 1965; *Living Language*, Autumn 1968. First stage production at the Arts Theatre, London, Sept. 1971.

REVIEWS: *Jewish Chronicle*, 1 Oct. 1971 (A.F.); *The Sunday Times*, 10 Oct. 1971 (Harold Hobson).

'The Price of a Bride': first broadcast, 22 Sept. 1966; *Living Language*, Autumn 1966 (opening only); *Here Now and Beyond*, Oxford University Press, 1968.

'The Head of Gold': first broadcast 21 Sept. 1967.

'The Coming of the Kings' (*The Coming of the Kings*): first broadcast 17 Nov. 1967; *Listening and Writing*, Autumn 1967. First stage production at the Arts Theatre, London, 4 Nov. 1972.

REVIEW: *Stage and Television Today*, 9 Nov. 1972 (H.G.M.)

Seneca's 'Oedipus': Arion 7, Autumn 1968. First performance by the National Theatre Company at the Old Vic, 19 March 1968, produced by Peter Brook.

REVIEWS: *Daily Mail*, 20 March 1968 (Peter Lewis); *The Daily Telegraph*, 20 March 1968 (Eric Shorter); *Guardian*, 20 March 1968 (Philip Hope-Wallace); *Illustrated London News*, 30 March 1968; *Lady*, 4 April 1968 (J. C. Trewin); *Londoner*, 6 April 1968 (Roger Baker); *Plays and Players*, May 1968 (Martin Esslin); *The Sunday Times*, 24 March 1968 (Harold Hobson); *The Times*, 20 and 23 March 1968 (Irving Wardle).

'Sean, the Fool, the Cats and the Devil' (*The Coming of the Kings*): first broadcast 2 May 1968; *Living Language*, Summer 1968. First stage production and reviews as for 'Beauty and the Beast'.

'Orpheus' (*The Tiger's Bones*): first broadcast 29 Jan. 1971; *Listening and Writing*, Spring 1971, Spring 1974.

Orghast: performed by Peter Brook's Experimental Theatre Co. at the Shiraz Festival 1971; 'The Birth of Sogis' in *Performance*, Dec. 1971. The fullest account of this work is *Orghast at Persepolis* by A. C. H. Smith, Eyre Methuen 1972.

REVIEWS, INTERVIEWS AND COMMENT: *The Daily Telegraph*, 17 Sept. 1971 (A. C. H. Smith); *Drama*, Winter 1971 (Ossia Trilling); *Drama and Theatre* 10, 1971 (Jean Richards); *The Financial Times*, 14 Sept. 1971 (Andrew Porter); *Guardian*, 7 Sept. 1971 (Henry Popkin); *The Observer*, 12 Sept. 1971 (Richard Findlater); *Performance*, Dec. 1971 (Geoffrey Reeves); *The Sunday Times*, 29 Aug. 1971 (A. C. H. Smith); *Theatre Quarterly*, Jan.–Mar. 1972 (Ossia Trilling); *Times Literary Supplement*, 1 Oct. 1971 (Tom Stoppard).

The Story of Vasco. Opera by Gordon Crosse first produced by Sadler's Wells at the London Coliseum, 13 March 1974.

REVIEWS AND COMMENT: *Birmingham Post*, 15 March 1974 (John Falding); *Country Life*, 11 April 1974 (Hugo Cole); *Daily Mail*, 14 March 1974 (David Gillard); *The Daily Telegraph*, 14 March 1974 (Peter Stadlen); *Eastern Daily Press*, 16 Feb. 1974 (C.V.R.); *Evening Standard*, 14 March 1974 (Christopher Grier); *The Financial Times*, 15 March 1974 (Ronald Crichton); *Guardian*, 13 March 1974 (Lee Langley); *Jewish Chronicle*, 22 March 1974 (Arthur Jacobs); *The Listener*, 14 March 1974 (Stephen Walsh); *Music & Musicians*, March 1974 (Stephen Walsh); *Musical Opinion*, May 1974 (L.S.); *Musical Times*, March 1974 (Hugo Cole), May 1974 (Winton Dean); *New Statesman*, 22 March 1974 (Bayan Northcott); *Observer*, 10 March 1974, 17 March 1974 (Peter Hayworth); *Opera*, March 1974 (Bayan Northcott), May 1974 (Harold Rosenthal); *The Scotsman*, 15 March 1974 (Conrad Wilson); *Spectator*, 23 March 1974 (Rodney Milnes); *Stage and Television Today*, 21 March 1974 (A.M.); *The Sunday Telegraph*, 17 March 1974 (Jeremy Noble); *The Sunday Times*, 17 March 1974 (Desmond Shawe-Taylor); *Tatler*, May 1974 (David Fingleton); *Tempo*, June 1974 (John Andrewes); *Times Educational Supplement*, 26 April 1974 (Patrick Carnegy); *Tribune*, 22 March 1974 (David Simmons); *Yorkshire Post*, 15 March 1974 (Ernest Bradbury).

5. RADIO TALKS

'Capturing Animals' (*Poetry in the Making*), first broadcast 6 Oct. 1961;

The Listener, 19 Oct. 1967. See Recordings.

Writing a Novel: Beginning' (*Poetry in the Making*), first broadcast 20 Oct. 1961; *Listening and Writing*, Autumn 1961.

'Writing a Novel: Going On' (*Poetry in the Making*), first broadcast 24 Nov. 1961; *Listening and Writing*, Autumn 1961.

'Meet My Folks!' (*Poetry in the Making*), first broadcast 30 March 1962.

'The Poetry of Keith Douglas': 31 May 1962; *The Listener*, 21 June 1962. The version in the *Critical Quarterly*, Spring 1963, is slightly different.

'Wind and Weather' (*Poetry in the Making*), first broadcast 2 Nov. 1962; *Listening and Writing*, Autumn 1962.

'Learning to Think' (*Poetry in the Making*), first broadcast 10 May 1963; *Listening and Writing*, Summer 1963. See Recordings.

'The Rock': 11 Sept. 1963; *Listener*, 19 Sept. 1963; *Writers on Themselves*, B.B.C. 1964; *Worlds*, Penguin 1974.

'Writing about People' (*Poetry in the Making*), first broadcast 22 Sept. 1963; *Listening and Writing*, Autumn 1963.

'Moon Creatures' (*Poetry in the Making*), first broadcast 25 Oct. 1963.

'*Voss*: by Patrick White': 23 Jan. 1964; *The Listener*, 6 Feb. 1964.

'Writing About Landscape' (*Poetry in the Making*), first broadcast 1 May 1964; *Listening and Writing*, Summer 1967 (as 'Water and Landscape').

'The Poetry of Vasco Popa': 24 Oct. 1966; *Critical Survey*, Summer 1966.

'Words and Experience' (*Poetry in the Making*), first broadcast 24 Jan. 1967.

'Sylvia Plath's *Crossing the Water*: Some Reflections': 5 July 1971; a revised version was published in the *Critical Quarterly*, Summer 1971.

6. ESSAYS AND INTRODUCTIONS

'Leonard Baskin', programme for an exhibition of Baskin woodcuts and engravings at the Royal Society of Painters in Water-Colours, London, May 1962.

Introduction to *Here Today*, Hutchinson 1963.

'The Genius of Isaac Bashevis Singer', *New York Review of Books*, 22 April 1965.

'The chronological order of Sylvia Plath's poems', *Tri-Quarterly*, Fall 1966; reprinted in *The Art of Sylvia Plath*, ed. Newman, Faber 1970.

Introduction to Vasco Popa's *Selected Poetry*, Penguin 1969.

'Myth and Education', *Children's Literature in Education* 1, 1970.

Introduction to *Children as Writers* 2, Heinemann, 1975.

'Myth and Education', *Writers, Critics, and Children*, ed. Fox, Hammond, Jones, Smith and Sterck, Heinemann 1976. This is a different essay from the one with the same title listed above.

7. REVIEWS

Weekend in Dinlock by Clancy Segal, *Nation*, 2 July 1960.

The Wesker Trilogy, *Nation* 19 November 1960.

The Loch Ness Monster by Tim Dinsdale, *New Statesman*, 2 June 1961.

Nimrod Smith by Alan Wykes, *New Statesman*, 23 June 1961.

The Cat in the Hat Comes Back by Dr. Seuss; *Barnaby and the Horses* by

Lydia Pender; *Timba* and *Gringolo* by Lilli Keenig; *The Cricket in Times Square* by George Selden; *Born Free* by Joy Adamson, *New Statesman*, 10 Nov. 1961.

The Nerve of Some Animals by Robert Froman, *New Statesman*, 23 March 1962.

Man and Dolphin by Dr J. C. Lilly, *New Statesman*, 23 March 1962.

Primitive Song by C. M. Bowra, *The Listener*, 3 May 1962.

One Fish Two Fish Red Fish Blue Fish by Dr Seuss, *New Statesman*, 18 May 1962.

The Cat's Opera by Eilis Dillon, *New Statesman*, 18 May 1962.

The Otter's Tale by Gavin Maxwell, *New Statesman*, 18 May 1962.

Everyman's Ark by Sally Patrick Johnson, *New Statesman*, 9 November 1962.

Here Come the Elephants by Alice Goudey, *New Statesman*, 9 November 1962.

I, Said the Sparrow by Paul West, *Guardian*, 8 Feb. 1963.

Rule and Energy by John Press, *New Statesman*, 9 August 1963.

Vagrancy by Philip O'Connor, *New Statesman*, 6 September 1963.

Emily Dickinson's Poetry by Charles R. Anderson, *The Listener*, 12 Sept. 1963.

Folk Tales of Japan, *Folk Tales of Israel*, *The Listener*, 12 December 1963.

Myth and Religion of the North by E. O. G. Turville-Petre, *The Listener*, 19 March 1964.

The Collected Poems of Wilfred Owen, *New York Times Book Review*, 16 April 1964.

A Selection of African Prose, ed. W. H. Whiteley, *The Listener*, 28 May 1964.

The Heroic Recitation of the Bahima of Ankile, *Somali Poetry*, ed. B. W. Andrzejewski and I. M. Lewis, *The Listener*, 28 May 1964.

The Three Christs of Ipsilanti by Milton Rokeach, *New Statesman*, 4 September 1964.

The Letters of Alexander Pushkin, ed. J. T. Shaw, *The Listener*, 1 Oct. 1964.

Astrology by Louis MacNeice, *New Statesman*, 2 October 1964.

Ghost and Divining Rod by T. C. Lethbridge, *New Statesman*, 2 Oct. 1964.

Shamanism by Mircea Eliade, *The Listener*, 29 October 1964.

The Sufis by Idries Shah, *The Listener*, 29 October 1964.

Mysterious Senses by Vitus Droscher, *New Statesman*, 27 November 1964.

Heimskringla by Snorri Sturluson, *The Prose Edda*, *Gods, Demons and Others* by R. K. Narayan, *New York Review of Books*, 31 December 1964.

The Faber Book of Ballads, *Guardian*, 14 May 1965.

Men Who March Away, ed. I. M. Parsons, *The Listener*, 5 August 1965.

Literature Among the Primitives, *The Primitive Reader* by John Greenway, *New York Review of Books*, 9 December 1965.

Selected Letters of Dylan Thomas, *New Statesman*, 25 November 1966.

Folktales of Chile, *Hindoo Fairy Legends*, *The Glass Man and The Golden Bird*, *The Black Monkey*, *New Statesman*, 24 May 1968.

The Environmental Revolution by Max Nicholson, *Spectator*, 21 March 1970. (A longer version of this essay appeared in *Your Environment* No. 3, Summer 1970.)

Imaginary Beings by Borghese, *Guardian*, 26 November 1970.

A Separate Reality by Carlos Castaneda, *The Observer*, 5 March 1972.

8. MISCELLANEOUS

'Ted Hughes Writes', *Poetry Book Society Bulletin*, 15, 1957.
'Context', *London Magazine*, February 1962.
Note in *Poet's Choice*, ed. Engle and Langland, Dial Press 1962.
Introduction to *Here Today*, Hutchinson, 1963.
'The Poet Speaks', XVI, British Council, 1963.
'Sylvia Plath', *Poetry Book Society Bulletin*, 44, 1965.
'Desk Poet', *Guardian*, 23 March 1965.
Biographical Notes, *Poetry International* '67 *Programme*.
'Ted Hughes' Crow', *The Listener*, 30 July 1970.
'Ted Hughes and Crow' an interview with Egbert Faas, *London Magazine*, January 1971.
Introduction to *Fiesta Melons* by Sylvia Plath, Rougemont Press, 1971.
Note in *Winter Trees* by Sylvia Plath, Faber, 1971.
Letter in *Times Literary Supplement*, 19 Nov. 1971.
Letter in *The Observer*, 21 Nov. 1971.
Letter in *Times Literary Supplement*, 17 Nov. 1972.
Sleeve note for Shusha, *Song of Long-Time Lovers*, TGS 114, 1972.
Blurb for *On the Coast* by Wayne Brown, Andre Deutsch, 1972.
Blurb for *Noth* by Daniel Huws, Secker and Warburg, 1972.
Introductory note to *Stones* by Paul Merchant, Rougemont Press, January 1973.
Sleeve note for *The Battle of Aughrim* by Richard Murphy, Claddagh, CCT 7.
Sleeve note for *Crow*, Claddagh, CCT 9–10, 1973.
Note in *Let the Poet Choose*, ed. Gibson, Harrap 1973.
Notes in *Worlds*, ed. Summerfield, Penguin 1974.
Notes on *Cave Birds* and *Lumb's Remains* in the Ilkley Festival programme, May 1975.
'A conversation with Ted Hughes about the Arvon Foundation', Arvon Press, 1976.
Argument of *Gaudete*, National Theatre Platform Performance programme, 18 July 1977.

E. HUGHES ON RECORD

Listening and Writing, BBC Records, RESR 19M 1971. Two talks by Ted Hughes, 'Capturing Animals', transmitted 6 October 1961, and 'Learning to Think', transmitted 10 May 1963. In the course of these talks Hughes reads 'The Thought-Fox', 'Pike', 'View of a Pig', and 'Bare Almond Trees' by D. H. Lawrence.

Poets Reading No. 5 Jupiter jep OC27. Recorded Spring 1962. Hughes reads 'The Thought-Fox', Soliloque of a Misanthrope', 'Mayday on Holderness' and 'Pibroch'.

The Poet Speaks No. 5 Argo PLP 1085. Recorded 29 August 1962. Hughes reads nine poems from *Wodwo*.

Here Today Part 1 Jupiter JUR OOA6. Recorded Autumn 1962–Spring 1963. Hughes reads 'View of a Pig'.

Jupiter Anthology of 20th Century English Poetry Part III Jupiter JUR OOA8. Recorded 1963. Hughes reads 'The Hawk in the Rain' and 'Hawk Roosting'.

Poetry 1900 to 1965 34155 (Longman) 1967. Hughes reads 'Hawk Roosting', 'Humming Bird' by D. H. Lawrence and 'Vergissmeinnicht' by Keith Douglas.

The Battle of Aughrim by Richard Murphy. Claddagh CCT 7 read by C. Day Lewis, Cyril Cusack, Niall Toibin, Ted Hughes and Margaret Robertson.

Crow Claddagh CCT 9–10 1973. Hughes reads all but three of the poems in the first English edition of *Crow*.

The Poetry and Voice of Ted Hughes, Caedmon TC 1535. Hughes reads 'The Thought-Fox', 'The Jaguar', 'Wind', 'Six Young Men', 'Mayday on Holderness', 'The Retired Colonel', 'View of a Pig', 'Sunstroke', 'Pike', 'An Otter', 'Hawk Roosting', 'Icecrust and Snowflake', 'Sheep 1', 'His Legs Ran About', 'Bride and Groom' and twelve poems from the Epilogue of *Gaudete*.

F. SETTINGS

Meet My Folks!, Gordon Crosse, O.U.P., 1965, First performed, 1964. Recorded HMV XLP 40001, 1965.

Three Choruses, Hugh Wood, Universal Edition, 1967. Includes setting of 'The Hawk in the Rain'.

The Horses, Hugh Wood, Universal Edition, 1967. Settings of 'The Horses', 'Pennines in April' and 'September'. First performed 13 Nov. 1967. Broadcast 24 Oct. 1971. Recorded Argo ZRG 750, 1974.

Smoke Blackened Walls and Curlews, Graham Collier. First performed Bradford University, 25 Feb. 1970.

Water-Song (*Crow*), Stanley Myers. Recorded by Shusha, *Song of Long-Time Lovers*, Tangent TGS 114 1972.

The New World, Gordon Crosse, O.U.P. First performed 30 August 1972. Recorded Argo ZRG 788, 18 Sept. 1974.

Six *Crow* Poems: 'Two Legends', 'Lineage', 'Examination at the Womb Door', 'The Door', 'Crowego' and 'Crow's Last Stand', Barbara Winrow. First performed Ilkley Literature Festival, 25 May 1975.

G. CRITICISM

(see also the list of reviews in section A)

Abbs, Peter, 'The Revival of Mythopoic Imagination: A Study of R. S. Thomas and Ted Hughes', *Poetry Wales* 10, 4, 1975.

Abse, Dannie, *Corgi Modern Poets in Focus*, 1971.

Backström, Lars, 'Ted Hughes och månskräcken', Lyrikvännen 11, 1964.

Bedient, Calvin, 'On Ted Hughes', *Critical Quarterly*, Summer 1972, reprinted in *Eight Contemporary Poets*, Oxford, 1974.

Bouson, J. Brooks, 'A Reading of Ted Hughes's *Crow*', *Concerning Poetry* 7, 1974.

Combecher, Hans, 'Ted Hughes: "The Thought-Fox" ', *Literature in Wissenschaft and Unterricht* 4, 1971.
Cox, C. B., 'The Violence of Ted Hughes', *John O'London's Weekly*, 13 July 1961.
Cox, C. B. and Dyson, A. E.: *Modern Poetry*, Arnold 1963. Contains a chapter on 'The Casualty'.
Dyson, A. E., 'Ted Hughes', *Critical Quarterly* 1, 3, 1959.
Fernandez, C. V., '*Crow*: a Mythology of the Demonic', *Modern Poetry Studies* 6, Autumn 1975.
Ferns, John, 'Over the Same Ground: Ted Hughes' "Wodwo" ', *Far Point* 1 (Univ. of Manitoba), 1968.
Fowkes, Rosalind, 'Pass, Crow: A Discussion of Ted Hughes' Last Published Collection of Poetry', *UNISA English Studies* 11, June 1973.
Gibson, John, 'A Thematic Analysis of the Poetry of Ted Hughes's Major Works', Ph.D., University of Northern Colorado, 1974.
Gifford, Terry, 'A Return to the Wound', *Kingfisher* 1, nos. 2 & 3, 1978.
Gitzen, Julian, 'Ted Hughes and Elemental Energy', *Discourse*, Autumn 1970.
'Ted Hughes and the Triumph of Energy', *Southern Humanities Review*, Winter 1973.
Grant, A., 'Ted Hughes' in *Criticism in Action*, ed. M. Hussey, Longman, 1969.
Grubb, F., 'Thinking Animal: Ted Hughes' in *A Vision of Reality*, 1965.
Hahn, Claire, '*Crow* and Biblical Creation Narratives', *Critical Quarterly*, Spring 1977.
Hainsworth, J. D., 'Extremes in Poetry: R. S. Thomas and Ted Hughes', *English*, Autumn 1963.
'Ted Hughes and Violence', *Essays in Criticism*, July 1965.
Hamilton, Ian, 'Ted Hughes' *Crow*, in *A Poetry Chronicle*, Faber, 1973.
Harrison, Martin, 'A Note on Ted Hughes', *Granta*, Easter 1972.
Heaney, Seamus, 'Now, and in England', *Critical Inquiry*, Summer 1977.
Hedetoft, Ulf, 'Ted Hughes, "Pennines in April": the Universal Poem in the 20th Century', *Language and Literature* 2, iv, 1974.
Hirschberg, Stuart, 'Myth and Anti-Myth in Ted Hughes' *Crow*', *Contemporary Poetry* 2, i. 1975.
Hoffman, 'Talking Beasts, The Single Adventure in the Poems of Ted Hughes', *Shenandoah*, Summer 1968.
Holbrook, David, 'The Cult of Gunn and Hughes', *The Poetry Review*, Summer 1963.
'Ted Hughes' *Crow* and the Longing for Non-Being' in *The Black Rainbow*, ed. Peter Abbs, Heinemann, 1975.
'From "Vitalism" to a Dead Crow: Ted Hughes' Failure of Confidence' in *Lost Bearings in English Poetry*, Vision, 1977.
James, G. Ingli, 'The Animal Poems of Ted Hughes: A Devaluation', *Southern Review*, 1967.
Jennings, Elizabeth, *Poetry Today*, Longman, 1961.
John, B., 'Ted Hughes: Poet at the Master-Fulcrum of Violence', *Arizona Quarterly*, Spring 1967.
Kano, Hideo, 'Ted Hughes no Shi-Gendaishi no ichi-men', *Oberon* 14, 1973.

Kimball, Arthur S., 'Ted Hughes' *Crow*: Chaos and the Fool', *UNISA English Studies* 13, i, 1975.
Kirkham, Michael, 'Ted Hughes' *Crow*', *Sphinx* 3: 51–6, 1975.
Kreutsch, Wilfried, 'A Reading of Ted Hughes' "Thrushes" ', *Literature in Wissenschaft und Unterricht* 9, 2, 1976.
Lewis, P. E., 'The New Pedantry and "Hawk Roosting" ', *Stand* 8, 1, 1966.
Libby, Anthony, 'Fire and Light: Four Poets to the End and Beyond', *Iowa Review*, Spring 1973.
'God's Lioness and the Priest of Sycorax: Plath and Hughes', *Contemporary Literature*, Summer 1974.
Lodge, David, '*Crow* and the Cartoons', *Critical Quarterly*, Spring 1971; reprinted in *Poetry Dimension* 1, Robson, 1973.
Lundkvist, Artur, 'En Stark vind; Om Englands nye poet, Ted Hughes', *Ord och Bild* 71, 1962.
May, Derwent, 'Ted Hughes' in *The Survival of Poetry*, ed. M. Dodsworth, 1970.
Mitgutsch, Waltraud, 'Zur Lyrik von Ted Hughes: Eine Interpretation Nach Leitmotiven', Saltzburg Inst. für Eng. Sprache & Lit., 1974.
Mollema, A., 'Mythical Elements in the Poetry of Ted Hughes', *Dutch Quarterly Review* 1, 1972.
Novak, R., 'Ted Hughes' *Crow*: Incarnation of the Universe', *Windless Orchard* 21, Spring 1975.
Okubo, Naoki, 'On Ted Hughes' Animal Poems', *Studies in Eng. Lit.* (Japan), 1974.
Oppel, Horst, 'Ted Hughes' "Pibroch" ', in Oppel (ed.): *Die Moderne Englische Lyrik: Interpretationen*, Berlin, 1968.
Peel, Marie, 'Black Rainbow', *Books and Bookmen*, Feb. 1971.
Poole, Richard, 'Dylan Thomas, Ted Hughes and Byron: Two Instances of Indebtedness', *Anglo-Welsh Review* 25, liv.
Porter, David, 'Beasts/Shamans/Baskin: The Contemporary Aesthetics of Ted Hughes', *Boston University Journal*, Fall 1974.
'Ted Hughes', *American Poetry Review* 4, 5, 1975.
Press, John, 'Metaphysics and Mythologies' in *Rule and Energy*, 1963.
Probyn, Hugh, *Ted Hughes' Gaudete*, Harris Press, Preston, 1977.
Rawson, Claud, 'Ted Hughes: A Reappraisal', *Essays in Criticism*, Jan. 1965.
'Rejoinder', *Essays in Criticism* 15, 1966.
'Some Sources and Parallels to Poems by Ted Hughes', *Notes and Queries* 15, 1968.
Ries, L. R., 'Hughes' "The Hawk in the Rain" ', *Explicator* 33, Dec. 1974
Wolf Masks: Violence in Contemporary Poetry, Kennikat, 1977.
Rife, David, 'Rectifying Illusion in the Poetry of Ted Hughes', *Minnesota Review*, 1970.
Riley and Harte, eds., *Contemporary Literary Criticism*, Vol. 2, Gale 1974.
Rosenthal, M. L., *The New Poets*, 1967.
Sagar, Keith, *Ted Hughes*, Longman for the British Council, 1972.
An Exhibition in Honour of Ted Hughes, Ilkley, 1975.
'Leonard Baskin and Ted Hughes' in *Leonard Baskin*, Hobson Gallery, Cambridge, 1978.

Sinnige-Bread, Afra, 'Plucking Bark: an Interpretation of Ted Hughes' "Wodwo" ', *Dutch Quarterly Review* 1, 1972.
Smith, Stan, 'Wolf Masks: the early poetry of Ted Hughes', *New Blackfriars*, Sept. 1975.
Sonne, Jørgen, 'Natur, Dyr, Djaevelskab: Om Ted Hughes' Lyrik', in his *Horisonter, Introduktioner og Essays*, Copenhagen, 1973.
Strauss, P. E., 'The Poetry of Ted Hughes', *Theoria* 38, 1972.
Swinden, Patrick, 'English Poetry' in *The Twentieth Century Mind*, ed. C. B. Cox and A. E. Dyson, Oxford, 1972.
Tabor, Stephen, *Ted Hughes: A Bibliography 1957–1975*, UCLA, 1977.
Tamura, Einosuke, 'Ted Hughes', *Oberon* 32, 1968.
Thurley, Geoffrey, 'Beyond Positive Values: Ted Hughes', in *The Ironic Harvest*, 1974.
Thwaite, Anthony, *Poetry Today 1960–1973*, Longman, 1973.
Wakeman, John, ed., *World Authors 1950–1970*, Wilson, 1975.
Walder, Dennis: *Ted Hughes, Sylvia Plath*, Open University Press, 1976.
Watt, Donald J., 'Echoes of Hopkins in Ted Hughes' *The Hawk in the Rain*', *Notes on Contemporary Literature* 2, 1972.
Weatherhead, A. K., 'Ted Hughes, *Crow*, and Pain', *Texas Quarterly*, Autumn 1976.

H. OTHER BOOKS USED

Alvarez, A., *The Savage God*, Weidenfeld and Nicholson, 1971.
Baskin, Leonard, *Sculpture, Drawings and Prints*, Braziller, 1970.
Beckett, Samuel, *Waiting for Godot*, Faber, 1956.
Endgame, Faber, 1958.
Beer, John, *Blake's Visionary Universe*, Manchester University Press, 1969.
Campbell, Joseph, *The Hero with a Thousand Faces*, Pantheon, 1949.
Myths to Live By, Souvenir Press, 1973.
The Masks of God, Souvenir Press, 1973.
Castaneda, Carlos, *The Teachings of Don Juan*, Penguin, 1970.
A Separate Reality, Bodley Head, 1971.
Journey to Ixtlan, Bodley Head, 1973.
Tales of Power, Hodder and Stoughton, 1974.
Conquest, Robert, ed., *New Lines*, Macmillan, 1956.
Dodds, E. R., *The Greeks and the Irrational*, University of California, 1951.
Eliade, Mircea, *Myths, Dreams and Mysteries*, Fontana 1968.
The Sacred and the Profane, Harcourt Brace, 1959.
Shamanism, Routledge, 1964.
Eliot, T. S., *Collected Poems*, Faber, 1963.
Euripides, *The Bacchae*, trans. Vellacott, Penguin, 1954.
Frazer, J. G., *The Golden Bough*, Macmillan, 1957.
Golding, William, *Lord of the Flies*, Penguin, 1960.
Graves, Robert, *The White Goddess*, Faber, 1961.
The Greek Myths, Penguin, 1960.
Grene, Marjorie, *The Knower and the Known*, Faber, 1966.
Harner, Michael J., ed., *Hallucinogens and Shamanism*, Oxford, 1973.

Ionesco, Eugene, *The Killer*, Plays Vol. 3, Calder, 1960.
The Chairs, Plays Vol. 1, Calder, 1958.
Jung, Carl, *Answer to Job*, Routledge, 1954.
Man and His Symbols, Aldus and Jupiter, 1964.
Psychology and Alchemy, Routledge, 1953.
Psychology of the Unconscious, Kegan Paul, 1921.
Psychological Types, Routledge, 1964.
Kafka, Franz, *The Trial*, Penguin, 1953.
The Castle, Penguin, 1957.
The Diaries, Penguin, 1964.
Kerenyi, C., *The Gods of the Greeks*, Thames and Hudson, 1951.
Prometheus, Pantheon, 1963.
Eleusis, Routledge, 1967.
Koestler, Arthur, *The Ghost in the Machine*, Hutchinson 1967, Pan, 1970.
Laing, R. D., The Politics of Experience and The Bird of Paradise, Penguin, 1967.
Larousse Encyclopaedia of Mythology, Batchworth, 1959.
Lawrence, D. H., *The Rainbow*, Penguin, 1950.
Women in Love, Penguin, 1950.
St Mawr, Penguin, 1950.
Selected Poems, Penguin, 1972.
Fantasia of the Unconscious, Penguin, 1971.
Apocalypse, Heinemann, 1972.
Phoenix, Heinemann, 1936.
Phoenix II, Heinemann, 1968.
Collected Letters, Heinemann, 1962.
Leavis, F. R., *Revaluation*, Chatto and Windus, 1956.
Lindsay, David, *A Voyage to Arcturus*, Gollancz, 1963.
Mabinogion, ed., Lady Charlotte Guest, 1848.
Nietzsche, Friedrich, *The Birth of Tragedy*, Doubleday Anchor, 1956.
Thus Spoke Zarathustra, Penguin, 1961.
Owen, Wilfred, *Collected Poems*, Chatto and Windus, 1963.
Plath, Sylvia, *Ariel*, Faber, 1965.
The Bell Jar, Faber, 1966.
The Colossus, Faber, 1967.
Letters Home, Faber, 1975.
Plato, *Phaedrus*, Penguin, 1973.
Radin, Paul, *The Trickster*, Bell, 1956.
Richards, I. A., *Beyond*, Harcourt Brace Jovanovich, 1974.
Russell, Bertrand, *A History of Western Philosophy*, Allen & Unwin 1946.
Sartre, J. P., *Nausea*, Penguin, 1965.
Seneca, *Oedipus*, Penguin, 1966.
Hercules Furens, in Tragedies 1, Heinemann, 1960.
Sharkey, John, *Celtic Mysteries*, Thames and Hudson, 1975.
Sophocles, *The Theban Plays*, trans. Watling, Penguin, 1947.
Tain, trans. Kinsella, Oxford, 1970.
Thomas, Dylan, *Collected Poems*, Dent, 1952.
Tibetan Book of the Dead, ed. W. Y. Evans-Wentz, Oxford, 1960.

Watts, Alan, *The Way of Zen*, Penguin, 1962.
Beyond Theology, Wildwood House, 1974.
Weston, Jessie L., *From Ritual to Romance*, Doubleday, 1957.
Whitman, Walt, *Complete Poetry*, Nonesuch, 1938.
Wolfram von Eschenbach, *Parzival*, Knopf and Random House.
Yeats, W. B., *Selected Plays*, Macmillan, 1966.
Collected Poems, Macmillan, 1955.

INDEXES

A. THE WORKS OF TED HUGHES

B. GENERAL